The UNIX
Text Processing System

D1617296

This book was typeset using the
typesetting tools of the UNIX Operating System.

The UNIX†
Text Processing System

KAARE CHRISTIAN

The Rockefeller University
New York, New York

†UNIX is a trademark of Bell Laboratories.

A Wiley-Interscience Publication

JOHN WILEY & SONS

New York • Chichester • Brisbane • Toronto • Singapore

Library of Congress Cataloging in Publication Data:

Christian, Kaare, 1954-
    The UNIX text processing system.

    "A Wiley-Interscience publication."
    On the title-page the trademark symbol for
a dagger follows UNIX.
    Bibliography: p.
    1. UNIX (Computer operating system) 2. Text
processing (Computer science) I. Title.
QA76.76.063C47 1987   005.4'3   87-10450
ISBN 0-471-85581-2

Printed in the United States of America

10 9 8 7 6 5 4 3 2 1

For Edward Josiah Bunker and Mary Piersol Bunker

Contents

Preface

The astounding price/performance revolution in laser printers has legitimized the UNIX document preparation tools. Until suitable output devices appeared at reasonable prices, few users could readily harness the power of troff and the other UNIX typesetting tools. Today most multiuser UNIX systems are equipped with a laser printer, and even many single-user UNIX work stations are laser equipped.

Most laser printers on UNIX systems are supported by software that lets them perform most of the functions of a true typesetter. Like typesetters, laser printers can print using various type styles and sizes. Special characters are available including many for setting mathematics. Laser printer resolution is usually less than that of a true typesetter, but for many purposes a laser printer is an adequate typesetting system.

In the summer and fall of 1982 I typeset my first book *The UNIX Operating System*. That summer I first learned how many quotes and dashes are in a typographer's tray. That experience readied me for typesetting my second book, and then this one, my third. Each time I've grown more adventurous and used more of the UNIX typesetting tools. Once you've experienced the feeling of total control over your manuscript, it's hard to go back to letting someone else do the typesetting.

This book is a comprehensive guide to the UNIX document preparation tools. Chapters 2 and 3 cover vi, the UNIX system's most popular text editor. Chapter 4 shows how vi can be retrofited as a rudimentary word processor—for simple jobs only! nroff and troff, the standard formatters, are covered in Chapter 5. I have carefully chosen the topics in Chapter 5 so that you can learn what is necessary without encountering unnecessary details. -ms and -mm, the two most popular macro packages, are covered in Chapters 6 and 7. The commands made available by these two macro packages are the focal point for most document preparation tasks. eqn, an aid for typesetting mathematics, was the first preprocessor. It is covered in Chapter 8. The `tbl` preprocessor, an aid for typesetting tables, is covered in Chapter 9. `refer`, an aid for typesetting and managing references, is described in Chapter 10. The UNIX system's latest preprocessor is `pic`, an aid for typesetting line drawings. It is discussed in Chapter 11. Various standard UNIX utility programs that aid document preparation are discussed in Chapter 12. Few readers will need to master all of these topics, so choose your reading strategy carefully. More guidance for selecting appropriate topics is in Chapter 1.

You should note that this book does not cover basic UNIX topics. If you aren't familiar with the UNIX system, you will also need one of the many general purpose introductory UNIX books. I often recommend my book, *The UNIX Operating System*. The other omission from this book may seem surprising—I don't cover `troff` in great depth. If you want to write your own macro package, this isn't the book for you. However, most people don't need to know `troff` esoterica. The existing macro packages and the preprocessors are much more important, so that's what I cover in depth.

Originally I planned to cover this material in the revised edition of my book on the UNIX system. As deadline after deadline slipped, I eventually realized that my document preparation material would never fit between the covers of my already bulging UNIX book. With the guidance and assistance of Maria Taylor, we decided that this material deserved a separate book. Once that decision was made, even more deadlines slipped, as all of the chapters expanded once again.

Many people helped to create this book. Maria Taylor, my editor at John Wiley, was always there when she was needed. Sandra Renner and Jenet McIver at John Wiley were also helpful. Thanks also go to Glen Gunsalus and Dan Ts'o of the Rockefeller University for their useful suggestions. Julie Dollinger created many of the sample documents in the chapter on the -mm macros, and she also did most of the secretarial work for the book. Many of the eliminated typos were discovered by Julie. Please write to me at the Rockefeller University, 1230 York Ave., New York, NY 10021, or to cmcl2!rna!kc on the UUCP network if you discover additional typos or have any comments.

I thoroughly enjoyed writing this book. It's fun to tell others how to do something that has been so satisfying to me. It was also fun to discover after months of work on the revision of my UNIX book that I had created something unexpected—a book on the UNIX text processing tools. An unexpected book is a gift few writers ever receive.

KAARE CHRISTIAN

New York, New York

The UNIX
Text Processing System

CHAPTER 1

UNIX Text Processing Tools

The advent of the laser printer has brought forth a new era in UNIX document preparation. Before the day of cheap, high-resolution laser printers, the UNIX text processing tools were too powerful for ordinary printers, yet typesetters were too expensive for ordinary users. Today even a personal UNIX system may be hooked up to a laser printer, and most multiuser UNIX systems are (or will be shortly) equipped with a powerful laser printer. Low-cost, near typeset-quality laser printing lets everybody take advantage of the UNIX text processing tools.

The UNIX text processing tools were designed to control the features of a typesetter. Over the years the system has evolved, but still the emphasis is on power, not ease of use. The full system is overkill for standard letters or short documents, but it works beautifully for technical manuscripts, books, and articles.

Surprisingly, the UNIX system has never had a standard word processing system for casual users. By *word* processor I mean an easy-to-use software system for producing simple documents. The term *text* processor, as used in this book, denotes a more powerful system, one where ease of use may be sacrificed for total control of document format.

Several word processors are commercially available for the UNIX system. You should choose one if you need a simple software package for writing letters or other short documents. (Several techniques for using vi as a simple word processor are presented in Chapter 4.)

UNIX text processing is performed in two steps. First the document is created using a text editor. The document contains plain text plus special codes that control the formatting process. The ed text editor was originally used, but today the more convenient vi (pronounced *vee-eye*) text editor is usually used. The second step is printing the document using a text formatter. The text formatter interprets the codes embedded in the document so that it is printed according to your specification. Note that a text editor can't format your document, and a text formatter doesn't help you edit

1

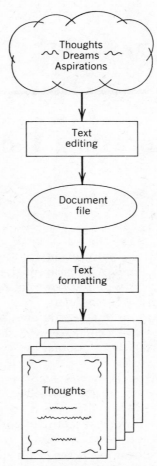

Figure 1.1. UNIX text processing is a two step process.

your text. These two functions are performed separately by the standard
UNIX tools. The structure of this book follows the structure of the process.
Chapters 2 through 4 discuss vi, the most commonly used text editor, and
Chapters 5 through 12 discuss the most important text formatting tools.

The original UNIX system text formatter was roff. Like its historical
brethren from earlier systems, roff used *embedded* formatting commands.
An embedded formatting system works with document text interspersed
with formatting commands. When the formatter is printing the document,
it has to distinguish the formatting commands from the document text.
The traditional method for separating commands from plain text is to put
the commands alone on a line beginning with a period. This works because
most documents don't contain lines starting with a period. (However, a

document describing a text formatter contains many lines beginning with periods!)

When a text formatting program encounters a line that begins with a period, it performs the given command. For example, when roff encounters a line containing the command .sp it outputs a blank line.

As many users realized, there are some severe limitations to the roff style of text formatting. One major limitation is flexibility. A roff-like system is good for a given class of documents, but it fails to work adequately for all styles of documents. Another aspect of flexibility regards documents (or a large part of a document) that are used in several different settings. For example, a document might start out as a proposal, then become a report, and then become part of a journal article. With a roff-like system, the document would need to be modified to produce the different formats.

The trouble with roff-like formatting systems is that roff commands describe the *actions* that you want the formatter to perform. In a more flexible system, you specify the *type* of text (e.g., paragraph, footnote, section heading) within the document, and you specify the *format* of each type of text outside the document. For example, you can put the command .SH inside the document to specify that a section heading follows, and then elsewhere you can specify the type style, spacing, numbering conventions, etc., for a section heading. This lets you adjust the style of your document without changing the document, and it lets you print the document in various styles by supplying suitable external style definitions.

When roff was replaced by nroff (pronounced *en-roff*), the major improvement was flexibility. nroff is a much lower level system than roff. The only sensible way to use nroff is to use a *macro package*, a prepared nroff program that translates your result-oriented commands (e.g., start new section, start new paragraph) into nroff's primitive command set. Although the general level of nroff is more primitive than that of roff, it has many features that make it more programmable. For example, nroff has variables that can store text or numbers, it has procedures (called macros) that can accept parameters, it has conditional statements, and it has arithmetic operations. Most of these added features aren't very useful to anyone but a programmer, but a skilled nroff programmer can use these features to create a macro package that produces documents in a wide variety of styles.

Fortunately, you don't need to be a programmer to use nroff (although it helps). A good macro package provides a much more result-oriented interface, thereby insulating you from nroff's intricacies. Sometimes one of the standard macro packages needs to be extended for specialized documents, but few people ever write a complete macro package from scratch.

From the start, nroff was designed to produce output for ordinary printers. Because of nroff's success, its author, Joe Ossanna, extended the program to handle typesetting equipment. While retaining nroff's noted programmability, Ossanna created `troff` (pronounced *tee-roff*) by adding features for managing type sizes, type faces, and variable-width characters. Although `nroff` and `troff` are separate programs, they accept the same commands, and most of the source code is the same. Throughout this book the word `troff` usually refers to both `nroff` and `troff`. I will try to be more explicit when discussing features that are handled differently by the two programs.

Another problem with `roff`-like systems is the user interface. Although programmers are used to symbolic commands, many users of a document preparation system are familiar with more visceral interfaces. For example, you generate blank lines with a typewriter by rolling up the carriage. The effect is immediately visible. Because document preparation systems are often used by people who are accustomed to nonsymbolic interfaces, many commercial developers created systems where the final format of the document is displayed on the screen as the document is entered. Such systems are often called WYSIWYG (pronounced *whiz-e-whig*), which stands for "What You See Is What You Get."

WYSIWYG systems are superior for many applications, and in time improved WYSIWYG systems may be superior for almost all document preparation. However, many of the currently available WYSIWYG systems have important drawbacks. One limitation concerns large documents. For a two-page letter or a short report, WYSIWYG can be ideal. However, for large manuscripts or books many people find that WYSIWYG systems are cumbersome and inefficient. This seems to happen because the command oriented interface of `troff` is ideal for standardizing style in a large document stored in multiple files.

Another problem is portability. Although there are several WYSIWYG systems that run on UNIX systems, none has gained universal acceptance. Any document created with a UNIX WYSIWYG word processor will, in general, need to be converted to plain ASCII text (thereby losing its format information) before it can be moved freely from one UNIX system to another. However, a document prepared with `troff` can be sent to any UNIX system and printed on any printer. That's why virtually all the documentation that describes UNIX software is in `nroff/troff` format; it is a universal format in the UNIX world.

Although almost anyone can be trained to use `troff`, it is clearly inappropriate for many users. For many short documents that don't need complex formatting, `vi` is an adequate "word processor." Many people find it easier to center the date at the top of a letter by inserting blank space rather than using `troff` commands. Business letters and other secretarial correspondence are ideal jobs for a commercially available UNIX WYSIWYG product.

Although `troff` is the only universally available UNIX text formatter, there are several less commonly used systems that work with the UNIX system. Perhaps the best known is Donald Knuth's T_EX (pronounced *tech*).

T$_E$X's page formatting is more sophisticated than troff's, it has a better understanding of character shapes and the rules for positioning one character next to another, and it features an advanced hyphenation algorithm. T$_E$X has more savvy while making tradeoffs to produce a pleasing page appearance, whereas troff obeys a uniformly rigid set of rules. Nevertheless, troff is the most often used UNIX formatter, because it was available first, and because it has been significantly extended over the years to handle specialized jobs.

nroff is used when the output device is a simple mechanical printer. Vanilla UNIX versions come with support for about a dozen printers, and drivers for various other printers are available within the UNIX community. You can produce a list of the supported printers on your system by listing the contents of the '/usr/lib/term' directory. When you run nroff you must tell it which printer you are using with the -Ttermname command line option, unless your local nroff has been modified so that its default matches your printer.

The original version of troff (the typesetter program) worked solely with the Graphic Systems typesetter. Breaking from the UNIX device independent style of programming, code to support the Graphic Systems typesetter was hard-coded throughout troff. Because many sites lacked the appropriate typesetter, several output filters were developed to translate the typesetting codes of the Graphic Systems device into the codes for other output devices. Although output filters add the desired functionality, they add an additional layer of complexity to an already complex process. The Graphic Systems codes are a serious limitation—output devices with more resolution or more sophisticated features are handicapped, because troff only knows about the limited features of the Graphic Systems device. Typesetters with less functionality are handicapped, because troff is unable to compensate for their weaknesses.

Because of these problems a new version of troff, called ditroff (the *di* stands for *device independent*), was developed by Brian Kernighan. ditroff outputs a generic page printer control language. Output filters are used to translate the ditroff output language into the codes needed by the various page printers. The new ditroff also circumvents many of the original limitations that were designed into the Graphic Systems typesetter and hence into the original troff. From a user's vantage point, the major difference between the new ditroff and the original troff is that ditroff allows more fonts to be used on a single page.

For most users, the choice between using nroff and troff is based on the available output devices, and the audience for the document. nroff must be used with ordinary printers, and it is preferable when the document (e.g., a business letter) should look as though it had been typed on a typewriter. The troff formatter is used when you have a printer that supports proportional-width fonts, various character sizes, and various fonts. Many

sites have laser printers with these features, and some sites have true typesetters that can be controlled by troff.

1.1 MACRO PACKAGES

The commands that are built into troff are designed to control specific features of the output device. To be used conveniently, troff capabilities
should be accessed via a *macro package*. A macro package is a program,
written using troff primitives, that tells troff how to format your pages,
headings, paragraphs, lists, and displays. Most macro packages can be customized, so that within some limit the format can be adjusted to suit your
preferences.

The first macro package to gain wide acceptance was -ms, the manuscript
macros. -ms was first distributed with Version 7 UNIX, and it is also available in Berkeley UNIX systems. It is not officially available as a standard
part of System V, but it is compatible with System V, and many System V
sites do have a copy.

-ms was originally developed at AT&T Bell Laboratories by Mike Lesk,
and it contains many vestiges of the style of documentation favored at the

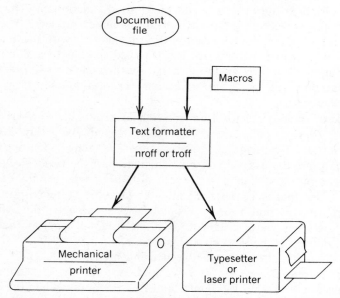

Figure 1.2. Macros provide the detailed instructions that enable nroff or troff to
format your document.

Labs. Some of -ms is devoted to features that can only be used by employees of AT&T Bell Laboratories. For example, there are macros to print the addresses of several AT&T facilities. Some of these extraneous features have been stripped away in newer versions of -ms.

The original version of -ms supported several paragraph styles, multicolumn output, ordinary or numbered section headings, easy-to-manage page headers and footers, displays (blocks of text that are kept together), and footnotes. You can exert some stylistic control over most of these features by altering troff number registers or strings. Perhaps the largest omission from the original -ms is support for generating a table of contents, but this feature has been added by Bill Tuthill for the Berkeley distribution, and it is described here. The -ms macro package is described in Chapter 6. -ms is also noteworthy because it works, as supplied, with the refer reference bibliography system.

The currently supported System V macro package is -mm, the memorandum macros. It is not available as a standard feature on Version 7 systems, or on Berkeley systems, although versions of -mm are often available on those systems. -mm was designed to "do everything" of the earlier systems. Thus it has almost all features found in -ms, including table of contents. The major additional feature is an elaborate set of macros for managing lists. -mm was the result of a conscious design effort to make the package robust. Whereas many simple errors in -ms lead to mystifying results, an attempt is made in -mm to produce informative error messages. Another improvement is the additional control of document format that -mm provides. Some -mm macros exist solely to tell -mm how to format your pages, headings, footnotes, etc. -mm also is easy for an advanced user to customize. Many of the -mm macros automatically invoke a user-definable macro, allowing easy extension of the package. The drawback of this amount of elaboration is obvious—the -mm macros are more than twice the size of -ms. The -mm macro package is described in Chapter 7.

Yet another general-purpose macro package, developed by Eric Allman at Berkeley, is -me. (The name -me, like the names of the other macro packages, is suggestive of its origins. All macro package names start with an 'm' because -m is the troff flag that says to load a macro package, and the 'e' is Eric's first initial.) -me is available mainly on Berkeley systems. Although its table of contents support is primitive and its support for lists is much less grand than that of -mm, -me nevertheless has advantages over its rivals. Unlike -ms and -mm, -me lets you automatically generate indexes. I admire -me, because it produces attractive documents with the least fuss. Its default format is attractive and easy to change, and there are few surprises. The names of the macros are nicely chosen, and the documentation is clear.

Several specialized macro packages are available. Perhaps the most common of these is man, a macro package for producing entries for the printed and the on-line UNIX manual. man has macros that produce the customary manual page and paragraph headings, and it supports the common list format that is often used to describe options and features of UNIX programs.

1.2 PREPROCESSORS

troff used with one of the general-purpose macro packages mentioned above is an adequate system for typesetting ordinary documents. You can control the appearance of pages, paragraphs, lists, and similar material. However, the power of troff plus a macro package is limited. troff allows you to set tabs, but it isn't set up for analyzing the widths of columns in a table, so it can't set column widths automatically. troff has some support for drawing lines and boxes, but the feature is hard to access directly, and the macro packages mentioned above are only capable of boxing a given chunk of text. And although troff has commands for local motions and it allows you to access mathematical symbols, the do-it-yourself style of typesetting mathematics is too odious with plain troff, and the general-purpose macro packages don't help.

But of course there is a solution—you can use *preprocessors* to extend the power of troff. A preprocessor is a program designed to address a specific typesetting specialty. The preprocessor translates parts of your document into primitive troff commands and leaves the rest alone. For example, tbl is a troff preprocessor. When tbl encounters tabular data in a document, it analyzes the column widths, prepares the headings according to your specifications, etc. The result is that your relatively simple table description is translated into primitive troff commands for typesetting the table. If you ever look at the output of tbl (or any of the other preprocessors), you'll get some idea of how much work they save you.

Preprocessors work with troff using ordinary UNIX pipes. For example, if your document contains tables, you process it with tbl and pipe tbl's output to troff, and troff then prints the entire document. The UNIX shell command to print a document containing tables looks like:

```
$ tbl mydoc | troff
$ _
```

Extending troff by providing separate programs to handle various specialty tasks has several advantages. One plus is training. If you don't typeset mathematics, you can safely ignore the eqn preprocessor. Your ignorance will never bite, unlike systems where you must learn enough about everything to avoid the features you don't want to use. Another advantage is execution time. troff is already a big, slow program; adding major

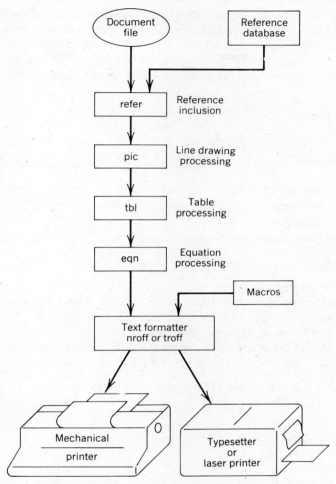

Figure 1.3. Preprocessors extend the range of the UNIX **nroff** and **troff** text format-ters. Shown above are all four preprocessors that are detailed in this book. Most documents do not need the four stages of preprocessing shown in this diagram.

features directly into **troff** would only enlarge it and make it run even slower. With separate preprocessors, you only need to execute software that you are really going to use. Typesetting is one area where the UNIX system's tools philosophy has worked well.

There are four often used and almost universally available **troff** preprocessors—**tbl** for managing tabular data, **eqn** for typesetting mathe-matics, **refer** for inserting scholarly references, and **pic** for creating line drawings.

The `tbl` preprocessor translates a description of a table into the `troff` commands that will actually implement the table. Tables can be boxed and can have horizontal or vertical lines. Columns can be centered, left-adjusted or right-adjusted, numeric, etc. Additional controls are available for managing sophisticated tables. The following contains a sample table description on the left and the generated table on the right.

```
.TS
center box;
C S
RI L.
Text Preprocessors
.sp .3v
tbl      Tables of data
eqn      Equations
refer    References
pic      Line Drawings
.TE
```

Text Preprocessors	
tbl	Tables of data
eqn	Equations
refer	References
pic	Line Drawings

`tbl` is discussed in Chapter 9.

The `eqn` preprocessor translates a description of an equation into the `troff` typesetting codes that actually format the equation. Very simple equations can be done by hand, but most people whose documents contain equations should learn eqn. Here is an example equation specification:

```
.EQ
int { { e sup {i omega t} + e sup {-i omega t} }
     over {2 pi} }
.EN
```

Here is the typeset equation:

$$\int \frac{e^{i\omega t} + e^{-i\omega t}}{2\pi}$$

eqn is discussed in Chapter 8.

Refer is a reference management system. It is useful for people whose documents contain numerous citations. The refer system has programs to maintain a data base of references. The `refer` preprocessor, which is just one component of the refer software, can take an informal citation, look up the reference in a data base, and then insert the citation into the text. The `refer` preprocessor can produce end notes or footnotes, and the exact format of the reference and the citation can be controlled by a macro package.

For example, I have a data base containing references for all of Darwin's books. In a paper I can place the following citation:

```
Darwin's work on orchids
.[
darwin orchids
.]
is not widely discussed today, but it represents
an important stage in his intellectual development.
```

In my document the output will be the following, plus the footnote that appears at the bottom of the page.

> Darwin's work on orchids[1] is not widely discussed today, but it represents an important stage in his intellectual development.

The refer software is discussed in Chapter 10.

The pic preprocessor converts a description of a line drawing into troff commands. pic line drawings are composed of circles, ellipses, arcs, lines, boxes, and text. The following figure contains a picture description on the left and the output picture on the right.

```
.PS
box ht .4 wid .6
box ht .6 wid .8 with .c at last box.c
PC: box ht .3 wid 1 with .n at last box.s
"PC" at PC.c + (-.35,0)
box ht .15 wid .3 at PC.c
box ht same at PC.c + (.3,0)
.PE
```

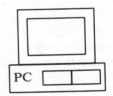

pic is discussed in Chapter 11.

1.3   STUDY GUIDE

This book covers the vi text editor, the nroff/troff formatters, the -ms and -mm macro packages, and four common preprocessors. Few readers will need to master all of these topics. Most people will use only one or two of the preprocessors, and almost everybody will use only one of the two macro packages. Many people will already be familiar with vi or another text editor, so they will be able to skip those chapters.

This book does not cover basic UNIX system usage such as file management. If you are not familiar with UNIX, you should first learn the basics, perhaps from my book *The UNIX Operating System* or from any of a dozen other general UNIX titles. You should be familiar with logging in; the general utility programs such as date, who, and cd; the file management

---

1. C. Darwin, *The Various Contrivances by Which Orchids Are Fertilized by Insects,* John Murray, London (1862).

commands such as ls, rm, mv, cp, and mkdir; and basic usage of the shell, including I/O redirection and pipelines.

Chapters 2 and 3 (Text Editing with vi and Advanced vi Editing) concentrate on the vi text editor. The commands presented in Chapter 2 are enough to get by, but you should invest the time to learn the more advanced usage discussed in Chapter 3 if you plan to spend much time editing.

Chapter 4 (vi Word Processing) shows you how to do simple word processing using vi. The first part of the chapter discusses a pair of vi features that are useful for making vi into a passable word processor, and the remainder of the chapter shows how to do simple paragraph and page formatting with vi. These techniques may be useful to you if you occasionally need a simple word-processing system for short documents or letters. You should skip Chapter 4 if most of your work will be on longer documents.

Chapter 5 (nroff and troff) focuses on the UNIX text formatting programs. The level of coverage is not especially detailed, because most users should interact with the formatters via a macro package (and possibly via preprocessors). What is presented in Chapter 5 is the part of troff that you may need to use with a macro package.

Chapters 6 and 7 (*The* -ms Macro Package and The -mm Macro Package) are mutually exclusive. Most people will want to learn one or the other, depending on their environment. -ms is the older of the two packages, it is available on Berkeley and Version 7 Systems, and it was used to produce most of the original UNIX documentation. The -mm macro package is newer, it is available on System V systems, it is somewhat more robust (better messages when you make a mistake), it has elaborate support for lists, and it has been proclaimed to be the "standard" macro package by AT&T. Your choice between -ms and -mm should depend on what system you are using (Berkeley-derived or System V-derived) and what macro package your co-workers use. Another consideration is the refer preprocessor, which only works with the -ms macro package.

The four preprocessors (Chapters 8 through 11) should be learned if you routinely need those features in your documents. For example if your documents routinely contain equations you should learn the eqn preprocessor. The preprocessors are easy to use, and they all significantly extend the power of the UNIX text processing system.

CHAPTER 2

Text Editing with Vi

vi is a text-editing program. With it you create what is commonly called a marked-up document—a text file containing the document text interspersed with formatting codes. In this chapter and the next, you learn how to use vi to edit a text file. For now you can ignore troff formatting codes and concentrate on learning to edit text files with vi. Formatting codes for troff are discussed in Chapter 5.

vi was originally conceived of as a programmer's editor. University of California at Berkeley graduate student Bill Joy enchanced ed, the original UNIX text editor, to create vi. Although vi contains some features that are used only when you are writing programs, its flexibility and power are useful for all users. A few advanced features that turn vi into a rudimentary self-contained word processor are divulged in Chapter 4.

vi is actually the full-screen, display-oriented personna of a family of text editors. The other members of the family are edit—a simple line-oriented editor; ex—a powerful line-oriented editor; and view—a browsing (no-changes) editor. A display editor such as vi uses the screen of your display terminal to portray a portion of the document. A line editor shows you the lines in your document, but the lines displayed on your screen may not be in the same order as those in your document. Most people find visual editing more convenient than line editing, and the focus of these vi chapters is on visual mode commands.

You needn't master vi to use it successfully; in fact, enough basic vi is presented in this chapter for realistic use. However, if you are planning to work with it extensively, you should learn most of the more advanced features that are discussed in Chapter 3. If you already know vi, you can skip this chapter and possibly the next. You should read the introduction to the third vi chapter, Chapter 4, to see if you need to learn to use vi as a simple word processor. Appendix I lists most vi commands.

The original vi document is *An Introduction to Display Editing with Vi* by William Joy, with revisions by Mark Horton. A related document is *Ex*

Reference Manual, also by William Joy and also containing revisions by Mark Horton. The ex manual describes the line-oriented command set of vi. People who want to master line editing can read any of the original UNIX ed documents or the extensive ed material in my book *The UNIX Operating System.*

2.1   UNIX TEXT EDITORS

Throughout the UNIX system's history there have been several common programs for editing text. The UNIX system's first text editor was ed. ed is a powerful program, but it is best used by programmers or other technically inclined people. Because it was the original text editor, ed has had a major impact on the entire UNIX system. Many UNIX programs contain a syntax or command language that has many similarities to ed's. Some examples are sed (a stream editor), lex (a programmer's utility), awk (a programmable text manipulation language), grep (a text-searching program), and the edit/ex/vi family of text editors. Because of ed's enduring legacy, most serious UNIX users learn it. However, both System V and Berkeley UNIX contain the vi program, and it is recommended as a better general-purpose editing program.

Another common UNIX text editor is Emacs. First developed at MIT by Richard Stallman, Emacs is a flexible and powerful text-editing program. Most versions of Emacs support windowing, so that several documents can be displayed and edited simultaneously. Emacs can be programmed to behave one way for one user and another way for someone else. This is Emacs' strength and weakness—there are many versions, all slightly different, and then once customized the many versions become a dense forest of different editors. If you want to program your editor so that it behaves as you think an editor should, then Emacs is for you. Many versions of Emacs are available for the UNIX system including Warren Montgomery's version, Jove (Jonathan's Own Version of Emacs), Gosling's Emacs, and GNU Emacs (a recent version produced by Stallman for his GNU project).

Some editors are touted as ''modeless,'' meaning that all commands are accessible at all times. Emacs is a good example. You don't need to go into a text entry mode to enter text; you just need to start typing. The drawback is that all of Emacs' commands are control sequences, which some people find hard to type. Bill Joy had more freedom to design vi's command structure because of its different modes of operation. (Perhaps more importantly, vi was based on the ed text editor, which has always had two basic modes of operation. vi has, by my count, five modes of operation if you don't count the shell escape as a separate mode.)

2.2 CHECKING YOUR TERMINAL TYPE

vi is called a visual (or screen-oriented) editor because it portrays, on your terminal's screen, a picture of part of the file being edited. Because there are a multitude of different terminals, each with its own control codes, vi must know what model of terminal you are using. It is possible to start vi and then specify the terminal, but it is much better to specify the terminal type in your login script so that you can use vi conveniently.

vi learns the name of your terminal from the $TERM environment variable. Ordinarily the system administrator makes sure that $TERM is set correctly when your account is created. On personal UNIX systems the $TERM variable may be set correctly during the standard procedure for creating a user account. You can check to see if $TERM is set correctly by entering the command

```
$ echo $TERM
vt100
$ _
```

In the example shown above, the word vt100 is the name of the terminal. If the answer is a blank line, or if the answer is wrong, then you must go through the procedure specified below to tell the UNIX system the name of your terminal. If the $TERM variable is set correctly, skip the following section and proceed to Section 2.4.

2.3 SETTING THE TERMINAL TYPE

Each time you log into the UNIX system, your shell executes a *login* script. If your standard shell is the Bourne or Korn shell, the login script is a file in your home directory named '.profile', and if you are using the c-shell the login script file name is '.login'. For your convenience you should put the commands to set $TERM in your login script so that the terminal type is set correctly each time you log in. You can do that with vi once you learn to use it, but for now you can set $TERM using simple UNIX commands.

You should enter the following command to set the $TERM variable. Ideally, this command should be placed in your login script so that you can forget about this messy side of the UNIX system. You needn't understand all of the following right now; it will become clearer when you learn more about the shell.

Each model of terminal has been assigned a short name. Like your login name, terminals' names are generally in lowercase, they never contain spaces, and they don't usually contain punctuation. Typically, a terminal's UNIX name consists of a few identifying characters followed by a model number. The easiest way to find the UNIX name for your terminal is to ask your system administrator.

Here is the command to tell the UNIX system that your terminal is an adm3a:

```
$ TERM=adm3a ; export TERM
$ _
```

or if you are using the Berkeley csh command interpreter, the command would be

```
% setenv TERM adm3a
% _
```

Once you know how to use vi, place the command in your login script.

2.4 STARTING VI

Once the name of your terminal is stored in the $TERM environmental variable, you can start vi. Enter the command vi. The screen should clear, vi will print the message "new file" at the bottom of the screen, and the cursor will be left flashing at the top left corner of the screen. This event is portrayed in the following pictures:

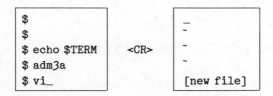

The picture on the left shows a portrayal of a miniterminal (5 short lines) before a <CR>C has been struck to tell the system to execute the vi command. The screen on the right portrays the screen once vi has started. The <CR> between the screens indicates that a carriage return was struck to advance from the situation on the left to the situation on the right. The _ in each screen symbolizes the cursor. The tildes (~) below the cursor on the right screen are vi's indication that there is no text on those lines.

If your result is a garbled screen, or if vi prints a warning message and then prompts you with a :, your $TERM variable is set incorrectly. Section 2.3 shows how to set $TERM correctly.

Another possibility is that $TERM will be set, but set to something other than the terminal you are using. If the terminal vi thinks you have uses very different control codes from what you actually have, then the screen will display a hash of control codes. This problem is easy to diagnose, and the fix is obvious: get $TERM set correctly. However, there are only a few families of terminals, and within a family the members usually have similar control sequences. This makes it possible for the name of your terminal to be slightly wrong, so that vi won't send an improper code except in some obscure situation. This problem is subtle, but the remedy is, as before, obvious: get the $TERM environment variable set correctly.

The hard part of portraying vi in a book is the fact that most commands have an effect, but the command characters themselves aren't directly displayed. Another problem is that most commands are carried out as you enter each keystroke. This is very different from your line-at-a-time interactions with the shell. You must be very careful while entering vi commands, because the keyboard is live—each keystroke is acted on immediately, and there is no way to take back an erroneous keypress. This immediacy of execution coupled with vi's refusal to echo your keystrokes on the screen makes for an interesting dialogue. You must (correctly) remember your keystrokes to deduce what went wrong when some command produces an unexpected result.

Of course you could proceed to edit text, but instead let's show how you depart from vi. For example, the command to quit vi is ZZ (capital Z struck twice).

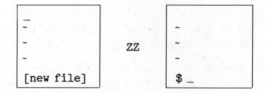

The diagram above, like all vi diagrams in this book, is read from left to right. The text between the screens indicates the keys that are struck to move from the situation shown on the left to the one shown on the right. In the diagram above, vi is running in the left picture, and the ZZ command is entered, causing the user to return to the shell command level of the UNIX system, as portrayed in the right-hand picture. Notice that the ZZ isn't displayed on the screen. You can see that you have returned to the shell by the characteristic shell prompt in the lower left-hand corner of the screen.

In the following section you will learn several vi commands for moving from one place to another in a file. For that exercise you need to have a file for practicing. Here's how to make one using vi. Carefully perform these simple steps:

1. Enter the shell command

   $ vi ex1

   The screen should clear, and the cursor will move to the upper left-hand corner of the screen.

2. Enter the vi command a to enter text entry mode. There will be no response on the screen. Only type the a once, and remember that there won't be any visual feedback.

3. Type the following list of words, one per line. While you are entering a word, you can use the backspace key to fix a typo, but don't bother to fix mistakes on any previous line. Remember that for the following section you only need a list of words; it doesn't matter if the words are spelled correctly. At the end of each word, hit return (enter) to advance to the next line.

```
John
has
seen
some
mice
and
men.
```

4. Strike the ESC key to return to vi command mode. Text entry will be explained in more detail in Section 2.6.

5. Strike ZZ to save your work, and return to the shell. vi should print a message about the size of the 'ex1' file, and then a shell prompt should appear on the bottom left of the screen.

Just as a check, you might want to display your newly created file using the UNIX cat command, a simple program that can display a file on your terminal.

```
$ cat ex1
John
has
seen
some
mice
and
men.
$ _
```

Now you are ready to learn how to move from one place in a file to another.

2.5   MOVING FROM HERE TO THERE

Now you are ready to use the 'ex1' file that you created in the previous section to learn the vi cursor movement commands.

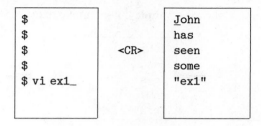

Note that the 'ex1' file is too large to fit on the screen of these little diagrams, but it will certainly fit onto the screen of your terminal. On our diagram screen the name of the file is shown on the bottom row, whereas the name and file length would be shown on a full-size screen.

Since most files are too large to be displayed on your terminal screen, vi actually presents a window that shows just a part of the file. For the miniscreen in our vi diagrams, the active part of the window is only four lines tall. Thus, just four lines of this seven-line file are visible. When vi is used with a normal 24-line terminal connected directly to a computer, the entire 24 lines are normally used. However, when your connection is via a telephone link, vi attempts to compensate for the slower communication speed by using a smaller window. This can improve the speed of screen updates, although the smaller viewing region is a drawback. When you edit the example file on your terminal, the entire file will probably be visible.

On some terminals, vi uses the terminal's arrow keys to move around in the file. However, some terminals don't have arrow keys, and even some that include arrow keys don't use them with vi. Therefore, vi has adopted the convention of using the hjkl keys for moving the cursor. Notice that on a standard keyboard layout the hjkl keys are next to each other. The h key moves one character left, j moves one line down, k moves one line up, and l moves one character right. Here is a picture of that region on the keyboard.

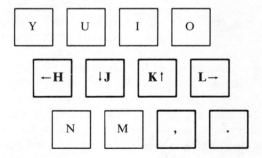

Here is an example showing simple cursor movement:

```
┌─────────┐       ┌─────────┐         ┌─────────┐
│ John    │       │ John    │         │ John    │
│ has     │       │ has     │         │ has     │
│ seen    │   j   │ seen    │   llk   │ seen    │
│ some    │       │ some    │         │ some    │
│ "ex1"   │       │ "ex1"   │         │ "ex1"   │
└─────────┘       └─────────┘         └─────────┘
```

Many commands can be performed repeatedly by supplying *numeric prefixes*. For example, the command 4j will move the cursor down four lines.

```
┌─────────┐           ┌─────────┐
│ John    │           │ has     │
│ has     │           │ seen    │
│ seen    │    4j     │ some    │
│ some    │           │ mice    │
│ "ex1"   │           └─────────┘
└─────────┘
```

On these miniscreens, moving down four lines causes the screen to scroll up one line, so that the line containing the cursor will be visible. Because your screen is larger, no scroll is necessary in this case.

Another way to move around is the G command. You can go to a specific line by typing the line number followed by G. Typing the command G without a numeric prefix will move to the end of the file. Note that the line number is not echoed on the screen as it is typed.

```
┌─────────┐       ┌─────────┐         ┌─────────┐
│ has     │       │ some    │         │ has     │
│ seen    │   G   │ mice    │   3G    │ seen    │
│ some    │       │ and     │         │ some    │
│ mice    │       │ men.    │         │ mice    │
└─────────┘       └─────────┘         └─────────┘
```

Another way to navigate in a text file is to use vi's page-forward command and its page-backward command. These commands move through a file in larger chunks, making them very useful for browsing. However, these commands are easier to demonstrate with a large file. So if you are still editing the 'ex1' file, use the ZZ command to exit from vi. On most systems there is a large dictionary of words in a file called '/usr/dict/words'. (If you don't have a copy of '/usr/dict/words' on your system, ask your system administrator for the name of a largish file to use for this exercise.) To make sure that you don't accidentally modify your practice file, you should use vi's -R "read-only" command line option. The read-only option makes it impossible to accidently modify the file.

Starting from a shell prompt, execute the following command:

```
$ vi -R /usr/dict/words
```

As usual, the screen will clear, and the first few lines of the '/usr/dict/words' file will appear on your screen. The commands to move forward and backward by screen-size chunks are control characters. You must hold down the *Ctrl* key and then strike the given letter. For example, the ^F command (the caret-F notation means control F) scrolls forward one screen, and ^B scrolls back one screen. Variants on these commands are ^D to scroll forward about a half screen, and ^U to scroll up about a half screen.

10th		4th		6th	
1st		5th		7th	
2nd	^F	6th	^D	8th	
3rd		7th		9th	
"words"					

Two additional commands for moving around in a text file are w to move forward one word, and b to move backward one word.

4th		4th		4th	
7th		7th		7th	
8th	w	8th	ww	8th	
9th		9th		9th	

vi considers '4th' to be two words, the '4' and the 'th'. That's why the first w command shown above moves the cursor from the '4' to the 'th' instead of all the way to the following line.

The commands e and E move to the end of a word. Similar to the w and W commands, the e command considers words to end at any boundary between letters and digits or between digits and punctuation. The E command considers a word to be any text delimited by white space.

Table 2.1 summarizes the movement commands that have been presented in this section.

2.6   ADDING AND INSERTING TEXT

Although moving from one place to another in a document is an important part of text editing, actually adding (and deleting—next section) text is really the heart of the matter. In this section we are going to show commands that are used to enter and leave vi's visual text entry mode.

Table 2.1. Basic **vi** Commands

Movement Commands

h	Left
j	Down
k	Up
l	Right
G	Go to a line
^F	Forward screenful
^B	Back screenful
^D	Down ½ screenful
^U	Up ½ screenful
w	Forward one word
b	Backward one word

Text Entry Commands

a	Append text following current cursor position
i	Insert text before current cursor position
o	Open up a new line following the current line and add text there
O	Open up a new line in front of the current line and add text there
<ESC>	Return to visual command mode

Text Deletion Commands

x	Delete character
dw	Delete word
db	Delete word backward
dd	Delete line
d$	Delete to end of line
d^	Delete to beginning of line
u	Undo last change
U	Restore Line

File Manipulation Commands

:w<CR>	Write work space to original file
:w file<CR>	Write work space to named file
:e file<CR>	Start editing a new file
:r file<CR>	Add a file to the work space
:q<CR>	Quit (a warning is printed if a modified file hasn't been saved)
:q!<CR>	Quit (no warning)
ZZ	Save work space and quit

To understand what happens when you insert text into a document, you must understand that the vi editor has several distinct modes, including a visual command mode (several of its commands were discussed above) and a visual text entry mode. In command mode, you can move the cursor, delete text, scroll through your document, etc. Everything that you type in command mode is interpreted as a command, including the commands that lead into text entry mode. (The two vi modes mentioned above aren't its only modes. There is also a line-oriented command mode similar to the ed editor and an open-line editing mode that lets you edit (somewhat) conveniently on a single line. These two vi modes are less used by most people, and they aren't discussed here.)

Although there are several ways to get into visual text entry mode, there is only one way out, the escape key (often labeled ESC). In the diagrams that follow, the escape key will be indicated using the <ESC> notation.

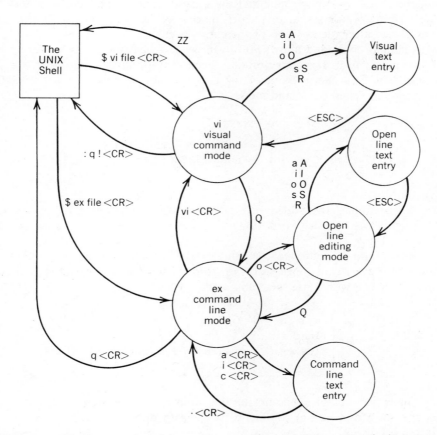

Figure 2.1. This diagram shows the major vi modes and the commands that cause mode changes.

When you see <ESC>, it means that you strike the escape key (without the angle brackets).

One simple way to add text to a document is with vi's *append* command. From visual mode, striking the a places you into visual append mode. From that point forward, everything you type will be added to the document as text, until you strike the escape key. Here is a simple example.

In the command illustrated above—a's<ESC>—the a is used to enter visual append mode, the apostrophe and the s are the added text, and the <ESC> is the terminator for visual text entry mode. Notice that the appended text was placed after the position of the cursor.

A similar command allows you to insert text in front of the cursor. The i key puts you in text entry mode. Then everything that you type will be inserted into the file in front of the cursor position, until you strike <ESC> to return to visual command mode.

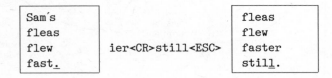

In this example, the added text is the letters er followed by a carriage return followed by the word still. Note that the screen scrolls up as necessary.

Both a and i modify text starting at the current position in the current line. However, sometimes you want to open up a new line and start there, for which you would use the o command.

The o (lowercase) opens up the line following the current line, but there is also an O (uppercase) command to open up the preceding line, as shown in the following.

```
┌─────────────┐              ┌─────────────┐
│ Sam's       │              │ Sam's       │
│ ne_w        │   Ofine<ESC> │ fin_e       │
│ fleas       │              │ new         │
│ flew        │              │ fleas       │
└─────────────┘              └─────────────┘
```

Whenever you are in one of vi's visual text entry modes, the only way back to command mode is by entering <ESC>. You should especially note the fact that the cursor movement commands discussed in the preceding section don't work while you are in text entry mode. If you want to move the cursor you must first return to command mode, and then you can use any visual mode command. When in doubt, strike the escape key. If you are already in visual command mode, the terminal's bell will sound after about a second, but if you are in a text entry mode, you will be returned to visual command mode.

2.7 DELETING TEXT

Some people can enter text once correctly and be done with it. Unfortunately, most of us need to revise our work, deleting the worst, adding new material, and changing the existing material. In this section we are going to cover several of vi's many text deletion commands.

The simplest vi text deletion command is x. The x command will delete text one character at a time. When you strike x, whatever is under the cursor is deleted, and material to the right of the cursor shifts to the left to fill in.

```
┌─────────────┐              ┌─────────────┐
│ Admiral     │              │ Admiral     │
│ John        │     3x       │ John        │
│ Paul        │              │ Paul        │
│ _Jones      │              │ _es         │
└─────────────┘              └─────────────┘
```

Remember that you can ususally type a number before a command to make the command repeat that many times.

Now that you can make deletions, you should know about vi's u undo command. By striking u, you can undo the last deletion, change, addition, etc. (More sophisticated methods of recovering deletions are discussed in Chapter 3.)

| Admiral
John
Paul
<u>e</u>s | kkk4x3x | _
John
Paul
es | u | <u>r</u>al
John
Paul
es |

Notice that there are two deletions, first four characters and then three characters. When vi executes the u command, it merely undoes the most recent deletion, so in the example above only the last three letters are recovered.

A variant undo command is executed when U (uppercase) is struck. Unlike u, which undoes the last change, the U command undoes all the recent changes to a given line. ("Recent" means since you last moved to the line. Once you move away from the line, the U command won't work.) Here is the example from above, redone using the U command.

| Admiral
John
Paul
<u>e</u>s | kkk4x3x | _
John
Paul
es | U | <u>A</u>dmiral
John
Paul
es |

vi's general purpose text deletion command is d. The d command can be used to delete any unit of text. For example, the command dw will delete the following word, db will delete the previous word, d$ will delete to the end of the line, d^ will delete to the beginning of the line, and dd will delete the entire line. Several other modifiers are available to instruct the d command how much to delete. In my work I use dw (delete word) and dd (delete line) more frequently than the other variants.

| <u>A</u>dmiral
John
Paul
es | dwj | <u>J</u>ohn
Paul
es | 2dd | <u>e</u>s
~
~ |

2.8 MANAGING FILES

One way to tell vi which file you want to edit is to supply that file name as an argument when you start vi. Thus the UNIX shell command

```
$ vi ch8.t
```

tells the system that you want to use vi to edit the file 'ch8.t'. (If the file doesn't exist, it will be created, and vi will print the *new file* message.) When you are done with your editing, you can use vi's ZZ command to save the changes and then exit from vi. This method is fine if all you want to do is edit a single file and then do something else, but it is clumsy if your needs are more complicated. vi contains several other file manipulation possibilities that you should know about.

2.8.1 Saving without Exiting

If you are working with a single file for an extended period of time, you should occasionally save your work. This helps to prevent a loss of data if the machine should crash or if you should make a disastrous mistake. The reason that periodic saves are a good idea is that while editing a file with vi you are actually working with a copy of the original file. The working copy is contained in vi's edit *buffer,* an internal storage area that vi uses when you are working on the file. If you've worked for half an hour, you should probably copy your changes back to the original file using the :w (write) command. When you invoke the :w command, the command itself is displayed on the bottom of the screen, and then when the update is complete, the size of your file is printed on the bottom line of the screen.

All vi commands that require the : prefix are more like ordinary UNIX shell commands than the vi commands that have been discussed above. Unlike other vi commands, the : commands are echoed on the bottom of the screen, they must be completed with a carriage return, and you can use the backspace or rubout key to correct typing errors.

The following dialogue shows the :w command in action. Not shown in the following dialogue is the beginning of the editing session, when vi was invoked to edit a file named 'f1'. vi remembers the name of the file being edited, and when you issue a :w command without explicitly specifying a file name, you will write the edit buffer to the original file. Unlike some editors, vi will not keep a copy of your original file under a different name. Once you perform the write operation, your original file will be replaced with the updated copy.

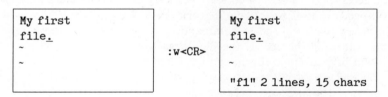

The :w command also allows you to specify a file name when you write the file. This allows you to make copies of your text in several different files.

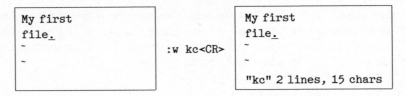

2.8.2 Quitting without Saving

Occasionally while editing you make a mess of the file. Your mistake might be an accidental deletion, an addition that you don't like, or some other change that is too pervasive to repair with the undo command. In these cases it is sometimes better to abandon the file without updating the original copy. The :q! command quits an editing session without saving the work. The exclamation point in the command says to vi, "Yes, I know what I'm doing," so vi won't question your action or print a warning message. Without the exclamation point, vi will warn you if the file has been modified and refuse to quit.

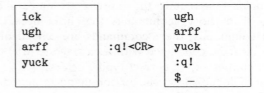

You should be very careful when you quit without saving your work. As a safety precaution you might save your work in a file with a different name, so that you have the original copy and the copy you are abandoning.

2.8.3 Editing a Different File

It isn't necessary to leave vi to start working on a completely different file. All you need to do is to save your work (:w) and then tell vi that you want to edit a new file using the :e command. You must supply the name of the new file following the :e. If the file doesn't exist, it will be created; otherwise it will be read in so that it can be edited.

If you haven't saved your previous work, the :e command will cause vi to print an error message, because the new file will overwrite the file, you have been working on. If you really want to start working on a new file without saving the changes to your previous file, you must use the :e! command to tell vi that you know what you're doing.

2.8.4   Adding One File to Another

The last file manipulation command in this section lets you take one file and insert it into the file that you are working on. Unlike the :e command, which starts a new editing session, the :r takes the text from a UNIX file and merges it into the file that you are editing. The text is added following the current line. One use of the :r is to add boiler plate text to a document.

```
The                                      The
rain                                     rain
in             :r news<CR>               Today
Spain                                    many
                                         "news"
```

2.9   VI'S COMMAND SYNTAX

At first glance, the vi command set appears to be a hopeless jumble. There are 128 separate codes in the ASCII character set, and vi has assigned a specific meaning to 100 of them. Although few people master all 100 commands, many people know most of them. The goal of this section is not to teach any particular commands but rather to help you understand how it is organized.

The overriding goal in the design of the vi commands was to make them mnemonic. With just a few exceptions, each command letter or symbol is reminiscent of the command name: a for append, i for insert, <ESC> to escape from text entry mode. Some of the exceptions have other organizing principles; for example, the hjkl keys have a layout on the keyboard that makes them easy to remember, and the < shift operator looks like what it does.

Another principle is that for most lowercase commands there is an uppercase variant. For example, the w command moves forward one word, but W moves forward one larger word. Another example is that both a and A lead into text entry mode; a adds text after the cursor position, and A adds text at the end of the current line. Once you have learned the lowercase commands, it is easy to remember their uppercase variants.

Many vi commands accept numeric prefixes. For most commands a numeric prefix means repeat the command that many times. For example, if you type 50j you will move the cursor down 50 lines. A few commands interpret the numeric prefix uniquely. For example, the unadorned G command goes to the end of the file, whereas 50G goes to line 50. (It would be pointless to go to the end of the file 50 times!) You should be careful, because not all commands accept a numeric prefix. For example, the intra-line search commands (f and variations) can be repeated with a prefix, but the full search command (/ and variations) cannot be repeated. Even stranger are commands whose ordinary form (e.g., d) can be repeated but whose uppercase variant (D) cannot. Commands that accept a numeric prefix are marked in Appendix I with a bullet.

There are six vi commands called *operators*. These six commands must be followed by a suffix that indicates a region of text to work on. The suffix can be any of the cursor movement commands, text search commands, or the go-to-marked-place command (Sections 1, 2, and 3 of Appendix I). But again you must be careful: the <, >, and ! operators can only take a suffix that indicates a range of lines, whereas the c, y, and d operators can take any suffix. One of the initially confusing aspects of operators is that each operator can be doubled when you want to operate on whole lines. For example, the command dd will delete the current line, cc will change the current line, and yy will yank the current line.

CHAPTER 3

Advanced Vi Editing

Although vi has hundreds of commands, one can get by with just a handful. In Chapter 2, I presented my personal selection of introductory commands, the commands I usually show to someone starting to learn vi. Now in this chapter I am going to present a second handful, a group of commands that will enable you to perform sophisticated text editing with vi. Appendix I summarizes most visual mode commands. Section 3.5 summarizes the most useful vi option settings; a more complete list is in Appendix II.

3.1 ESCAPING TO THE SHELL

Interruptions are a fact of life. The phone rings, and you need to look up a telephone number stored on the system. A co-worker wants to see the latest draft of an important business letter. Or perhaps lunchtime is approaching and you want the computer to display the time.

Of course you could save your vi file, exit from vi, and then attend to the interruption. However, it is usually easier to escape temporarily to a UNIX shell, do what needs to be done, and then resume your vi session where you left off.

There are two ways to escape to the UNIX command interpreter from within vi. The first method is used if you simply want to run a single UNIX command, such as the date command. From the vi visual command mode, enter :! followed by the UNIX command, followed by a carriage return. vi takes the UNIX command and hands it to a shell (command interpreter), the shell executes the command, and then vi continues.

```
┌─────────────┐           ┌─────────────┐           ┌─────────────┐
│ Flying      │           │ Flying      │           │ Roseland.   │
│ Roaches     │           │ Roaches     │           │ :!ls        │
│ Tonight at  │  :!ls     │ Tonight at  │  <CR>     │ ch1  ch1a   │
│ Roseland.   │           │ Roseland.   │           │ ch2  ch3    │
│             │           │ :!ls_       │           │ [Hit <CR>]_ │
└─────────────┘           └─────────────┘           └─────────────┘
```

In the example pictured above, the ls command is executed from within vi. When ls has finished listing the four files in the current directory, vi regains control, prompting the user to strike return to continue. When the carriage return is entered, vi erases the screen, redraws the display of the file being edited, and returns the cursor to the original position.

The second method of escaping to a shell from within vi is used when you are likely to want to execute several commands. From visual mode the command :sh<CR> starts a new shell that can be used as long as you want.

```
┌─────────────┐           ┌─────────────┐           ┌─────────────┐
│ Flying      │           │ Flying      │           │ Roaches     │
│ Roaches     │           │ Roaches     │           │ Tonight at  │
│ Tonight at  │  :sh      │ Tonight at  │  <CR>     │ Roseland    │
│ Roseland    │           │ Roseland    │           │ :sh         │
│             │           │ :sh_        │           │ $ _         │
└─────────────┘           └─────────────┘           └─────────────┘
```

The shell prompt in the right-hand frame indicates that a shell is running, waiting for commands. You can enter as many UNIX shell commands as you want, and then you can resume your original editing session by terminating the shell, either by entering the command exit or by striking ^D at the beginning of a line.

One common mistake in this situation is to attempt to resume the original vi editing session by entering the vi shell command. The problem with this is that you will be starting a fresh vi session, not resuming the original vi session. Because the UNIX system has multi-tasking, you can have multiple vi programs running concurrently. Sometimes you want to let one vi session lay dormant while temporarily using another vi session to do something else, but usually you want to use just one copy of vi. If you become confused about how many copies of vi are running, use the ps command.

3.2 SEARCHING FOR TEXT

vi has several ways to search for text patterns in your file. vi has a single-character search for moving from one place on a line to another, and it has a more sophisticated search command for locating a text pattern anywhere in the file.

The single-character search is a speedy way to maneuver on a line. The command f followed by a character will move the cursor to the next occurrence of that character on the current line. For example fa will move the cursor to the next *a* on the line. The F command will search backward from the cursor position, and the last f or F search can be repeated using the ; command.

Flying Roaches Tonight at Roseland.	ft	Flying Roaches Tonight at Roseland.	;	Flying Roaches Tonight at Roseland.
Flying Roaches Tonight at Roseland	Fg	Flying Roaches Tonight at Roseland	FT	Flying Roaches Tonight at Roseland

The general text search capability of vi is invoked by the / command. Following the / you enter the search target and then a carriage return. vi then moves the cursor forward (down) to the target or beeps to indicate that the target isn't found.

Flying Roaches Tonight at Roseland	/land<CR>	Flying Roaches Tonight at Roseland /land	/Ball<CR>	Roaches Tonight at Roseland Ballroom.

You can direct the search to start from the current location and proceed toward the top of the file by using the ? command. The last search can be repeated by using the n (next-occurrence) command, or it can be repeated in the opposite direction by using the N command.

Roaches Tonight at Roseland Ballroom.	?Ro<CR>	Roaches Tonight at Roseland Ballroom. ?Ro	n	Roaches Tonight at Roseland Ballroom. ?

Notice that the n command performs a reverse search if the previous search was a reverse search. In the dialogue shown above, the N command would have performed a forward search.

If the search target isn't found between the cursor location and the end of the file, vi restarts the search from the top of the file and searches down to the current location. (See the wrapscan setting in Section 3.5 to see how this behavior can be modified.) In long files you can save time by searching in the correct direction, and if there are multiple search targets, it is of course important to search in the correct direction.

Besides the literal searches described above, vi also can perform searches using a pattern-matching language. This lets you find text that meets some criteria. For example, you might search for the word *The* only if it appears at the beginning of a line, or you could search for a word in its capitalized or uncapitalized form, etc. You can avoid this capability by avoiding the characters *, [, ˆ, $, \, and . (period) in your target strings, or you can set the *nomagic* mode (see Section 3.5). Another way to make a special character lose its meaning inside a search target is to precede it with a backslash, and you must use a backslash in front of a literal / in a forward search (and you must use a backslash in front of a literal ? in a reverse search). Table 3.1 summarizes the usage of the magic characters.

3.3   FINE-TUNING YOUR SCREEN DISPLAY

Sometimes you want the current line to appear at a given point on the screen. Perhaps you want the first line of a paragraph to rest on the top line of the screen, or you might want one line in a list to appear in mid-screen so that you can see what comes before and after. vi has the z command to let you position your screen exactly as you wish. The z command requires one of three suffixes that specifies where (on the screen) the current line should be displayed.

z<CR>   move the current line to the top of the screen

z.   move the current line to the middle of the screen

z-   move the current line to the bottom of the screen

Another way to move your window to exactly where you want it is with the ˆE and ˆY commands. The ˆE command moves the window down one line (the text on the screen moves up one line). ˆE is similar to the ˆD command that scrolls down a half screenful, except ˆE moves just one line. The ˆY command is the opposite. It moves the window up one line (the

Table 3.1. vi's Pattern Matching Characters

---

^   A *caret* anchors a search target to the beginning of a line. Thus the pattern ^the will match the letters the at the beginning of a line. The caret is only magic when used as the first character of a target (or when used in a *character set*).

$ A *currency symbol* anchors a search target to the end of a line. Thus the pattern PP$ will match the letters PP only when they occur at the end of a line.

.   A *period* matches any character. Thus the pattern b.d will match bed, bid, bad, etc.

[A *left square bracket* introduces a *character set*. The end of the set is indicated by a right bracket. A character set matches any *one* of the characters in the set. For example, [aeiou] matches any single vowel. A hyphen may separate two characters to indicate that range of characters. For example, [0-9] indicates any one of the numerals. A caret as the first character of a character set means "the character set consists of all characters not explicitly mentioned." Thus the character set [^A-Z] matches anything other than a capital letter.

*   An *asterisk* matches zero or more repetitions of the previous single-character matching expression. The asterisk is often used after a period, to match anything, or after a character set, to match any number of occurrences of that set. Thus the pattern [aeiou][aeiou]* will match any sequence of one or more vowels.

\<   The pair of characters *backslash, less-than* anchors a pattern to the beginning of a word. This pattern is present in vi but not in ed.

\>   The pair of characters *backslash, greater-than* anchors a pattern to the end of a word. This pattern is present in vi but not in ed.

\   A *backslash* is used to escape the next character.

---

text moves down on the screen). The ^Y command is a relative of the ^U command that moves up a half screenful. Of course both the ^E and ^Y commands accept a numeric prefix to direct them to scroll just that many lines.

```
┌──────────────┐              ┌──────────────┐           ┌──────────────┐
│ Roaches      │              │ Ballroom.    │           │ Tonight at   │
│ Tonight at   │              │ Come see     │           │ Roseland     │
│ Roseland     │  ^E^E^E      │ a thriller.  │  2^Y      │ Ballroom.    │
│ Ballroom.    │              │ Wow!         │           │ Come see     │
└──────────────┘              └──────────────┘           └──────────────┘
```

You can move the cursor to the top of the screen with the H (home) command, to the middle line using the M (middle) command, or to the bottom line using the L (last) command. If the cursor is on the bottom line, it's easier to use the H command to move to the top than strike 22 k commands or enter the command 22k.

On some terminals vi would have to redraw a large part of the screen whenever a line was deleted. Fortunately, most newer display terminals are more sophisticated, and vi can insert or delete lines without redrawing from the cursor to the bottom of the screen. On terminals without appropriate commands, vi often places an @ on the left end of a blank line to indicate that the display is not quite up to date, especially when it is operating at speeds of 1200 baud or less. The @ isn't part of the file; it merely means that particular line of the screen should be disregarded. At some point vi may close up the gap, but you can force a screen update by entering the ^R command. vi lets you choose when you want the screen update, so that your typing isn't disrupted by massive screen redraws. If your screen begins to appear sloppy because of several @ lines, use the ^R command. (vi also places an @ in the left margin when a line that is longer than the screen width would be partially displayed at the bottom of the screen. Such lines aren't cleared up by the ^R command.)

```
┌──────────────┐              ┌──────────────┐           ┌──────────────┐
│ The          │              │ The          │           │ The          │
│ oft          │              │ @            │           │ Jones        │
│ belittled    │  2dd         │ @            │  ^R       │ antibody     │
│ Jones        │              │ Jones        │           │ has proven   │
└──────────────┘              └──────────────┘           └──────────────┘
```

Occasionally your editing screen is disrupted without vi's knowledge. For example, you might receive a broadcast message, or transmission line (phone line) problems might cause a display irregularity. In any case, you can tell vi to completely redraw the screen by entering the ^L command. The ^L command is a more powerful but slightly slower screen update command than ^R.

3.4 MORE WAYS TO MODIFY TEXT

In Chapter 2, I presented the basic commands for appending and inserting text (the a and i commands) and for opening lines (the o and O commands).

vi has several similar commands that are very useful for more specialized situations.

You often need to change one letter to another. One approach is to use the x command to delete the incorrect character, use the i command to go into insert mode, enter the replacement character, and then hit <ESC> to get out of insert mode. That process can be simplified using the r (replace) command. Following the r you must type the replacement character. The easiest way to split a long line in two is to move the cursor to a space and then enter the command r<CR> to replace the space with a line separator.

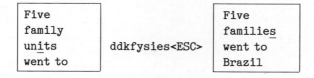

The first command shown above moves the cursor to the c (the fc command) and then replaces the c with a t (the rt command). The second command moves the cursor to the blank on the second line (the jbh command) and then replaces that blank with a line separator (the r<CR> command).

A slightly more powerful command is the s command. The s command replaces the text under the cursor with whatever is typed in. An <ESC> terminates the input. The s command is often used to form the plural of a word or to perform other simple chores in which one letter is replaced by a few letters.

```
┌─────────┐                    ┌─────────┐
│ Five    │                    │ Five    │
│ family  │                    │ families│
│ units   │  ddkfysies<ESC>    │ went to │
│ went to │                    │ Brazil  │
└─────────┘                    └─────────┘
```

In the dialogue shown above, the line containing the word *units* is deleted (the dd command), the cursor is moved up to the *y* on the previous line (the kfy command), and then the text *ies* is substituted for the *y* (the sies<ESC> command).

An even more powerful change command is the c command. The c command, like the delete command, requires a suffix that indicates how much text should be changed. For example, the command cw will change a word, cb will change the preceding word, c$ will change to the end of the line, c^ will change to the beginning of the line, and cc will change the entire line. Numeric prefixes can make the change affect that many text objects. I use cw and cc most often. After the change command is initiated, you type in replacement text, and then you hit the <ESC> key to terminate the change.

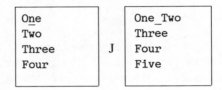

In the dialogue shown above, the cursor is moved to the beginning of the word *units* (the b-command), and then the word is changed to *members* (the cwmembers<ESC>). (In this particular situation the change command could have been cc, because the entire line is changed.)

Lines can be joined using the J command. Put the cursor on a line, and then strike J. The following line will be glued onto the first, and the cursor will be placed between the two parts.

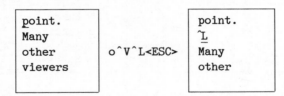

If you want to delete the (vi-inserted) space, you can immediately strike the x command. Any trailing white space on the top line, or leading white space on the bottom line, will be lost.

When you are in text entry mode, a control character can be entered into the document using the ^V prefix. For example, you can enter a Form-Feed into a document by striking ^V^L when you are in insert mode.

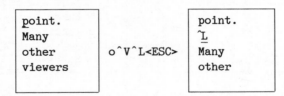

The ^V prefix is also useful when you are setting up macros or abbreviations (see Chapter 4). Note that ^V isn't a command. Striking ^V while in command mode has no effect. It is only used in text insert mode.

3.5 SELECTING YOUR PREFERENCES

vi has a limited ability to adapt to your needs and preferences. Many of its features are controlled by internal options that can be enabled and disabled using the set command. You can see a list of the settings that differ from the defaults by entering the command :set<CR>, or you can see the complete list of settings by entering the command :set all<CR>. Also note that many of the setting names have abbreviations.

Many of vi's settings are either on or off. For those settings the mode is enabled with the command :set modename<CR>, or unset by prefixing a no to the mode name—:set nomodename<CR>. The other options have values that are set using the command

   :set modename=modeval<CR>

The following list explains some of the more common options. You should consult Appendix II for more information about all vi options.

autoindent is often used for editing programs and other work that often contains leading white space. When autoindent is set, each newly appended line has the same amount of white space as the preceding line. You can add additional white space to the beginning of a line, thus causing all following lines to be similarly indented. Striking ^D at the beginning of a line will cause the indentation level to retreat to the left. The special input character sequence ^^D (a caret followed by a control D) will reset the indent to zero for a single line; the special input sequence 0^D will reset the indent to zero. (The default is noautoindent, and the abbreviation is ai.)

ignorecase causes vi to ignore case distinctions in searches and substitutions. (The default is noignorecase, and the abbreviation is ic.)

list causes vi to display tabs and end-of-line markers. list mode is useful in cases where the distinction between a tab and an equivalent number of spaces is important, and it is one of the easiest ways to discover white space dangling at the end of lines. (The default is nolist, and the abbreviation is li.)

magic mode enables the vi regular expression characters. When nomagic mode is turned on, only ^ and $ are magic. nomagic mode is often more convenient than using a backslash to escape the special characters. (The default is magic.)

number mode makes vi display the line number at the beginning of each line. (The default is nonumber, and the abbreviation is nu.)

shell contains the name of the shell to use for the :! and :sh commands. The value of this option is taken, if possible, from the shell environment variable $SHELL when vi starts to run. Setting shell to '/bin/csh' will make the c shell your default shell. (The abbreviation is sh.)

shiftwidth specifies the width of vi's software tab stop. This value is used by the shift commands and when autoindent mode is on. (The default is 8, and the abbreviation is sw.)

term is the name of the terminal. This setting may only be changed from ex line editing mode. The value of the term option is taken, if possible, from the $TERM shell environment variable when vi starts to execute. The following commands change to line editing mode, set term for a C.Itoh 500 terminal, and then change back to visual editing:

```
Q
:set term=cit500<CR>
:vi<CR>
```

wrapscan mode affects vi's text search strategy. Setting wrapscan forces vi to search the entire file before giving up. When nowrapscan mode is set, searches proceed from the current location to the end (or beginning) of the file and then stop. (The default is wrapscan, and the abbreviation is ws.)

wrapmargin sets the boundary at which vi automatically inserts a new line when you are entering text. When you get within wrapmargin characters of the right screen column during a text insertion, vi will attempt to break your line at a space character and continue on the next line. This mode is very useful when you are entering ordinary text, because you don't need to strike the return key at the end of every line. Some people find the wrapmargin-induced cursor movement disconcerting. Another hazard is that the new lines inserted by wrapmargin mode occasionally make it hard to use the delete key to erase the last few input characters (because the erase can't back up to the previous line). You can disable wrapmargin by setting it to zero. When enabled, wrapmargin is often set to 8 so that vi will wrap your lines when you get to about eight characters from the right edge of the screen. (The default is 0, and the abbreviation is wm.) The following command sets the wrapmargin to 8:

```
:set wm=8<CR>
```

Although any of these option settings (except for term, which can only be set outside of visual mode) can be changed while in visual mode, you might want to place your customary options into a '.exrc' start-up file so that they will be engaged each time you use the editor. Each time vi starts to execute, it reads and executes the commands stored in the '.exrc' file. The '.exrc' file can be in your home directory, your current directory, or both. Alternatively you can place a :set command in the shell environment variable $EXINIT. Most people set environment variables in their login session startup file, either '.profile' for Bourne shell users or '.login' for c-shell users.

3.6   MARKING TEXT

vi has numerous ways to identify lines of text. As in ed, you can identify a
line with a text pattern or with line numbers. Line numbers are easy to use
if you set the number option (see Section 3.5). You can always find out
what line you are on using the ^G command.

```
┌────────────────┐            ┌────────────────┐
│ cheese         │            │ cheese         │
│ fruit          │            │ fruit          │
│ grapes         │     ^G     │ grapes         │
│ flowers        │            │ flowers        │
│                │            │ line 6 of 12   │
└────────────────┘            └────────────────┘
```

Notice in this example that the top line visible on the screen is actually the
fifth line of the document.

Another method for identifying lines is the m (mark) command. vi can
remember up to 26 marked lines, each identified by one of the letters a
through z. For example, you can identify the current line with the label a
using the ma command. There is no visible feedback when you enter the
mark command.

Marks can make it easy to move from one place in the file to another, or
they can mark regions of text to be deleted or moved. When a mark is
placed, the particular marked *line* can be referenced using the ´ command (a
´ is a single quote), or the particular marked *character location* can be referenced using the ` command (a ` is a reverse single quote, which is sometimes
called an accent *grave*). Both the single quote and the reverse single quote
must be followed with a letter indicating the given mark. By itself, the
command ´a will move to the line marked as a.

```
┌────────────────┐            ┌────────────────┐            ┌────────────────┐
│ flowers        │            │ flowers        │            │ flowers        │
│ fertile        │            │ fertile        │            │ fertile        │
│ fragrant       │    majj    │ fragrant       │     ´a     │ fragrant       │
│ folly          │            │ folly          │            │ folly          │
└────────────────┘            └────────────────┘            └────────────────┘
```

The ´ command shown above interprets the given location as a *line* location
and returns to the beginning of that line. A similar feature, the ` com-
mand, interprets the given location as a *character* position, and moves to
that position.

```
flowers                    flowers                   flowers
fertile                    fertile                   fertile
fragrant    majj           fragrant      `a          fragrant
folly                      folly                     folly
```

Marks can be used with the d (delete) command to delete regions of text. In Chapter 2, I mentioned some of the variants of the d command, including d$, dw, and d^. In all of these commands the d is followed by an indicator of the region of text to be deleted. This feature also works with the ´ indicator; thus d´a will delete from the current line to the line marked a (in either direction), inclusive. The command d`a will delete from the current cursor position to the character position marked a, inclusive.

```
flowers                    flowers                   flowers
fertile                    fertile                   file
fragrant    mzlll          fragrant      d`z         fragrant
folly                      folly                     folly
```

The marks in a file last only for your current editing session. When you start a new session, all the marks are unset.

3.7 MOVING BLOCKS OF TEXT

Editing text with a computer is more efficient than working with a typewriter, because the revisions are easier. Some revisions are local, fixing the spelling of a word, revising a sentence, or adding or deleting snippets of text. However, the greatest benefit of text processing is making those much harder global changes, moving paragraphs from one place to another or moving text from one file to another.

vi's text movement capability works with several internal *buffers*. To move text from one place in a file to another (or even from one file to another; see Section 3.8), you yank the text into a buffer, move to the destination, and then pull the text out of the buffer and put it back in the text. You can't see what's in a vi buffer without pulling the text out, but since vi has an undo command, you can always put the contents of a buffer into your file, look at it, and then undo your modification. The best rule for working with buffers is "keep it simple." Although it is possible to load up a dozen buffers and keep track mentally (or on paper) of what's in each, it is usually better to use just one or two buffers at a time.

vi contains three sets of buffers, the *unnamed* buffer (it doesn't have a nicer name), 10 numbered buffers that contain the 10 most recent largish deletions, and 26 buffers identified by a through z.

The easiest way to move a chunk of text from one place in a file to another is to use the unnamed buffer. There are two ways to put something into the unnamed buffer: you can perform a deletion, or you can use the yank command. If you want to move text from one place to another, the easiest way is to delete it from one place, move to the destination, and then put the text back. However, you must be careful. Once you make a deletion, the text is in the unnamed buffer, but it vanishes from the unnamed buffer when you make another deletion. Thus a common mistake is to delete something you want to recover, then delete something trivial, thereby making it harder (but usually not impossible) to retrieve the original text.

Any of the text deletion commands, x, dw, d$, dd, etc., will place the deleted text into the unnamed buffer. The text in the unnamed buffer can be placed back into the text using the p command, which places the buffer text after the cursor, or using the P command to place the text before the cursor. When the deletion is a sequence of characters, the text is pulled back relative to the current cursor location in the file. When the deletion is of a group of lines, the text is pulled back relative to the current line, and the position of the cursor within the line doesn't matter. Both of these situations are shown in the following two examples.

Bruce
McGurk is
  a
  soda
	dwjh	Bruce
		McGurk
		  a
		  soda
			P	Bruce
				McGurk
				is a
				soda	

Bruce McGurk is a soda	ddj	Bruce is a soda jerk!	p	Bruce is a soda McGurk	

In the first example, a word is deleted on one line (dw) and then put back (P) on the following line. Since the original deletion wasn't a full line (or group of lines), the put-back text was inserted in front of the cursor. In the second example above, the deleted line (dd) is put back (p) following the current line, and the position of the cursor within that line is irrelevant.

Yanking text into the unnamed buffer is somewhat safer than deleting the text, because whatever is in the unnamed buffer (right or wrong) remains in the text. The y (yank) command is similar to the d (delete) command, in that following the y there must be an indication of how much text to yank. The suffixes w, $, ^, ′a, ‵b, and y mean word, to end of line, to beginning of line, to the line marked a, to the character position marked b, and full line, respectively.

Bruce		Bruce		McGurk
McGurk		McGurk		is a
is a	yyjj	is a	p	soda
soda		soda		McGurk

Notice that in this example the cursor must be moved down one more line (jj) than in the previous example to get to the line containing *soda*, because the line *McGurk* is yanked (yy), not deleted. With the cursor on the bottom line of the screen, putting the *McGurk* line into the text (p) causes the screen to scroll up.

3.8   MOVING TEXT FROM ONE FILE TO ANOTHER

There are two basic methods for moving regions of text from one file to another. The overall procedure is the same for both methods: the first file is edited with vi, the text is saved somewhere, the second file is edited, and then the saved text is inserted. The difference between the two methods is where the text is saved; in the first method shown below, the text is saved in a named buffer, whereas in the second it is saved in an intermediate file.

Since the last section talked about buffers, let's start with that technique. Once you understand moving text with the unnamed buffer, it's easy to extend your understanding to moving text from one file to another. First we need to talk about named buffers. Whenever a delete or yank command is prefixed with a " command, the indicated text is deleted or yanked into the named buffer. Thus the command "fdw will delete a word (dw) into the f buffer (the "f part). vi has 26 named buffers, but use of more than two or three at once is error-prone. Similarly, whenever the put command is prefixed with the " command, the extracted text will come from the named buffer. Thus, the command "fp will put the contents of the f buffer into the text.

Whenever you start to edit a new file, vi clears the unnamed buffer. Thus, it cannot be used to transfer text from one file to another. However, the named buffers aren't touched when you switch from one file to another, so they are ideal for moving text from one file to another. You should be careful here, because the named buffers are only maintained during your current session with vi. The named buffers are preserved when you switch from editing one file to another during one session, but their contents are lost if you exit from vi and then restart vi to start another editing session.

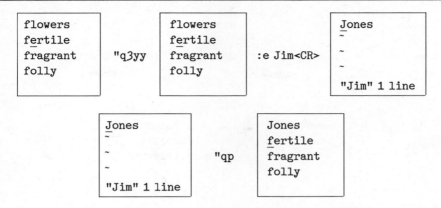

All five panels shown above form a complete sequence. The first command, "q3yy, tells vi to yank three lines (3yy) into the buffer named q ("q). The second command, :e Jim<CR>, tells vi to switch to the file named 'Jim'. As you can see from the screen's status line, the file 'Jim' has just one line. In the final command, "qp, the q buffer is placed into 'Jim'.

The second method for moving text from one file to another uses an intermediate file to contain the text. If you are familiar with ed, this technique will seem natural, because ed uses the same method for moving text. If you don't feel confident of your ability with buffers, use this method.

The vi write command will write the entire work space to a file by default, but by supplying line addresses you can write a portion of the work space to a file. The simplest line addresses are line numbers, which can be obtained by the ^G command (to learn the number of the current line) or by turning on the line numbers option (see the number setting in Section 3.5). In either case, a command of the form :n1,n2w filename<CR> will write lines n1 through n2 to the named file. Once the text to be transferred has been copied to an intermediate file, you can edit the second document file and use the read file command (see Section 2.8.4) to load in the intermediate file.

The following panels show how an intermediate file can be used to transfer text from one file to another. The write command shown assumes that the first line on the screen is actually the first line of the file. In practice you will have to determine line numbers as discussed above.

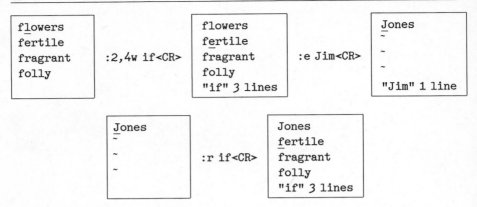

The first command in these five panels, :2,4w if<CR>, tells vi to write lines 2 through 4 to an intermediate file named 'if'. The message on the screen's status line confirms the write and mentions the fact that three lines were written. In the next command, :e Jim<CR>, the file named 'Jim' is edited. The final command, :r if<CR>, uses the vi read command to read in the intermediate file. The intermediate file will remain in your directory until it is removed, so you should plan to perform frequent housecleaning if you commonly use intermediate files to transfer text from one document to another.

vi will complain if you attempt to use the :w command to overwrite an existing file. If you really want to overwrite an existing file, use the :w! variant to tell vi that you know what you are doing and that you really want to overwrite the file.

3.9   LINE-EDITING COMMANDS

vi has multiple personalities—an asset or a fault, depending on your preference. The easiest vi personality to use is visual mode, and most of the commands discussed in this chapter and in Chapter 2 are visual mode commands. In addition, vi has a line-editing command set similar to the command set of ed, though it is somewhat more powerful. The line-editing command set is harder to learn than the visual command set, but it is much more powerful.

As shown in many of the examples in this chapter (and in Chapter 2), you can temporarily dip into the line-editing command set by prefixing a line-editing command with a : (colon). When you enter such a command, the cursor is immediately moved down to the bottom line of the screen (the status/command line), where you enter the remainder of the command. When you dip into the line-editing command set, you are immediately returned to visual mode when the command is completed.

If you are going to perform a sequence of line-editing commands, you can use the Q command to move from visual mode to line-editing mode. Once you have moved from visual mode to line-editing mode, the screen will scroll upward as lines are displayed on the screen, much as if you were using ed. One difference is that vi customarily prompts with a : in line-editing mode, whereas ed customarily doesn't print a prompt when it is waiting for a command. While in line-editing mode in vi, you can prefix your line-editing commands with a : as if you were in visual mode. The redundant : is allowed in line-editing mode because old habits die hard. When you are through entering line-editing commands, the command vi<CR> will return you to visual editing mode.

Other than the file-reading and writing commands, the line-editing commands aren't discussed extensively in this book. There are several good references for learning the powerful ex line-editing commands. A gentle introduction is the material on ed in my book *The Unix Operating System*. The ex commands are just an extension of ed, so learning ed will teach you most of ex. The ultimate reference for ex is *Ex Reference Manual* by William Joy with revisions by Mark Horton.

3.10   OPEN LINE EDITING

Besides the ability to work on a full screen, vi can perform most of its commands on a single line. This feature is useful on primitive terminals that don't have cursor addressing capability, and it can even be used reasonably on a printer terminal. If you start vi without first setting the TERM environment variable, it will complain that it doesn't know what terminal you are using and proceed to enter line-editing command mode. You won't be able to enter visual mode until you tell vi what kind of terminal you are using, but you can enter open line-editing mode immediately, because vi doesn't need to know anything about your terminal to use open line mode.

Open line editing can be invoked from line-editing mode by entering the command open<CR>. In open line mode, your cursor will always be on the bottom line of the screen (or on the only line of the printer). All of the vi visual commands will work, although only one line at a time will be visible. For example, if you enter the j command to move down one line, the screen will scroll up to make room, and then the next line will be displayed. When you enter the k command, the screen will also scroll up, and the preceding line will be displayed. Thus, the commands work, but the scene on the screen is a record of your previous line selections, not a window into the work space.

While in open line mode, you can use the : prefix to escape temporarily to line-editing mode. You can return to simple line-editing mode from open line mode using the Q command.

Table 3.2. More vi Commands

Shell Escapes

:!cmd<CR>	Escape to perform one command.
:sh<CR>	Start a subshell. You may enter commands, then exit from the subshell to return to vi.

Text Searches

fc	Intraline search forward for char c.
Fc	Intraline search reverse for char c.
;	Repeat last intraline search.
/pat<CR>	Forward search for pattern pat.
?pat<CR>	Reverse search for pattern pat.
n	Repeat last search.
N	Repeat last search in opposite direction.

Window Movement

z<CR>	Current line to top of screen.
z.	Current line to middle of screen.
z-	Current line to bottom of screen.
^Y	Scroll down one line.
^E	Scroll up one line.
H	Move cursor to top line of screen.
M	Move cursor to middle line of screen.
L	Move cursor to bottom line of screen.

Text Entry

r	Replace character under cursor.
s	Substitute the following text entry for character under cursor. <ESC> terminates text entry mode.
c	Change the given object. Suffixes w, b, c, $, and ^ have the usual meanings. <ESC> terminates text entry mode.

Marked Text

ma	Mark text with mark named a.
´a	Go to line marked a.
`a	Go to character position marked a.
^G	Report current line number.

Buffers

y	Yank text into buffer. (*Delete* also saves text in a buffer.)
p	Pull back text from buffer and place it after current line or character position.
P	Pull back text from buffer and place it before current line or character position.
"a	A prefix to yank, delete, or put to indicate that buffer named a should be used.

CHAPTER 4

vi Word Processing

The usual UNIX word processor is a text editor, often vi, combined with the nroff/troff document-formatting tools, and often combined with specialized preprocessors. Powerful indeed, often too powerful for routine letter writing or creating simple documents. For simple tasks, there are three approaches: use the standard tools (the baseball bat replacement for a fly swatter), use a commercially available word processor, or follow the advice given here to use vi as a passable word processor.

Although vi was conceived as a text editor, primarily for programmers, its unusual flexibility allows it to function as a simple word processor. If you need a general-purpose word processor for everyday use, you should probably buy one. Several are available. However, for occasional use, vi is a serviceable word processor.

The first two parts of this chapter introduce vi features that are useful when using vi as a word processor, and the closing sections show how it's done. If you simply want to know about vi macros and vi buffer filtering, read the first two sections. If you primarily intend to use the full UNIX text-formatting system, you can safely skip the last two sections of this chapter.

4.1   VI MACROS

A *macro* is one thing (usually small) that is expanded into something else (usually large). vi macros let you expand one or two keystrokes into a more complicated chain of keystrokes. vi has four flavors of macros that will be discussed below.

Buffer Macros allow you to place a series of vi commands into one of vi's 26 named buffers. To create a buffer macro, you type the desired vi command into your document, and then you delete that text into a named buffer. The command @*b* will execute the macro stored in buffer *b*, where *b* is any of the letters of the alphabet. Here is an example.

As a typical task, consider the job of entering the troff command to italicize a given word. As will be discussed in Section 5.3, any word in a troff document can be presented in italics (underline in nroff) by preceding it with \f2 and following it with \fP. If you have a document that needs to have key words italicized, it will save time to automate the process. But first let's see how the task would be done manually. First you would move the cursor to the beginning of the word, then you would use the i command to enter insert mode, then you would type \f2, then you would escape from insert mode, then you would move to the end of the word, and then you would go into append mode to add the text \fP, and finally you would return to command mode. A simple series of commands for a vi expert, but a grand total of 11 keystrokes.

To create an italicizing macro in vi, you open up a blank line in your input file and type the following 13 characters:

i \ f 2 ^V <ESC> E a \ f P ^V <ESC>

(A ^V stands for control V, and <ESC> is the escape key.) The i enters insert mode, the \f2 is the inserted text, the ^V allows a literal escape to be entered into the buffer, the escape terminates insert mode, the E moves to the end of the word, the a\fP appends the given text to the end of the word, and the ^V and escape terminate the append mode.

On your screen it will look like this when it is completely typed, because vi displays the escape code on screen as ^[.

i\f2^[Ea\fP^[

To put that text into a named buffer, you move the cursor to the beginning of the line and enter the vi command

"iD

which deletes the entire line (without the trailing linefeed) into the buffer named i. Then to insert italics codes around a word, you move the cursor to the word's beginning and type the command @i. The troff italics codes should instantly bracket the given word.

Maps allow you to assign a given command string to a given key on the keyboard. You enter a map using the :map *lhs rhs*<CR> command, or you can see a complete list of the current maps by entering the command :map<CR>. The *lhs* must be a single keystroke, the character sequence produced by a function key, or the notation #*n* to mean function key *n* (0-9). Remember that ^V can be used to quote the next character, so that control characters, escapes, carriage returns, and the like can appear in the *rhs*. (Note that you can put a ^V itself into the *rhs* by typing it twice. This lets you quote spaces or tabs.)

On a model VT100 terminal, function key 1 (labeled PF1) sends the three-character sequence <ESC>OP. You can assign it the italicizing macro described above by typing one of the three following **vi** commands:

```
:map #1 i\f2^V<ESC>Ea\fP^V<ESC><CR>
:map ^V<ESC>OP i\f2^V<ESC>Ea\fP^V<ESC><CR>
:map <PF1> i\f2^V<ESC>Ea\fP^V<ESC><CR>
```

The *lhs* of the third command was formed by striking the <PF1> key, whereas the *lhs* of the second was formed by typing in the exact character code manually.

On your screen these three commands will look like the following:

```
:map #1 i\f2^[Ea\fP^[
:map ^[OP i\f2^V<ESC>Ea\fP^[
:map ^[OP i\f2^V<ESC>Ea\fP^[
```

You can use any of the above commands; they all produce the same result. In a '.exrc' vi start-up file, the *#n* notation is preferred because it will work on any terminal's function keys. During an editing session, simply hitting the given function key is probably the simplest. You can assign a macro to any key, including the common **vi** command keys.

If your terminal doesn't have function keys, you have two choices: you can assign a macro to an ordinary key (including control keys), or you can assign a macro to a function key using the *#n* notation and then activate that macro by entering the two-character sequence *#n*. (On terminals with function keys, the *#n* notation can be used to enter a map, but it can't be used to activate a map.)

Given any one of the map definitions shown above, you can enter the **troff** codes to italicize a word by moving the cursor to the beginning of the word and then hitting the first function key.

A map can be disabled with the :unmap command.

Maps are also possible during insert mode, although the command used is map! instead of map. An ordinary map is not active while you are in text insert mode, and a text insert mode map isn't active while you are in visual command mode, although it is active while in line-oriented command mode. Like ordinary maps, insert mode maps should be assigned to a single keystroke or to a function key.

Let's set up two insert mode maps to make it easier to enter text containing **troff** italicizing commands. The plan will be to hit a function key to enter the start-italics command, then type in the word or phrase to be italicized, and then hit another function key to enter the code that cancels italics. Here are the two **vi** commands you would type to set up the two insert mode maps:

```
:map!  #1  \f2<CR>
:map!  #2  \fP<CR>
```

Pressing the given function keys while in insert mode will make the replacement text appear in your document.

Abbreviations are vi's fourth type of macro. An abbreviation is a word that, when it is recognized during insert mode, is replaced by some other character sequence. For example, you could make "ux" an abbreviation for "The Unix(tm) Operating System" using the following command:

```
:ab ux The Unix(tm) Operating System<CR>
```

When ux is typed as a word, it is replaced by the full phrase. However, typing a word such as flux will not trigger the replacement, and if the word ux already exists in the document, it won't be replaced. You can cancel an abbreviation using the :una command.

You must avoid using the abbreviation in the replacement text. For example, the following command is a disaster—whenever you type "Unix," the system will try repeatedly to substitute the whole phrase each time it encounters the word "Unix" inside the phrase.

```
:ab Unix The Unix Operating System<CR>
```

Avoid self-referential abbreviations.

4.2   FILTERING THE BUFFER

vi allows you to filter a portion of the edit buffer. Text from the edit buffer is routed into a UNIX pipeline, it is transformed by the pipeline, and then the output of the pipeline replaces the original text. The operation of a vi filter is shown schematically in Figure 4.1.

Filters have numerous applications. Programmers sometimes filter their work through cb, a C language formatting program. You can enter commands using vi and then send them to a command processor such as the shell or the bc arithmetic program. If you want to include the output of a UNIX command in a document, you can filter a single line of the buffer into that command. But for me the most common reason for filtering parts of the vi buffer is to send a paragraph through a simple paragraph formatter. More on that in the next section.

There are two approaches to filtering the vi edit buffer: you can use commands in visual command mode, or you can use ordinary line-editing commands. In either case the exclamation point is the command character. In visual command mode you enter ! followed by a suffix that selects a region of text. The suffixes must select whole lines; for example, suffixes such as w (word) are not accepted (see Section 2.7). The usual visual mode filter

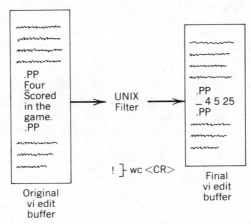

Figure 4.1. A paragraph being filtered by the wc (word count) program.

commands are !! to send one line into the pipeline, !} to send the remainder of the paragraph into the pipeline, and !]] to send the remainder of the section into the pipeline. Any of these may be preceded by a number meaning send that many items. In line-editing mode you enter the command

```
:n1,n2 ! command
```

Lines *n1* through *n2* will be sent to the pipeline, and its output will then replace those lines.

For example, you might suspect that one of the words on the current input line is misspelled. In visual mode you can enter the command !!spell<CR>. The output of the spell program, a list of possibly misspelled words (see Section 12.1), will replace the current line. Carefully examine the output for misspellings, then enter the command u to undo the buffer change, and then fix any incorrectly spelled words. This style of interaction with vi is more dangerous than any presented so far, because you don't really want to discard your original text and replace it with a list of incorrectly spelled words. Timely use of the undo command is essential; don't be too adventurous until you are confident of your abilities.

The same technique can be used to spelling-check an entire paragraph or an entire document. Occasionally you might want to pipe all (or part) of a document to wc for a word count, etc.

You can also use vi buffer filters with commands that don't read the standard input. For example, you might want to include today's date in a document. Open up a blank line, type the vi command !!date<CR>, and the date will appear on the given line. This technique is often used with ls, who, etc. to include their output in a file.

4.3   VI PARAGRAPH FORMATTING

Now that you understand vi macros and filters, you are ready to learn to use vi as a simple word processor. Our first concern is paragraph formatting. While you are entering text, it is relatively easy to keep a paragraph formatted (with a ragged right margin) by setting vi's wm (wrap margin) parameter. If you want a line length of about 72 characters, set the wrap margin to 8 on an 80 character-wide display. You can set the wrap margin by entering the :set wm=8<CR> command. When your entry text oversteps the 72 character boundary, vi will choose a break point and move everything past that point down to the next line.

Managing additions and deletions to paragraphs is trickier. If you insert a word or phrase on the left side of a line, its right-hand end will push too far to the right. Of course you can manually adjust the line breaks, but that doesn't qualify for word processing. A better way is to use a vi filter to reformat an edited paragraph. There are two options, depending on whether you are using a System V or Berkeley UNIX system.

On Berkeley systems there is a simple text-formatting program called fmt. If you send it a chunk of text, it will rearrange the lines so that they are all about the same length. For example, the vi command !}fmt<CR> will format from the current line in the paragraph to the end of the paragraph. fmt accepts numeric arguments to set the right margin. For example, the command !}fmt -50<CR> will format a paragraph with a line width of 50 characters. The first line of your paragraph should not be indented, or fmt will also indent the second line. If you want an indented first line you should start with a flush-left first line, then run fmt, and then indent the first line a few characters by hand. Another approach is to run fmt only on lines 2 through the end of your paragraph.

On System V there isn't a simple text-formatting program, so you must use nroff to format your paragraphs. The paragraph macro package shown in Figure 4.2 contains the necessary commands. Enter the text of Figure 4.2 into a file, and then have your system manager install the macros

```
.pl 1
.na
.if !\nW .nr W 66
.ll \nWm
.c2 '^E'
.cc '^E'
```

Figure 4.2.. This simple macro package tells nroff how to format a paragraph. The Ctrl-E characters in the last two lines can be entered using vi by striking Ctrl-V and then striking Ctrl-E. These commands should be placed in the '/usr/lib/tmac/tmac.p' file.

```
.pl 1
.if !\nW .nr W 66
.ll \nWm
.ad c
.c2 '^E'
.cc '^E'
```

Figure 4.3.. This simple macro package tells nroff how to center a line. Entering the Ctrl-E characters in the last two lines is explained in the legend to Figure 4.2. These commands should be placed in the '/usr/lib/tmac/tmac.pc' file.

in the '/usr/lib/tmac' directory using the name 'tmac.p'. Once the paragraph macros have been properly installed on your system, they can be accessed using the -mp option of nroff. You can format a paragraph by moving the cursor to its first line and then entering the !}nroff -mp<CR> command. nroff is a slower paragraph formatter than Berkeley's fmt program, but it works adequately.

You can tune the paragraph macros to suit your preferences. If you don't want hyphenation, insert the command .nh after the .ll command. If you would prefer a justified right margin to the ragged right, delete the .na command. Provisions have also been made for a variable line width. You can set the W number register on the nroff command line to control line width. For example, to format a paragraph with lines 50 characters wide, you would enter the !}nroff -rW50 -mp<CR> command.

Centered lines are often useful. A macro package for centered lines is shown in Figure 4.3. Place the centered-lines macros in a file named 'tmac.pc' in the '/usr/lib/tmac' directory. To center a line, you enter the !!nroff -mpc<CR> command. This technique applies to Berkeley UNIX system as well, because Berkeley's fmt program doesn't have centering capability.

The commands given above to format paragraphs using vi filters are too onerous to type by hand very often. It is much better to set up macros to do the work. You should experiment to determine the settings you like and then use vi macros to save keystrokes. Ideally, the macros should be in a '.exrc' start-up script so you don't need to re-enter them each time. Here is what my '.exrc' script looks like for System V:

```
$ cat .exrc
:set wm=8
:map #1 !}nroff -mp^M
:map #2 !}nroff -rW80 -mp^M
:map #3 !!nroff -mpc^M
:map #4 !!nroff -rW80 -mpc^M
$ _
```

On a system that has the fmt command, you should use it instead of nroff, because it is considerably faster. On a system with fmt, the '.exrc' file would be

```
$ cat .exrc
:set wm=8
:map #1 !}fmt^M
:map #2 !}fmt -80^M
:map #3 !!nroff -mpc^M
:map #4 !!nroff -rW80 -mpc^M
$ _
```

In either case, the first function key is set to format a paragraph with a normal (66 default) character width, the second will format a wide paragraph, the third will center a line, and the fourth will center a line on a wide page.

There are several caveats for using these functions. Although you can format several paragraphs at once (by entering a number before the command), you can only center one line at a time. Also, paragraphs must be single-spaced, and there must be at least one blank line between paragraphs. This system works best with flush-left paragraphs, although you can indent the first line by hand. Another shortcoming is that no provisions have been made for underlining, half-line motions, etc. On typical systems it takes about 5 seconds to invoke nroff for simple tasks such as formatting a paragraph. These techniques may be too slow to be useful on a very slow (overloaded) system.

4.4   PAGE FORMATTING

Once you have a document with formatted paragraphs, the next chore is to add page breaks. For a small document, subject to only minor revisions, there is little disadvantage to adding page breaks by hand. However, for larger documents you need a real formatting program, because manually added page breaks will be a major nuisance.

With a visually oriented editor, such as vi, it is easy to manually set page breaks because you can "proof" about a third of a page on a standard 24 line terminal. If your document is more than about 60 lines long, you need to add a page break. Enter the vi command 66G, which means move to line 66. Choose a page break point about five to eight lines above your cursor, move to that line, and then insert about 10 to 15 blank lines. Once again move to line 66. Now you should see white space (the page break) above and below the cursor. If you want a page header or footer, place it about three lines below (above) the cursor.

For documents longer than about 125 lines, you will have to repeat the process explained above in the vicinity of line 132, the second page boundary. The page boundary for the third page is line 198, and I'm not going to mention any further page boundaries, because you need a real text-formatting system for documents longer than four pages.

If you add text to the document, you may need to adjust the page breaks. One or two sessions adjusting page breaks manually will make a true believer out of many die-hard nroff avoiders.

CHAPTER 5

Nroff and Troff

nroff and troff are programs that *format* a text file. nroff is used when files are printed on ordinary typewriterlike printers; troff is used when documents are printed on typesetters, or on printers that have most of the features of true typesetters. Formatting involves numerous alterations to the file that make it easier to read. Perhaps the most basic chore of formatting is text filling. Text is collected word by word until there is enough to fill a line. Similarly, lines are collected to form paragraphs, and paragraphs are arranged to form pages. Pages usually acquire headers and footers, and in many documents there are typeface changes to provide added emphasis.

Although nroff and troff (referred to collectively as troff unless noted otherwise) are heavily used UNIX facilities, most users don't really need to know very much about them. In truth there is a great deal to know, but most UNIX text processing users are better off skipping the advanced information. The first key to using the UNIX text processing system is knowing that you should use a macro package. Yes, nroff or troff is used, but you don't need to know C to use UNIX utility programs, and you don't need to know COBOL to manage your bank account. Comparatively few users need to master the troff command set. Instead you should concentrate on one of the two major macro packages, -ms (Chapter 6) or -mm (Chapter 7). The overview of troff presented in this chapter is a useful introduction to either -ms or -mm. troff command line options are summarized in Appendix III, and the troff codes for specifying special characters are listed in Appendix IV.

The original troff was designed to control the Graphic Systems typesetter. Consequently it had several limitations that reflected the limits of that particular typesetter. Recently a new version, called ditroff, has been developed. The major goal for ditroff was to maintain compatibility with the original troff while lifting its most cumbersome restrictions. That goal has been met, and all of the material in this chapter applies to either version of troff.

The original `troff` document is the *NROFF/TROFF User's Manual* by
Joseph F. Ossanna. Ossanna's manual is authoritative and well organized,
and it serves beautifully as a reference. However, `troff` is a programming
language for managing a typesetter, and few people other than programmers appreciate Ossanna's manual. For those who insist on learning more
about `troff` than presented here, try the document *A TROFF Tutorial*, by
Brian W. Kernighan.

The goal of this chapter is to present basic `troff` knowledge that you will
need to use `troff` with one of the macro packages. You need to know how
to invoke `nroff` or `troff`, you need to know some of the basics of typography, and you need to know a handful of `troff` commands. The last section of this chapter shows you how to design your own macros, a level of
detail that most people can safely avoid.

5.1 COMMAND LINE OPTIONS

Although I have used `troff` extensively for a decade, I have only typed the
command

    $ troff ...

once or twice. That's because I've only once used `troff` with a Graphic
Systems typesetter. On most systems, users typically access the typesetter
(or laser printer) via a command script. `troff` command scripts are often
named to suggest the brand of printer that is used; thus, `qtroff` is used
with QMS laser printers, `itroff` is used with Imagen laser printers, etc.
Most `troff` command scripts allow you to use the usual command line
options, and many scripts also have local options that reflect needs in the
local environment. You should read the local literature and talk to your
system administrator to find out how to use `troff` on your system.
Throughout this book my command examples will refer to `troff`, although
most people will actually type some other name to access `troff`.

Four of the most commonly used command line options are -m*name*,
-n*N*, -r*AX*, and -o*pagelist*. The -m*name* option tells `troff` to use one of
the standard macro packages. The command line option -mm accesses the
memorandum macros, -ms accesses the manuscript macros, -me accesses the
-me macros, and -man accesses the manual page macros.

The command line option -n*N* is used to assign the page number *N* to
the first generated page. This is useful when you print a single document in
several pieces, although the same capability can be accessed inside a document using standard `troff` format commands.

The command line option -r*AX* enables you to assign any value *X* to any
internal `troff` number register with the single-character name *A*. For

example, the command line option -rG5 assigns the value 5 to the G number register.

The command line option *-opagelist* tells troff to print just the named pages. The *pagelist* is a comma-separated list of page numbers, or page groups. A *page group*, which indicates a group of sequential pages, is a pair of page numbers separated by a hyphen. You shouldn't have any spaces in a page list. For example, the option -o1,3,5,11-19 tells troff to print pages 1, 3, 5, and 11 through 19. Here is an example showing a different page list:

```
$ troff -o5,6,14 -ms visifld.t
$ _
```

The command shown above tells troff to print pages 5, 6, and 14, using the -ms macros, of the document 'visifld.t'.

At some sites, nroff is accessed using a supplied command script, at other sites you run nroff directly and pipe its output into a print spooler program, and at some sites you log in on a printing terminal and run nroff as you would any other command. Check with your system manager for more information.

nroff accepts the four options mentioned above plus several more. The *-Tprintername* option tells nroff what type of printer you are using. Your system administrator will know which printers are available. For printers that work at either 10 or 12 pitch, two separate names are usually available, so you can select the pitch you want to use.

Two output tuning command line options are also available for nroff. The -e option will produce equally spaced words using any microspacing capabilities of the output printer. The -h option will output tabs as appropriate, thereby speeding up printing on some terminals.

```
$ nroff -mm -T450-12 visifld.t | q450
$ _
```

The command shown above nroffs the 'visifld.t' document using the -mm macro package. Output is prepared for the 12 pitch version of the model 450 printer and then piped to the q450 print spooler.

5.2 TYPOGRAPHY

With the advent of cost-effective laser printers, increasing numbers of people are becoming aware of typographic issues. In the early 1970s, most technical documents were printed on a typewriter or on a printing terminal whose output strongly resembled a typewriter. A typewriter is an admirable machine for producing legible documents, but it lacks the features that typographers consider important for making a document easily readable.

In the recent past you could survive with a minimal knowledge of typographic issues, but today people who produce documents need at least some knowledge of typography.

The major difference between a typewriter and a typesetter is *fonts*. A font is a matched set of letters and symbols. A typesetter has a choice of fonts, each available in many sizes and several forms (plain, bold, italic, and sometimes slant). Well-designed typesetting fonts are easy to read, and the capability of switching from one font to another lets the typography reinforce the content of the material.

The primary typesetting fonts are *proportional,* meaning each character has an appropriate width. *Monospace* fonts, which means all characters have the same width, are also available on many typesetting systems. You should beware that most terminals display text in a monospace font. Thus, material that aligns vertically on your terminal's screen probably won't align in a typeset document, because the typesetter usually uses a proportional font.

The size of a typeface is measured in *points*, with one point equal to 1/72 of an inch. A common size for a manuscript typeface is 10 points, although other sizes are often used. Footnotes, captions, and page headings are often a point or two smaller than the text, and section headings are often a few points larger than the text. In a 10-point font, only extratall characters, such as a (are actually 10 points tall. When text is set in a 10-point font, lines are often spaced 12 points apart. In the trade, 10-point text printed on lines 12 points apart would be called "10 on 12." See Figure 5.1.

Typographers usually measure most dimensions on a page in units called *picas.* A pica is a sixth of an inch. Many technical books are printed on an area of about 30 by 45 picas, or about 5 by 7 inches. When describing horizontal gaps, such as the space between columns of a table, or the length of a paragraph indent, typographers often refer to *ems* or *ens.* An em is the apocryphal width of a capital M, and an en is about half that. Notice that ems and ens vary in size depending on the point size of the surrounding text. For 10-point text, an em is about the same as a pica, although for bigger fonts an em is correspondingly larger. Although 1 pica is mathematically equal to 12 points, you will never get respect from a typographer if you ask for a 1-pica (12-point) font or demand a 360-point (30-pica) page

[this text
is 10 on 12]

**[this text
is 10 on 12]**   10 points

12 points

Figure 5.1. Vertical spacing is the distance between baselines. Point size is the height of extra-tall characters, such as a square bracket.

width. However, troff is more relaxed than many typographers. With troff, measurements may be specified in points, picas, inches, centimeters, multiples of the current vertical line space, ems, or ens. The default troff units are multiples of the vertical line space for vertically oriented measurements, ems for horizontal measurements, and points for font size changes or line-spacing changes. See Figure 5.2.

Typical typographic fonts contain many more characters than a typewriter. Additional characters include bullets, daggers, degree symbols, square boxes, the copyright symbol, the registered symbol, and small case fractions. Also, most typesetters have an assortment of characters for setting equations, including Greek letters, mathematical symbols (e.g., equality, inequality, union), and characters that can be combined to form braces, integrals, summations, etc. In troff, all these special characters are contained in the *special* font, whereas in most other typesetting systems such a group of characters would be called a mathematics font.

You can access troff's special characters using four-character escape codes. The first two characters are \(, and the last two characters suggest the symbol's name. For example, the troff code \(rg, is the registered symbol ® , \(bu is a bullet ●, \(sq is a square □, \(*a is a Greek alpha α, etc. An exhaustive list of these coding sequences is found in Appendix IV.

Part of the confusion of preparing material for typesetting is management of these additional characters. On a typewriter you can produce an acceptable cent sign by overstriking a C with a /. In troff documents, you must input the special code \(ct to access the built-in cent symbol. (An acceptable cent sign in troff can be produced by overstriking reduced C and /, using the code \s-3\o'C/'\s0, but the result of this troff handywork, ¢, is harder to produce and slightly less appealing than the built-in cent symbol ¢.) Thus, although typography gives you great freedom to use

|◂——— Two inches (2i) ————▸|

|◂——— Six centimeters (6c) ———————▸|

|◂——— Two hundred points (200p)————▸|

|◂———Eighteen picas (18P) ——————————▸|

MMMMMMMMMMMMMMMMMMMMMMMMMMMMMM
|◂——— Thirty ems in 10-point text (30m) ——————————▸|

|◂——— Sixty ens in 10-point text (60n) ——————————▸|

MMMMMMMMMMMMMMMMMMMMMM
|◂——— Twenty ems in 16-point text (20m)——————————▸|

Figure 5.2. Common troff measurements.

appropriate symbols, it requires patience and understanding on your part to learn (and correctly enter) the codes for those symbols.

Another aspect of preparing materials for typesetting is management of dashes and quotes. On a typewriter there is just one width of dash, but in troff there are three common dashes—the hyphen (-), the 3/4 em dash (—), and the minus sign (−). You must enter the correct code for each. (troff's minus sign corresponds to the en dash that is available on many other typesetting systems.) Quotes are even more of a problem. On a type-writer you have double quotes (") and the apostrophe. On a typesetter, double quotes (" ") are customarily formed from pairs of single quotes (' '), single quotes (') are sometimes used, and the grave (`), the acute ('), and the typewriter-style double quote (") are needed occasionally. Thus, the three styles of quotes on a typewriter are just a thin reminder of the seven commonly used typesetting quotes.

In many fonts there are pairs or trios of letters that can be set closer together than usual. The most common example is 'fi', in which the 'i' can nestle under the top of the 'f' and still be quite readable. Such pairs or trios of letters are called *ligatures*. troff can cope with five ligatures, fi, fl, ff, ffi, and ffl. These letter sequences, printed without the decreased spacing are fi, fl, ff, ffi, and ffl.

Filled text is produced by collecting words of input until there are enough words for one output line. If those words are then output with one standard-width space between each, the right margin will be, *ragged*. If, however, those words are output on a line containing enough extra spaces to make the line end exactly at the margin, then the right margin will be *justified*. It is also possible using troff to produce an aligned right margin and a ragged left margin.

In the past, most formally typeset materials, books, journals, etc. have been produced with justified margins, and most letters, typewritten reports, etc. have been produced ragged right. Thus to most readers a justified right margin connotes a more formal, more "produced" document. Today the nearly universal access to word processors and text formatters makes it pos-sible for any document to be produced in any style, so you should try to choose a style that is most appropriate for your audience.

The common reaction of someone who first encounters the power of typesetting is to use these features recklessly. The motivation for these fea-tures is increased comprehension and less strain for the reader. Pundits observe that typesetting that stands out has failed its purpose. Typesetting is a subtle art; mere access to troff and a suitable page printer is little guarantee that professional-looking results will emerge. Besides learning enough about troff to control these features, you should develop your eye so that you can judge your results.

5.3   A FEW TROFF COMMANDS

For most documents you should choose a macro package and use the commands built into that macro package to control the format of your document.   However, some direct troff features are often necessary, and for some unusual document styles it's best (easiest) to go it alone.   This section is barely the beginning of an introduction to troff usage.   Of troff's 80 commands and 40 escape sequences, only 30 are discussed below.   For more information see the documents mentioned in the introduction of this chapter.

troff contains two different types of commands, *dot* commands and *embedded* commands.   Dot commands must stand alone on a line, and all dot commands have a period as the first character on the line, making them very distinctive.   Many dot commands accept one or more arguments, which give them more information about what to do.   For example, the dot command .sp without an argument will produce one extra line of space in the output.   With an argument (e.g., .sp 2), you can control how much extra space to leave (2 lines).   At least one space or tab must separate the arguments, and many commands require more than one argument.

Dot command arguments often refer to sizes of things.   troff accepts size specifications using any of the following units: inches (i), centimeters (c), picas (P), points (p), the current line spacing (v), ems (m), or ens (n).   Prepend the scale indicator as necessary to your numbers.   For example, 4P is 4 picas, 3i is 3 inches, and 2.5c is 2.5 centimeters.   By default, horizontal measurements are usually in ems, vertical measurements are in multiples of the current vertical spacing, and point size selections are in points.

troff maintains all numbers in an internal measure.   On the old version of troff, there are 432 internal units per inch, but the number per inch varies in the newer ditroff version.   Ther are 240 internal units per inch in nroff.   The scale indicator u is used when you want to specify a value in internal units; for example, the number 432u is an inch to the old troff (but just under 2 inches to nroff).   One rarely specifies something in absolute internal units.   However, troff often converts a value from some other scale into internal units.   When you use that value in a context in which some other scale is expected, you have to use the u to tell troff that the conversion has already been applied.

Embedded commands all start with a backslash, and they don't need to be alone on a line or placed at the beginning of a line.   Embedded commands are often used to access a special character or to access a number register or string.   Most embedded commands accept an argument, which must immediately follow the command without any intervening space.   Some features, such as point size changes or font changes, can be controlled by either a dot command or an embedded command.   However, most dot commands are used to control the global features of a document, and embedded commands are often used to control local features.

Sometimes you want to place remarks in a document that won't be printed. This is similar to placing a comment in a computer program. `troff` has a special dot command that starts a comment. Any text on a line starting with `.\"` will be ignored. It is often a good idea to place remarks at the beginning of a document to specify any special printing instructions. For example, the remark might show the full UNIX command to print the document. You can also place a remark on the end of a line that already contains a dot command. Simply put `\"` after the command, and then anything on the tail end of the line will be ignored by `troff`.

5.3.1 Spacing

The following commands allow you some control over the spacing in a document. The `.sp` and `.br` commands can usually be used with macro packages, although the macro packages make them redundant. The codes for half-line motion and the space codes are often useful for fine-tuning the appearance of documents. Many of the other commands discussed in this section may interfere with a macro package; they are best used in simple documents that aren't formatted with a macro package.

`.sp`   controls vertical spacing. By itself, the `.sp` command will insert an extra line space in the output. Arguments can be supplied; for example, `.sp 1i` will produce a 1-inch space, and the command `.sp 3c` will produce a 3-centimeter space. The command can be used to move upward on the page by supplying a negative size; for example, `.sp -2` will move upward two lines. Absolute motion is also possible; for example, `.sp |3i` will move to the page position 3 inches from the top, or `.sp |-4i` will move to the position 4 inches from the bottom. (The | is the absolute position indicator.) The `.sp` command will not produce any extra space when *no-space* mode is in effect. For example, most macro packages turn on no-space mode after printing page headings, so that any top-of-the-page space requests will be ignored, thus making the first line of text on all pages start at the same place. The command `.rs` is often placed in front of `.sp` commands when you always want to produce the space.

`.vs`   controls the vertical spacing, the space between one line and another. The vertical spacing is typically set to about 20 percent more than the point size, so for 9-, 10-, or 11-point text the vertical space would often be set to 11, 12, or 13 points, respectively. For example, `.vs 12p` will set the vertical space to 12 points.

`.ls`   controls the line spacing. For example, the command `.ls 2v` will cause double spacing, because a double dose of vertical space will be output to advance to the next line. `.ls 3v` is triple spacing, `.ls 4v` is quadruple spacing, etc.

.ne   tests to see how much space is left between the current location on
the page and the next trap, which usually signifies the end of text on
the page. For example, .ne 2v tests to see if there are at least two
lines of space remaining on the page. If there isn't enough space,
the vertical position on the page is advanced to the next trap, which
usually prints the page footer and then advances to the next page.
.ne is used to prevent a widow, the first line of a paragraph isolated
on the last line of a page.

.in   controls the indent. All following text will be indented by the stated
amount; for example, .in 5m will indent all the following text by 5
ems.

.ti   controls the (temporary) indent for the following line. The value
may be positive or negative, but you can't indent to the left of the
left margin. Indentation is usually controlled by the macro package.

.br   causes a break in the text-filling process. The following line of text
will start on its own line. For example, the .br command is often
used in the greeting part of a letter.

```
Alice B. Toklas
.br
The West Bank
.br
Paris, France
.sp 2
Dear Alice,
```

Without the .br commands, Alice's three-line address would be output on a single line, but with the .br commands each line of the
address will appear on a separate line of the output document. Both
.sp and .br are usually safe to use within macro packages, but they
aren't often used, because spacing can usually be controlled adequately by the macro package.

.bp   forces troff to start a new page. Any bottom of current page footers or top of following page headers will be produced normally.

.ta   sets the tab stops. You must supply a list of tab-stop positions as
arguments. For example, the commands

```
.ta 8n 16n 24n 32n 40n
.ta .5i 1i 1.5i 2i 2.5i
```

set five tabs at eight-character intervals, or at half-inch intervals.
Tab settings will remain in effect until changed, so they only need to
be set once in theory. In practice, you should set the tabs every time

you use them, because the standard macro packages and the preprocessors are constantly changing the tabs.

\u   and \d are used to produce half-line motions. For example, a superscript (n*) can be produced as n\u*\d. For any given line, the ups and the downs must be balanced, so the net vertical motion is zero. Ignoring this rule can cause subtle havoc. The distance traveled depends on the given point size, so you should expect that e\u\s-2x\s0\d will produce a different effect from e\s-2\ux\d\s0 (the first is e^x; the second is e^x). You should never code something similar to e\s-2\ux\s0\d, because the vertical motion is not balanced.

\| and \ˆ are narrow-space codes. The \| is 1/6 em; the \ˆ is 1/12 em. Here is a familiar phrase printed using the narrow space, and then the very narrow space: xxxoooxxx vs. xxxoooxxx. A *digit width* space can be produced with \0, but it is wider than the usual interword space. The construction \(space) (a backslash followed by a space) is an *unpaddable* space; i.e., it won't be expanded when troff is inserting extra interword space to justify a line.

\c   is the end-of-line continuation marker. Ordinarily a line break is equivalent to a space, but when a line ends in \c, the line break (and the \c) vanish. This has the effect of gluing the following line onto the current without an intervening space.

5.3.2 Filling and Adjusting

The following commands aren't often needed if you use a macro package, because the same result can be produced using display macros. Occasionally these commands are useful within a display to create a hybrid—for example, one with both no-fill and filled text. These commands are also very useful for simple documents that aren't produced using a macro package.

.na   and .ad control the adjustment of the margins. The command .na (which stands for *no adjust*) causes troff to stop adjusting the margins. Input words will still be collected to form an appropriately long output line, but interword spaces won't be added to make the margins align exactly. The .ad command tells troff to resume adjustment. By default both margins are adjusted. The .ad command accepts four arguments: l (letter ell) means adjust the left margin only, r means adjust the right margin only, c means center all lines, and b (or n) means adjust both margins. Without an argument, the previous adjustment mode is restored.

.nf   and .fi control the troff text fill mode. .nf (which stands for *no fill*) causes troff to stop collecting input lines to produce appropriately long output lines. `.fi` restores the `troff` filling process. No-fill mode is a simple way to force `troff` to make the output page layout the same as the input page layout. For example, the greeting part of the letter shown above can be done with `.nf` instead of `.br`.

```
.nf
Alice B. Toklas
The West Bank
Paris, France
.fi
.sp 2
Dear Alice,
```

`.nf` is often placed at the top of a simple document, so that `troff` refrains from altering the page layout. This allows `troff` to manage font changes and to be used for simple spacing requests without the elaboration of full `troff`.

`.ce`   centers the following input line(s). Each input line becomes one output line, much as if no-fill mode were in effect. An optional numeric argument specifies how many input lines will be centered; the default is 1, and the command `.ce 0` will turn off centering. (`troff` commands such as `.sp` don't count.)

5.3.3   Fonts

`.ft`   is used to switch from one font to another. Historically, `troff` has used the numeral 1 to refer to the standard Roman-style font, 2 to refer to the italic version of that font, and 3 to refer to the bold version. Thus, reference to these numbers provides a generic way to refer to fonts. Fonts can also be referred to by one- or two-character names. For example, on the Graphic Systems typesetter that `troff` was originally designed to support, the members of the standard Roman font family were named R, I, and B. Although all `troff` typesetting systems have at least one Roman font family, the plain Roman font is not always named R. For example, on the typesetter I usually use, there are two Roman font families, one named `tr` (times Roman) and one named `mr` (modern Roman). Historically, many `troff` documents use the font name R to refer to whatever Roman font is mounted. However, it's better to use the font position number 1 when you want to select whatever Roman font is being used, because the main document font, whatever its name, is mounted on position 1. Font names are best when you need a particular font, or in the `.fp` commands when you tell `troff` to mount a named font on a given position.

\fn   is another way to to switch fonts. For example, the `troff` input `\f1plain\f2italics\f3bold\f1` will produce plain*italics***bold**. Many macro packages provide macros to switch from one font to another.

.fp   tells `troff` what font to mount on the typesetter. For example, on the typesetter I normally use, the three default Roman fonts are called `tr`, `ti`, and `tb`. To use the alternate modern Roman fonts, named `mr`, `mi`, and `mb`, I place the following commands at the start of my document:

```
.fp 1 mr
.fp 2 mi
.fp 3 mb
```

`troff` font names are always one or two letters long, and your selection of fonts depends on how your typesetter is equipped. Many `troff` scripts provide command line options that allow you to choose a font family. For example, the `qtroff` command file accepts the command line option `-Fmr` to choose the modern Roman font family.

.ps   sets the point size for the following text. For example, `.ps 8` will set the point size to 8, `.ps -2` will decrease the point size by 2, and `.ps` without specifying a size will restore the previous point size. Here is how you would print the phrase NROFF/TROFF using these commands. (The `\c` tells `troff` to join the ensuing text without adding an extra space. Without the `\c` commands, the phrase would print as four words rather than as one.)

```
.ps 10
N\c
.ps -2
ROFF/\c
.ps
T\c
.ps -2
ROFF
.ps
```

\sn   controls the point size using embedded commands. For example, `\s8` will set the point size to 8, `\s-2` will decrease the point size by 2, and `\s0` will restore the previous point size. The construction `N\s-2ROFF\s0/T\s-2ROFF\s0` is an alternative way to produce the phrase NROFF/TROFF.

5.3.4 Number Registers and Strings

.nr is used to assign a value to one of troff's internal number registers. The -ms and -mm macro packages allow you to exert some control over spacing and layout by placing values into number registers. For example, in the -ms macro package, a number register called PI (all number register names, like all troff names, are 1 or 2 characters long) contains the amount of the paragraph indent. The standard paragraph indent is 5 ens, but the command

        .nr PI .5i

will change the standard paragraph indent to a half inch. The values in number registers often control the parameters in macro packages.

\nx or \n(xx is used to interpolate the value of the x (or xx) number register into the text. For example the troff input

        The paragraph indent is currently set to \n(PI units.

will print out the current paragraph indent in internal units in a -ms document. You can place a + or a - following the \n to indicate that the number register should be automatically incremented or decremented before interpolation.

.ds is used to define a value for a string. troff strings are like number registers, except they contain text instead of numeric values. Although much more sophisticated options are available, strings are often used for saving keystrokes. A commonly used phrase can be placed in a string, and that string can be interpolated into the text as necessary. For example, it takes 25 keystrokes to type NROFF/TROFF because of the embedded point size changes. The command

        .ds NT N\s-2ROFF\s0/T\s-2ROFF\s0

places the full phrase into the string named NT.

*x or *(xx is used to interpolate the contents of a string named x or xx into a document. If the string assignment shown above had been executed, then the troff input

        The \f2*(NT User's Manual\fP is an excellent document

will produce the sentence

    The *NROFF/TROFF User's Manual* is an excellent document

The string shown above saves 20 keystrokes, but most importantly it reduces the chance of error.

5.3.5   Hyphenation

troff occasionally hyphenates a word at the end of a line. Hyphenation makes the text appear to have more uniform density, but occasionally troff, like any automated hyphenator, makes mistakes.

.nh   turns off automatic hyphenation.

.hy   enables automatic hyphenation. It accepts a numeric argument that disables hyphenation for certain situations. If the argument is 2, hyphenation is disabled for the last line on a page; if the argument is 4, the last two characters in a word will never be split off; and if the argument is 8, the first two characters in a word will never be split off. These numeric values are additive; for example, 6 means last lines won't be hyphenated and the last two characters in a word won't be split off.

.hw   allows you to manually specify desired hyphenation points for a small group of words. A hyphen in each word shows the desired hyphenation points. Here is an exceptions list that I used for a recent paper:

.hw de-vice proc-ess cata-logue un-known trans-portable

.ht   allows you to specify a hyphenation threshold. Every candidate word in a document is scanned by troff, and each will only be hyphenated when the threshold is exceeded. In many versions of troff, the default is 160, and specifying a threshold of about 300 will make hyphenation occur less often.

\%   allows you to control the hyphenation of a single word in the input. Placing \% before a word prevents troff from hyphenating that word; placing \% inside a word shows troff where to hyphenate that word. The difference between the .hw command and the \% control is that the .hw list can be effective for the entire document, whereas \% affects a single word at a time.

.hc   allows you to select the hyphenation character, which was described in the previous paragraph. The default is %.

5.3.6   File Switching

troff has two commands that let you switch from one input file to another.

.so   switches from the current file to the file named as an argument. When the inserted file is completely read, troff switches back to the original file at the point following the .so command. .so commands may be nested.

.nx   switches from the current file to the file named as an argument. All processing stops when the inserted file is completely read. Any text following a .nx command will not be processed by troff.

5.4 ENTERING TROFF DOCUMENTS

troff converts your document, stored as a text file, into a format suitable for printing on a typesetter or printer. For the most part, the format of the output depends on the format codes that you enter in the document. Line breaks and line lengths in the input are usually ignored. However, there are some aspects of the input document that are important to troff. For example, any line that starts with a blank will cause a *break*. A break is an interruption in the text-formatting process. Any partially collected line will be forced to the output, and then text output will start afresh on the next line. The text immediately before the break won't align at the right margin, as if it were the last line in a paragraph. Breaks can be caused explicitly using the .br command (discussed above), which is usually preferable to leaving a break-causing blank at the start of a line.

Another character to watch out for at the beginning of a line is the period. troff conventionally uses a period at the beginning of a line to mean that the line contains a troff command. Another troff convention is that unrecognized commands are ignored, so that a line starting with a period will be either executed as a troff command or ignored. The single quote is also treated specially at the beginning of a line. The single quote is troff's secondary command character, and lines starting with a single quote are also presumed to be commands. Since the period and the single quote don't normally appear at the beginning of a line, they were chosen to indicate the start of troff commands. If your input data does have ordinary text lines that begin with a single quote or a period, you can use a zero-width placeholder to occupy the first position on the line. The zero-width placeholder, \&, vanishes in the output, but it can help to clarify your input. For example, the following table of numbers will print as expected, because the \& placeholder keeps the period away from the beginning of the line:

```
10,578.90, 321.05, 8.1,
\&.0076, .0067
```

The zero-width placeholder is also often used in embedded commands to separate them from the following text.

A similar problem exists with producing backslashes in the printed output. Whenever a backslash is encountered in the input, troff assumes that the following few characters have some special significance. If you really want to print a backslash, use the \e code.

Although tabs or spaces are often used in documents prepared manually to control horizontal positioning, they are less useful for most people in a `troff` document. Tabs can be used to great advantage in a `troff` document, but they must be set correctly before they are used. Columns of text that align on your terminal screen because of tabs or spaces probably won't align in the printed document. Most material that would benefit from judicious use of tabs (e.g., tables) is better handled by the `tbl` preprocessor. In fact, the most common use of tabs in `troff` documents is as column separators in a `tbl` specification.

Ordinarily, `troff` understands that a line break in the input text should be represented as an interword space in the printed output. Occasionally you want `troff` to make the last character on one line flush with the first character on the following line. If an input line ends with \c, then `troff` will read the following line as a continuation of the current, without an intervening space.

Lines in your input document shouldn't exceed a few hundred characters. The internal limit in `troff` is over a thousand characters, but that generous margin exists because macro preprocessors such as `tbl` and `eqn` sometimes produce very long input lines. You should beware that most versions of `vi` will let you enter text with lines much longer than `troff` can accept gracefully.

Figure 5.3 shows how `troff` can mangle a document if the caveats presented above are ignored. The first problem is that the input contains four backslashes and two lines that start with a period. All six of these errors cause missing text in the output. The code \e must be used to produce a literal backslash in the output, and lines that start with a period should be protected with a \& placeholder. Another problem is the third line, which starts with a space. Unless you really want to cause a break, all lines should start flush left. The final problem is the small summary table. Because `troff` normally fills lines, the table is processed as if it were a paragraph. No-fill regions must be identified to `troff`, either by macros provided by a macro package or by the `.nf` and `.fi` built-in commands.

Most errors in Figure 5.3 are shown corrected in Figure 5.4. The backslashes are coded correctly, the leading periods are protected, the inadvertent break on line 3 has been fixed, and the table is processed in no-fill mode. The only remaining problem is the table—since `troff` uses a proportional-width font, the columns don't line up properly. The only remedy is to learn to use and set tabs in `troff`, or to use the `tbl` preprocessor.

INPUT:

<pre>
                              DOS Pathnames

     Unlike UNIX pathnames, DOS pathnames use the \ to separate the
     elements of the path. For example the path C:\DOS31 leads
     from the root directory on drive C to the DOS31 directory.

     Like UNIX, the DOS parent directory has the special name
     .. (pronounced dot dot) and the current directory has the
     name . (pronounced dot). Thus the pathname

     ..\JONES

     refers to the JONES directory in the parent directory.

     Summary:
                     DOS   UNIX
     Separator   \   /
     Parent   ..   ..
     Current   .   .
</pre>

OUTPUT:

DOS Pathnames

Unlike UNIX pathnames, DOS pathnames use the to separate the elements of the path.
For   example   the   path   C: root directory on drive C to the DOS31 directory.

Like UNIX, the DOS parent directory has the special name name . (pronounced dot). Thus the pathname

refers to the JONES directory in the parent directory.

Summary:
           DOS   UNIX Separator   / Parent   ..
.. Current   .   .

Figure 5.3. Input text to be processed by **troff** must be prepared with **troff** in mind.

INPUT:

DOS Pathnames

Unlike UNIX pathnames, DOS pathnames use the \e to separate the
elements of the path. For example the path C:\eDOS31 leads
from the root directory on drive C to the DOS31 directory.

Like UNIX, the DOS parent directory has the special name
\&.. (pronounced dot dot) and the current directory
has the name . (pronounced dot). Thus the pathname

\&..\eJONES

refers to the JONES directory in the parent directory.

Summary:
.nf

	DOS	UNIX
Separator	\e	/
Parent	..	..
Current	.	.

.fi

OUTPUT:

DOS Pathnames

Unlike UNIX pathnames, DOS pathnames use the \ to separate the elements
of the path. For example the path C:\DOS31 leads from the root directory
on drive C to the DOS31 directory.

Like UNIX, the DOS parent directory has the special name .. (pronounced
dot dot) and the current directory has the name . (pronounced dot). Thus the
pathname

..\JONES

refers to the JONES directory in the parent directory.

Summary:

	DOS	UNIX
Separator	\	/
Parent	..	..
Current	.	.

Figure 5.4. Properly prepared **troff** input documents contain control codes so that
troff can format correctly.

5.5 MACROS

The troff typesetting language is programmed by creating *macros*. A
macro constructs a new facility by repackaging existing facilities. Macros
are similar in function to the subroutines that are used in many general-
purpose programming languages.

It is easier to write macros if you understand how they work. A macro
is a text substitution device. When a macro definition is encountered in
your document, the body of that macro is stored somewhere inside troff,
and troff remembers its name. Whenever the name is used as a command,
troff retrieves the stored macro body and reads through it once again.

Each time troff scans through a chunk of text, it is actively looking for
commands. troff goes through ordinary (nonmacro) text just once, but
macro text is scanned at least twice, once when it is defined and once when
it is used. We will see below that multiple scanning has a major impact on
how macros are written.

Simple macros are constructed by enclosing a block of text within .de
and .. commands. The .de command also requires an argument that is the
name of the macro, a two-character troff-style name. Here is a simple
macro that prints a centered message:

```
.de HI
.ce
Have a nice day!
..
```

You can use the command

```
.HI
```

to print the message. (The command .HI should not appear in the document before its definition.)

Macros often require arguments. Inside a macro a supplied argument
can be accessed by \$1 for the first argument, \$2 for the second, etc.
Because macro bodies are scanned at least twice, you need to put another
backslash in front of the argument reference, so that the argument will be
accessed when the macro is used, not when it is defined. Here is a simple
remake of the previous example.

```
.de HI
.ce
Have a \\$1 day!
..
```

You can use this macro to print a variety of messages:

```
.HI great
```

produces

Have a great day!

However, you need to be careful. The following will not produce the desired result:

```
.HI truly great
```

because the word truly is the first argument. To make a string of words containing blanks into a single argument, you should surround it with double quotes. The command

```
.HI "truly great"
```

will produce

Have a truly great day!

A literal double quote can be produced within a quoted macro argument by coding a pair of double quotes.

Besides references to arguments, many other references need to be delayed by inserting leading backslashes. For example, the command \n(XY within a macro will be expanded, as the macro is defined, into the current value of the XY number register. If you need the value of XY when the macro is actually used, you need to place an extra backslash in front of the reference to the number register.

```
.nr XY 10
.de A1
The XY number register is: \n(XY
..
.de A2
The XY number register is: \\n(XY
..
.nr XY 100
.A1
.A2
```

The output is:

The XY number register is: 10
The XY number register is: 100

Although most macros are invoked explicitly, as with any other troff command, it is also possible to automatically invoke a macro at a given point on the output page. This facility is usually used to produce page headings and footers. The .wh command tells troff where to invoke a given macro. For example, the command

```
.wh 7i QQ
```

will automatically invoke the QQ macro when the output gets to the point 7 inches from the top of the page. On an 11-inch page, the position -4i would be equivalent to the one above, because negative measures are interpreted as distance from the bottom of the page. The measurement zero is the top of the page.

5.6 TROFF LIMITATIONS

Although troff has become a defacto standard in the UNIX community, it has several limitations. Perhaps the most important limitation is troff's primitive concept of page layout. troff uses an inflexible set of rules for managing page layout. For example, if all but the last line of a paragraph fits on a page, troff doesn't know how to squeeze the preceding vertical spaces to make the last line fit. Any material that doesn't fit is forced to the following page, even if relatively minor adjustments of the vertical spacing would allow it to fit. Sometimes the first line on a page is the last line of a paragraph, an inauspicious start.

A related problem is the bottom page margin. Each time a paragraph or section is encountered, the controlling macro executes a .ne (need) request to make sure that the output isn't too near the end of the page. This is necessary because it is undesirable to start a major document feature, such as a new section, too close the bottom of a page. Unfortunately, when the output is too close to the bottom of the page, troff starts the section on the top of the following page, but the preceding page's bottom margin won't align with the bottom margins of the other pages. A better page layout routine would try harder to make all pages the same length by adjusting the vertical spacing.

Although the output from laser printers is impressive when compared to that of most impact printers, it is inadequate for some purposes. Many people have discovered that troff documents print somewhat differently on different output devices. The problem is that different printers have different fonts, and each font has slightly different widths for each character. This is particularly disheartening when someone tweaks a document so that page layout is ideal on one printer and then discovers that those tweaks don't work on another printer. This makes it hard to use a laser printer to preview the results you will attain using a commercial typesetter.

There are two ways to circumvent this problem. You can get your commercial typesetters to send you their width tables and use those widths when you print (and tweak) your document on your laser printer. This will let your laser printer previews have the same page layout as the eventual commercially typeset output, but your previews will look awkward, because your font and width table will be mismatched.

Another option is to use a utility program that converts troff documents to PostScript format and then print them on a PostScript printer. (Post-Script is a page layout system created by Adobe, Inc.) When your document is finished, you send your PostScript file to the commercial typesetter for higher-quality output. The commercially typeset version will have the same page layout as your laser printer previews, because PostScript files are guaranteed to print identically on different printers.

Another problem with troff is hyphenation. troff uses a relatively primitive algorithm—it finds hyphenation points by looking at the sequence of vowels and consonants. In the past decade several researchers have created much better hyphenation algorithms. Some commercial troff service bureaus have modified troff to hyphenate more intelligently, but none of them have made their modifications available to others.

CHAPTER 6

The -ms Macros

-ms was the UNIX system's first widely used general-purpose troff macro package. It is available on Berkeley UNIX and on Version 7. Although -ms is officially unsupported on System V (because -mm is the official System V macro package), it is available on many System V installations. The -ms macro package is summarized in Appendix V.

The original description of -ms is *Typing Documents on the UNIX System: Using the -ms Macros with Troff and Nroff*, by Mike Lesk. Most -ms features are described in just six pages of text, and six additional pages contain tables and examples. (Contrast that with Western Electric's 80-page description of -mm in their *Document Processing Guide*.) A few features were added to -ms at Berkeley; they are described in *A Revised Version of -ms*, by Bill Tuthill. The Berkeley enhancements should probably be avoided if you plan to format your document on both Berkeley and System V systems.

6.1 USAGE

Whenever you place -ms commands in a document, you must also use the -ms command line option with nroff or troff. For example, the following will nroff a document called 'maypicnic' for a model 300 printer and send the output to the lpr2 print spooler:

```
$ nroff -ms -T300 maypicnic | lpr2
$ _
```

If you forget the -ms command line option, your document will print, but all of your formatting instructions will be ignored.

6.2   PAGE LAYOUT

The default page layout of -ms is very sensible. One-inch margins are provided on the top, left, and bottom, the lines are 6 inches long, the page
header (for pages 2 onward) is the centered page number, and in nroff the
page footer is the date (in troff the page footer is blank). This default
setup is usable for many documents.

Most of these parameters can be changed by changing the values in various number registers. The page header and page footer sizes are controlled
by the HM and FM number registers. The 1-inch default can be changed
using the .nr command; for example, the command

    .nr FM 4i

will make the footer margin 4 inches. On 8½ by 11 paper, a 4-inch bottom
margin combined with a 1-inch header margin will make the text on the
page 6 inches long.

The distance of the text from the left margin is controlled by the PO
(page offset) number register, the length of each line of text is controlled by
the LL number register, and the title length is controlled by the LT number
register. The title length refers to the length of three-part titles, such as
those in page headers and footers, and it is unrelated to the width used
when you are printing your title on the first page of a paper. Figure 6.1
demonstrates these page layout features. Appendix V summarizes the -ms
number registers.

INPUT:

```
.nr HM 4.5i
.nr FM 4.5i
.nr PO 3.25i
.nr LL 2i
.LP
The commands given above will produce a very
small printed region, two inches on a side,
in the center of an ordinary piece of
8½ x 11 paper.
Most people don't adjust these parameters to such
extremes, but the option is always there.
```

Figure 6.1. Values contained in number registers control page formatting in -ms.

Ordinarily your text is printed with both margins justified. If you prefer
a ragged right to a justified right, you can put the command

    .na

OUTPUT:

The commands given above will produce a very small printed region, two inches on a side, in the center of an ordinary piece of 8½ x 11 paper. Most people don't adjust these parameters to such extremes, but the option is always there.

in your document. You can switch back to aligned margins using the

    .ad

command.

-ms can be used to produce multicolumn output. The command .2C engages two-column mode, and the command .1C starts a new page and reverts back to one-column mode. The column width is controlled with the CW number register, and the space between the columns is controlled with the GW (gutter width) number register.

You can customize the page headers and footers by placing text into the LH, CH, RH, LF, CF, and RF (left, center, right; header and footer) string registers. In a page header or footer the percent character (%) is replaced by the current page number. For example, if you want the page number centered in the footer, you could do the following:

    .ds CH
    .ds CF - % -

The first string assignment clears the CH string, thereby removing the page number from the centered part of the page header; the second string assignment places the page number character into the centered part of the page footer.

The Berkeley version of -ms gives you additional control over page headers and footers. You can specify one type of header (or footer) for even pages and another for odd pages. This feature is often useful for material that is printed on both sides of the paper. It lets you set up headers (or footers) so that some information, often the page number, is farthest from the binding.

There are four macros that let you manage even and odd headers and footers.

    .EH 'L'C'R'
    .OH 'L'C'R'
    .EF 'L'C'R'
    .OF 'L'C'R'

The E and O stand for even and odd, and the H and F stand for header and footer. Each macro lets you specify the left, center, and right part of the header or footer. A % in the header or footer text will be replaced with the current page number. If these macros are used, then the six header and footer string registers discussed above will not be used in the headers or footers.

It is confusing that the way you control the headers that appear on all pages, setting string registers, is different from the way Berkeley manages the headers that appear only on odd or even pages, macro calls.

6.3 PARAGRAPHS AND SECTION HEADINGS

-ms has several different styles of paragraphs. For most purposes, the .PP command is best. It produces a paragraph with an indented first line. Use .LP to start a paragraph with a flush-left first line. The .IP command creates a paragraph whose entire body is indented. You can supply a label, or a label plus an indentation to override the default indentation. A fourth paragraph style, accessed with .QP, has both the left and the right margins indented. .QP is useful for setting off a paragraph of text that is a quotation from another source. Figure 6.2 is an example showing all of these styles.

Two other paragraphing features are often useful: .RS and .RE. The .RS (right shift) command will shift the following text to the right about one paragraph indent, and .RE (retreat) will shift everything back. They are useful for outlines, and they are also useful when you want to indent a group of paragraphs.

Berkeley added *exdented* paragraphs to the -ms repertoire. An exdented paragraph has all lines indented, except the first, which is flush left. Exdented paragraphs are often used for making lists, because they make it very easy to read the first word on the first line. For example, exdented paragraphs are often used in bibliographies.

There are two number registers for tuning paragraph appearance, PI and PD. The PI number register contains the standard paragraph indent; the default is 5 ens. PD controls the spacing between paragraphs; the default is one-third of a line.

Section headings, such as the one at the beginning of this section, help the reader to understand the organization of a document. The above heading is called a *level 2* heading, because the number has two parts, the chapter number and the section number. A level 3 heading has three numbers, etc. In this book there aren't any level 1 heads; the titles at the beginning of each chapter serve that purpose. However, many documents aren't organized into chapters; the level 1 headings present the major features, level 2 headings adorn the subsections, etc.

The -ms command .NH is used to introduce a numbered heading. The .NH command takes a numeric argument that specifies the level of the heading, and then the heading text follows on the next line (or lines, if necessary). The heading is terminated by an ensuing paragraph command or heading command. Headings are customarily printed in bold.

In -ms the numbered headings are numbered automatically. Each time you insert a heading, the numbering of that level is increased by 1, and the numbering of lower levels is reset. Figure 6.3 demonstrates the -ms numbered headings. If you want unnumbered section titles, use the .SH command.

INPUT:

```
.LP
As Celia and Fay walked down Sixty-sixth Street they
noticed a gaudy green storefront where, for three dollars,
you could have your palms read or your fortune told.
In front of the window was a freestanding sign,
securely chained to a gutter pipe.
.PP
"I've always wondered why fortune tellers use locks,"
mused Celia.
"Can't they get up in the morning, look at
their palms, realize that today some bum is going to
rip off their sign, and not put it out that day?"
.IP 1
"Perhaps that's exactly what they did," said Fay, "and
that's why the lock is on it."
.IP 2
"Or maybe they can't read their own fortunes, like doctors
never treat themselves.
Imagine knowing everyone else's
future, but never having a clue about your own!"
.LP
"That sounds just like my life," laughed Celia.
.QP
As the two girls walked past the storefront, they passed a
heavyset middle-aged woman slowly shuffling down the street.
Fay and Celia walked left onto crowded First Ave.,
as the woman, pausing in front of the palmistry shop,
cautiously looked up and down the street.
Then she took a
heavy ring of keys from her pocket and unlocked the trio of
deadbolts guarding her parlor door.
```

Figure 6.2(a). A sample input text showing four different kinds of paragraphs.

6.4 CHARACTER FORMATS AND ACCENT MARKS

There are several ways to choose character styles and sizes. In the previous chapter I discussed several troff commands for choosing font styles and point sizes. The macros provided in -ms for this purpose are .LG for increasing the point size by 2, .SM for decreasing the point size by 2, .NL for resetting the point size to normal, and .R, .I and .B for selecting plain

OUTPUT:

As Celia and Fay walked down Sixty-sixth Street they noticed a gaudy green storefront where, for three dollars, you could have your palms read or your fortune told. In front of the window was a freestanding sign, securely chained to a gutter pipe.

"I've always wondered why fortune tellers use locks," mused Celia. "Can't they get up in the morning, look at their palms, realize that today some bum is going to rip off their sign, and not put it out that day?"

1   "Perhaps that's exactly what they did," said Fay, "and that's why the lock is on it."

2   "Or maybe they can't read their own fortunes, like doctors never treat themselves. Imagine knowing everyone else's future, but never having a clue about your own!"

"That sounds just like my life," laughed Celia.

As the two girls walked past the storefront, they passed a heavyset middle aged woman slowly shuffling down the street. Fay and Celia walked left onto crowded First Ave., as the woman, pausing in front of the palmistry shop, cautiously looked up and down the street. Then she took a heavy ring of keys from her pocket and unlocked the trio of deadbolts guarding her parlor door.

Figure 6.2(b). Sample output from the input in Figure 6.2(a).

Roman, italic, or bold. All five of these commands are temporary. For example, the sequence

```
.SM
.B
.LP
This is small point, bold paragraph.
```

will not work, because the .LP command resets everything to its default value. Placing the paragraph start command before the two other commands

```
.LP
.SM
.B
This is small point, bold paragraph.
```

will produce the desired result:

This is small point, bold paragraph.

I often find it easier to use **troff**'s in-line escape codes to make font changes or point size changes (see Section 5.3.3). This is especially true

INPUT:

```
.NH 1
How I Spent My Summer Vacation
.LP
Last summer was the best yet.
And when I get to be a teen-ager summers will
be even more exciting.
I can't wait.   . . .
.NH 2
June
.NH 3
Jones' Beach
.NH 3
Walter's Party, Hey Hey Hey
.NH 2
July
.NH 3
Bar Harbor\(emA Vertical Adventure
.NH 3
Seal Island
.NH 2
August\(emCamp WoeIsMe
```

OUTPUT:

1. How I Spent My Summer Vacation

Last summer was the best yet. And when I get to be a teen-ager summers will be even more exciting. I can't wait.   . . .

1.1. June

1.1.1 Jones' Beach

1.1.2. Walter's Party, Hey Hey Hey

1.2. July

1.2.1. Bar Harbor—A Vertical Adventure

1.2.2. Seal Island

1.3. August—Camp WoeIsMe

Figure 6.3. Text demonstrating the numbered heading commands of -ms. In this example, the text that would normally follow each heading is shown only for the first heading.

when just a single word or phrase is in the alternative style. For example, I find it hard to read the following, because my eyes can't skim text containing intrusive left-margin commands.

```
.LP
Jan's first book
.I
The Joy of Pottery
.R
won
.B
.LG
rave
.NL
.R
reviews in most magazines.
```

For me, it's easier to read the following, although people who are not accustomed to troff's strange-looking in-line codes may disagree.

```
.LP
Jan's first book \f2The Joy of Pottery\fP won
\f3\s+2rave\s0\fP reviews in most magazines.
```

For either input the output is the same:

Jan's first book *The Joy of Pottery* won **rave** reviews in most magazines.

Many languages use accent marks to indicate an altered meaning or pronunciation for a letter. The original version of -ms contained definitions for seven accent marks. Each accent mark is invoked by typing a three-character code *in front* of the letter to be accented. The following table shows the seven original -ms accent marks:

NAME	INPUT	OUTPUT	NAME	INPUT	OUTPUT
acute	*'e	é	grave	*`e	è
circumflex	*^o	ô	tilde	*~n	ñ
haček	*Cc	č	cedilla	*,c	ç
umlaut	*:u	ü			

In some versions of ms you produce a haček using the code *v instead of the code shown above.

One improvement made by Berkeley is its vastly increased set of accent marks and foreign characters. If you want to use the improved Berkeley accent marks, you must place the macro .AM at the beginning of the document. The codes for the improved accent marks must be placed *after* the letter to be marked, which is the opposite of the original accent marks. The new accent marks and foreign symbols are detailed at the end of Appendix V.

6.5 KEEPS, DISPLAYS, AND FOOTNOTES

A *keep* is a block of text that won't be split by page breaks. Text within a keep is handled normally, filled paragraphs are still filled, etc. An -ms *display* is a region of text that is processed no-fill mode. That means the text's original line breaks are retained. The -ms package contains displays that are also keeps (so that they won't be split up), and displays that can be split onto separate pages.

An ordinary keep is produced by bracketing a region of text with the commands .KS and .KE. If a page break would ordinarily fall in the middle of the keep, the entire keep is moved to the next page, leaving a blank region at the bottom of the original page. A floating keep is produced by bracketing a region of text with the commands .KF and .KE. If the floating keep can't fit on the current page, it is temporarily set aside, the text following the keep is brought onto the current page until the page break occurs, then the saved keep is placed on the top of the next page, followed by the next text. Thus a floating keep floats down through the text, as necessary, to a place where it won't be split by a page break. In an ordinary keep the order of the material is preserved, but blank regions may be left at the bottom of the page, whereas a floating keep never leaves behind large blank regions, but the order of the text is not preserved.

```
.KS
This extremely long sentence will never be split across a
page boundary because of the "keep start" and "keep
end" commands that bracket it, just as asides,
observations, and other literary devices often bracket
sentences constructed by Henry James, an author known for
sentences numbering five hundred words or more.
.KE
```

-ms has seven types of displays. Let's first discuss the four displays that are keeps. An ordinary display, bracketed by .DS and .DE, will be slightly indented and kept together. The alternatives:

- The .DS L command starts a flush left display.

- The .DS C command starts a line-by-line centered display.

- The .DS B command starts a display centered as a whole.

Figure 6.4 contains all four display flavors.

Because the displays discussed above are kept all on one page, they aren't appropriate for a long chunk of text that should be presented verbatim, with the troff formatting turned off. For that -ms provides three additional forms of display:

INPUT:

```
.DS L
A left-adjusted display is truly
a joy to behold.
.DE

.DS
But sometimes
a touch of indentation
can change the atmosphere
slightly.
.DE

.DS C
Please come to my
New Year's Eve
Party!
December 31 @ 10 till whenever.
R.S.V.P.
.DE

.DS B
Bruce and Sarah are giving a
New Year's Eve Party!
Please come.
Starting at eight.
Ending whenever!
.DE
```

Figure 6.4(a). A sample showing four **-ms** displays.

- The display starting command `.CD` produces a display, with each line centered, that will not be kept on a single page.

- The display starting command `.LD` starts a flush left display that will not be kept on a single page.

- The display starting command `.ID` starts an indented, possibly split display.

You shouldn't mix displays and keeps in one region of your document. However, you can use both features in one document, so long as there is enough intervening text that the displays are flushed out before you start a keep, or vice versa.

Footnotes are produced by bracketing the footnote text with the **-ms** commands `.FS` and `.FE`. It is up to you to provide the footnote indicator.

OUTPUT:

```
A left-adjusted display is truly
a joy to behold.

   But sometimes
   a touch of indentation
   can change the atmosphere
   slightly.
                          Please come to my
                            New Year's Eve
                               Party!
                  December 31 @ 10 till whenever.
                            R.S.V.P.

                   Bruce and Sarah are giving a
                   New Year's Eve Party!
                   Please come.
                   Starting at eight.
                   Ending whenever!
```

Figure 6.4(b). Sample output from the input in Figure 6.4(a).

```
Until Mahler, no one had seriously studied the potential
of musical groups with a thousand players.[7.]
.FS
[7.] \f2Mahler, the Man and his Amazing Legacy\fP,
B. S. Horn, Musical Trivia Publishing, Vienna 1931.
.FE
```

The footnote is shown at the bottom of this page.

The Berkeley version of -ms has a special string called ** that will auto-matically number footnotes. When you place ** in the text, it will print as a numerical superscript, and it will increase by 1 each time it is used. You should not use ** in the footnote; the macros will automatically put the reference in for you. Another feature of Berkeley's enhanced footnotes is that the .FS command takes an argument that will label the footnote. One caution: when you use **, *all* following .FS commands will include an automatic footnote number, unless you supply an argument to replace the automatic footnote number.

[7.] *Mahler, the Man and his Amazing Legacy*, B. S. Horn, Musical Trivia Publishing, Vienna 1931.

```
After Mahler no one seriously considered using
musical groups with a thousand players.\**
.FS
\f2Mahler\(emHis Effect on Music\fP,
O. Beau, Avant Garde Press, Paris 1961.
.FE
```

The sentence above will produce the output:

> After Mahler no one seriously considered using musical groups with a thousand play-ers.[1]

The footnote is shown at the bottom of this page.

The footnote mark should not be separated from the preceding word by an ordinary space, because a line break might move the footnote mark to the following line. Place the mark adjacent to the preceding text (as shown above), or use an unpaddable space code separator.

6.6   TABLE OF CONTENTS

The Berkeley version of -ms can produce a table of contents. There are three macros that collect the data for the table of contents, and one that prints it all out. For documents that are printed in one pass, you can collect the information in the original document and then print it out at the end of the document. However, for documents that are stored in separate files and printed in separate pieces, you need to put the table of contents information in a separate file and update that information as your original document changes.

An item for the table of contents should be bracketed by the macros .XS and .XE. If an argument is supplied to .XS then it will be used as the page number when the table of contents is printed; otherwise the current page number will be used. Thus, when you keep your table of contents information in a separate file, you should supply a page number argument to .XS but when you put the .XS in the original document, you don't need to use an argument. To simplify table of contents specifications in separate files, there is the .XA macro, which allows you to specify another table of contents item within a .XS .XE pair. Like .XS the .XA command accepts an optional argument that specifies the page number.

You can output the stored table of contents using the .PX command. Note that the .XS, .XA, and .XE commands don't actually output anything; rather they store the information so that it can be printed when .PX is encountered at the end of your document. Figure 6.5 shows a sample table of contents specification and the resultant output.

---

[1] *Mahler—His Effect on Music*, O. Beau, Avant Garde Press, Paris 1961.

INPUT:

```
.XS 1
Chapter 1\(emThe U\s-2NIX\s0 Text-Processing Tools
.XA 6
1.1 Macro Packages
.XA 7
1.2 Preprocessors
.XA 10
1.3 Study Guide
.XE
.XS 13
Chapter 2\(emText Editing with \f2vi\fP
.XE
.XS 14
2.1 U\s-2NIX\s0 Text Editors
.XE
.PX
```

OUTPUT:

Table of Contents

Figure 6.5. The Berkeley additions to -ms to produce a table of contents.

6.7 THE FIRST PAGE

You can get started with -ms knowing just a few commands and then expand your knowledge to produce more sophisticated looking documents. Unfortunately, the initial hurdle with -ms is rather high, because it is hard to produce an unsurprising first page. That's why the discussion of the first page has been postponed till here, the last section of the chapter.

The original design of -ms was to have the first line in a document indicate the overall format of the document. Accordingly, the original -ms macro package contained about a half dozen format styles, hardwired into the system. Most of these format styles related to the internal needs of Bell Laboratories, and many of these styles caused the Bell System logo to be printed somewhere on the first page.

If you use one of the supplied formats, it is easy to produce documents with a truly impressive massif on the first page. However, most people don't work in the Bell System, and the -ms-supplied formats aren't generally useful. For most people it is better to tune the first page manually and then use standard -ms features in the body of the text.

At the very top of a document you should put any commands to initialize the page layout. These commands were discussed in Section 6.2. After the page layout commands it's best to put one of the -ms paragraph commands, followed by a slight amount of blank text to force out the paragraph. This bit of magic gets the -ms macros humming, so that you can then exert some control of your own. Once started, you can design your own first page. Here are some of the ingredients I often use to format the first page:

.CD   will start a line-by-line centered block (that is terminated by .DE). It is used for page titles, authors, etc. on a manuscript, or for the date (plus your own address when you don't use letterhead stationery) at the top of a letter.

.LD   will start a left display. Because the individual lines aren't filled to form paragraphs, this type of display is often used for the destination address at the top of a letter.

.LG,   .NL, and .SM are used to control sizes. .LG is often used above the titles of a manuscript to enlarge the title.

.R,   .I, and .B are used to control fonts, especially in the title, or author headings of a manuscript.

.sp   is used to leave space as necessary.

.br   is used to force a line break without inserting extra space.

Figure 6.6 shows the boiler plate text for a business letter. The .LP command at the beginning of the document and the \0 code on the next line are used to force out a paragraph, which initializes -ms. Without these two codes, the following text might format unpredictably. Any commands to change the default page margins should be made before the first .LP command. The amount of space specified in the .sp commands is variable; it depends on the size of the letter. For a longer document, I would probably decrease the space above and below the date. If you are using nroff (not troff) for a short letter, you will need to add the -ms command .ND to remove the date from the page footer. By default, in either nroff or troff the page number will be centered in the heading for page 2 through the end.

The troff input text in Figure 6.7 shows how you can produce a title page for a manuscript. As in the first example, the first two commands, .LP and \0, are used so that -ms gets started properly. After that there is a centered display, containing the title in large bold, the investigator's name

in normal-size italics, the investigator's institution, and the title for the
abstract. Following that are a quoted paragraph containing the abstract,
the first numbered heading, and the first paragraph of the paper.

INPUT:

```
.LP
\0
.sp 1i
.CD
March 17
.DE
.sp .5i
.LD
CGI Compatibles
One Flattery Drive,
Phoenix, Az.
.sp
.DE
Dear Sir or Madam,
.sp
.LP
I am writing an article for a nationwide magazine about hobbyists
who are building their own personal computer systems.
As a result of your advertisements in the March issue of Byte
magazine I see that you are selling several products in this
area.  My purpose in writing this letter is twofold: I want to
evaluate several of your products in my article, and I would
like to get in touch with several hobbyists who have successfully
built personal computers using your products.
.PP
Please respond as quickly as possible because my deadline
is just three weeks from today.  I look forward to your reply.
.sp
.DS B
Yours,
.sp 3
Laura
.DE
```

OUTPUT:

March 17

CGI Compatibles
One Flattery Drive,
Phoenix, Az.

Dear Sir or Madam,

I am writing an article for a nationwide magazine about hobbyists
who are building their own personal computer systems. As a result
of your advertisements in the March issue of Byte magazine I see
that you are selling several products in this area. My purpose in
writing this letter is twofold: I want to evaluate several of your
products in my article, and I would like to get in touch with several
hobbyists who have successfully built personal computers using your
products.

Please respond as quickly as possible because my deadline is just
three weeks from today. I look forward to your reply.

Yours,

Laura

Figure 6.6. A 1-page business letter.

INPUT:

```
.LP
\0
.sp 1i
.CD
.LG
.B
Interpersonal Relations
between
Pedestrians and Cab Drivers
in New York City
.NL
.I
.sp 2
Wilson B. Frank, Ph.D.
.sp .5
Cindy Lou Whooper, Ph.D.
.sp 2
.R
City University Hospital
New York City, N.Y.  10022
.sp 2
.I
Abstract
.DE
.QP
.SM
```

In the course of a working day in New York City there are tens of
thousands of verbal incidents involving pedestrians and cab drivers
(who are also known as hacks). Very little is known about these
potentially violent interchanges, and even less is known about how to
reduce the chance of conflict. This paper is a survey of current
thinking on this vital urban issue, and a plan for future research.

```
.NH 1
```

Introduction

```
.LP
```

The original street plan for New York City set aside certain paved
areas, called streets, for motor vehicles, and other paved areas,
called sidewalks, for pedestrians. Unfortunately this harmonious
design fails to adequately separate these two factions because
(1) pedestrians often need to cross the streets and (2) vehicles
(especially cabs) occasionally travel on the sidewalks. Thus there
is an ongoing conflict between the two groups.

OUTPUT:

Interpersonal Relations
between
Pedestrians and Cab Drivers
in New York City

Wilson B. Frank, Ph.D.

Cindy Lou Whooper, Ph.D.

City University Hospital
New York City, N.Y. 10022

Abstract

In the course of a working day in New York City there are tens of thousands of verbal incidents involving pedestrians and cab drivers (who are also known as hacks). Very little is known about these potentially violent interchanges, and even less is known about how to reduce the chance of conflict. This paper is a survey of current thinking on this vital urban issue, and a plan for future research.

1. Introduction

The original street plan for New York City set aside certain paved areas, called streets, for motor vehicles, and other paved areas, called sidewalks, for pedestrians. Unfortunately this harmonious design fails to adequately separate these two factions because (1) pedestrians often need to cross the streets and (2) vehicles (especially cabs) occasionally travel on the sidewalks. Thus there is an ongoing conflict between the two groups.

Figure 6.7. The first page of a manuscript.

CHAPTER 7

The -mm Macros

-mm is the UNIX system's most flexible troff macro package. It was designed to do everything that -ms could do, and then some. -mm was also designed to provide informative error messages and to be easily extensible. These goals have been attained, although a certain price has been paid.

In this chapter I am going to present -mm's -ms-*like* subset. In some areas, such as user programmability, -mm goes well beyond the capabilities of -ms. However, I am only going to delve into one -mm extension, its support for flexible lists. The -mm macro package is described in Appendix VI, and the mm and mmt command line options are summarized in Appendix VII.

-mm is described at great length in the *Document Processing Guide*. In the guide, discussions of trivial matters are often drawn out, and other discussions seem too short. Overall there are too few examples. Confronted by a package of this size, it is an author's responsibility to organize and codify so that the reader is sheltered from the details. Exactly the opposite tack seems to have been taken.

-mm is confusing for several different reasons. Unfortunately, the term mm refers to two separate UNIX facilities: there is the -mm macro package, and there is a UNIX command named mm that helps you to format your document using -mm (the macros). Most of this chapter is about the -mm macros, although the mm command is also mentioned. Another problem with -mm is its bulk—there are about 100 macros and accessible strings, and another 50 visible number registers. Few documents need all of these features, but each of these features is needed by some document somewhere. Another difficulty with -mm is the documentation. Eighty pages is too long to browse through, but without an index, browsing is the only way to locate some features. Examples would help, but the manual contains only two nontrivial ones.

This chapter tries to present the most useful aspects of -mm, with ample portions of examples. I've tried to organize this chapter so that related features are discussed together. Overall the organization of this chapter parallels that of the -ms chapter, so that you can flip from one chapter to the other to see how each macro package handles similar features.

7.1 USAGE

Documents can be formatted using the nroff or troff formatters and the -mm macros in several different ways. The traditional approach is to supply the flag -mm when running nroff or troff.

```
$ nroff -mm -T450-12 sandy.let
```

— The Document is printed on the terminal —

```
$ _
```

In UNIX System V, the process of formatting a document using the -mm package has been considerably speeded up by supplying a *compacted* version of the macros. Compaction is to a macro package as compilation is to a true programming language. You can use either the compacted or the uncompacted version of the -mm macros. The results should be identical, so the compacted versions should be used wherever they are available, unless there is some reason to do otherwise. The compacted macros are accessed using the -cm flag instead of the -mm flag.

```
$ nroff -cm -T450-12 sandy.let
```

— The Document is printed on the terminal—

```
$ _
```

Compacted macros aren't usually available on Berkeley or Version 7 UNIX systems.

A convenience offered on System V is the mm program that will print -mm documents. mm is really just a disguise for nroff. Its purpose is to simplify the process of running the UNIX formatting software, but the disadvantage is that it presents yet another interface that must be learned.

We are going to start with mm, the nroff formatter interface. Usually with nroff you must specify the terminal type with the -T*term* option. That option may also be used with the mm program, or you can permanently specify the terminal by setting the environment variable $TERM to the name of the terminal. Using the environment variable works only if you are formatting documents onto your own terminal; you will need to use the -T*term* option if you are sending your output to a print spooler. (You shouldn't simply set $TERM to the name of the destination printer, because then programs such as vi that use the terminal will not work correctly.) Three other useful options are the -12 option, which will format documents in 12 pitch; the -y option, which will use the noncompacted macros instead of the compacted; and the -E option, which will invoke the -e equal-width spacing option of nroff. The preprocessors tbl and neqn can be invoked with the -t and -e options, respectively. mm will pass unrecognized option arguments along to nroff for it to peruse. If the environment variable $TERM is set to 450, then the following document formatting command is equivalent to the one shown above.

```
$ mm -12 sandy.let
```

   —The Document is printed on the terminal—

```
$ _
```

mmt is a simplified interface to the troff processing system. It accepts the -y option to access the noncompacted macros, the -e option to preprocess with eqn, and the -t option to preprocess with tbl. Like mm, mmt will pass along unrecognized options to troff for it to handle.

One of the most important things to understand about -mm is that 11 number registers governing the overall format of a document must be set *before* the actual -mm commands are processed. Thus they must be set 1) on the command line (using the -rA*X* flag) or 2) in a .nr command that precedes the inclusion of the -mm package. These special -mm number registers are listed in the following table.

A	Suppress Bell logo on first page	O	Specify left margin offset
C	Specify copy type for footer	P	Specify page number
D	Set debug mode	S	Specify point size and spacing
E	Specify fonts for first page	T	Printer specific features
L	Specify physical page length	U	Specify underlining in headers
N	Specify page-numbering style	W	Specify page width

(Note that the P number register may also be specified within the document.)

You can set any of the above number registers using the -rA*X* command line flag of nroff, troff, mm, and mmt. For example, setting the N number register to 2 makes -mm output page headings that are similar to the -ms page headers — no page number on the first page and centered page numbers at the top of pages 2 through the end. (The N number register settings are discussed in the next section.) The following command shows how the N number register could be set to 2 on the command line.

```
$ mm -12 -rN2 sandy.let
```

   —The Document is printed on the terminal—

```
$ _
```

If correct printing of your document relies on several command line number register assignments, you should place a troff comment at the beginning of the document that lists those assignments.

The other method is to embed the number register assignment in the document followed by a file inclusion command that reads in the -mm macros. When you use file inclusion (the .so native troff command) to read in the -mm macros, you cannot use the mm or mmt programs to format the document. Instead, you must use nroff or troff directly, and you must remember to omit the -mm or -cm command line flag. The advantage of this technique is that the register assignments are embedded in the document, so they can't be forgotten or accidently omitted from the command line.

The following dialogue shows what you would need to place in the first few lines of 'sandy.let' to assign 2 to the N number register and then include the -mm macros. (Note that head is a Berkeley UNIX program that displays the first few lines of a file.) The second part of the following dialogue shows the command to print the file. Note there is no command line reference to -mm and no use of the mm (or mmt) program.

```
$ head -8 sandy.let
.\' nroff -12 sandy.let
.nr N 2
.so /usr/lib/tmac/tmac.m
.DS C
December 11, 1987
.DE
Hi! I'm sending you this quick note because
I just found out that the arrangements we made
$ nroff -12 sandy.let
```

> *—The Document is printed on the terminal—*

```
$ _
```

7.2   PAGE LAYOUT

Unlike -ms, the default -mm page layout is, to my eye, unattractive. The default left and bottom page margins are smaller than those on the top and right. In -mm the left margin is controlled by the O (letter oh) number register, and the line length is controlled by the W number register. The default values of .75 inch and 6 inches makes the text on 8½ by 11 paper look heavy on the left. Assigning the value of 1 inch to the O number register improves the appearance.

```
$ mmt -12 -rO1i sandy.let
$ _
```

For troff, the value for the O or W number register must be a scaled value, as shown above. In nroff, the number must not have a scale suffix, and the value is in units of character positions. For example, with nroff you would set the O number register to 10 (on a 10-pitch printer) to get a 1-inch left margin.

-mm uses a curious macro called .VM to provide some control over the sizes of the page headers and footers. .VM takes two arguments, the number of lines to lengthen the header and the number of lines to lengthen the footer. Although the default header is acceptable, the default footer seems too small. The following command lengthens the footer by five lines.

```
.VM 0 5
```

The .VM command should appear before any document text, paragraph commands, headings, etc. if the specification is to apply to the first page.

-mm's default right margin is justified when using the troff formatter and ragged when using the nroff formatter. However, you can control the appearance of the right margin using the .SA macro. The command .SA 0 will turn off justification; the command .SA 1 will turn on justification. Without an argument, the .SA command will restore whatever style you chose when you last supplied an argument to .SA, or to the default.

Automatic hyphenation is controlled with the Hy number register. By default the Hy number register has the value zero, meaning automated hyphenation is disabled. You can enable automated hyphenation by setting the Hy number register to 1.

The point size and vertical spacing for your document are set using the .S command. You can change the point size and vertical spacing throughout your document. The .S command accepts two arguments: the first controls the point size, and the second controls the vertical spacing. You can supply a signed number (e.g., -2) to increment or decrement the current value, or you can supply an ordinary number (e.g., 10) to set the point size or spacing to that value. Three other arguments can be used—D, which means restore the default; C, which means maintain the current value; or P, which means revert to the previous value. The default point size is 10 and the default vertical spacing is 12.

-mm has two macros for forcing output to start on a new page. The .SK command will skip to a new page. With a numeric argument .SK will skip that many pages. The related command .OP will skip to the top of the next odd-numbered page. .OP is used to place important material, such as the beginning of a chapter, on a right-hand page (odd-numbered pages are traditionally right-hand pages). A .SK command issued at the top of a page will do nothing, as will a .OP command issued when you are already at the top of an odd-numbered page.

You can leave extra vertical space in your document with the .SP command. The argument to .SP specifies how many lines (in nroff) or half lines (in troff) to leave in the output. The advantage of using .SP instead of troff's built-in command .sp is that several requests for space with .SP don't accumulate; rather the largest is used.

-mm's default page-numbering style is a centered page number on all pages. Although this is appropriate for a line-printer style program listing, most documents will require an alternative style. For letters and similar documents, page 1 should be devoid of headers and footers, and pages 2 through the end should have a centered page number. This is -mm page-numbering style 2. Many technical or scholarly documents benefit from a centered page number on the bottom of the first page, plus centered page numbers at the top of 2 through the end, which is -mm's numbering style 1.

Setting the N number register controls what style of page number will be placed into the headers and footers, what will appear on page 1, what will appear on subsequent pages, whether level 1 sections will start on new pages, and how tables, figures, exhibits, and equations will be numbered.

Here is a complete list of the -mm page-numbering codes.

Register N Page Header Codes

Value	Page 1 Head	Page 1 Foot	Pages 2FF Head	Pages 2FF Foot
0	Page No.		Page No.	
1		Page No.	Page No.	
2			Page No.	
3		Section No.		Section No.
4				
5		Section No.		Section No.

The difference between styles 3 and 5 is that in style 5 the automatically generated numbers for figures, tables, exhibits, and equations are reset each time there is a level 1 section heading. For styles 3 and 5, each level 1 section heading will start on a new page. Style 4 suppresses any automatic page numbering, but you can supply your own page headers for pages 2 through the end using the .PH macro.

As explained above, the N number register must be set before -mm is processed. Hence it is often set on the command line:

```
$ mm -12 -rN2 sandy.let
```

—The Document is printed on the terminal—

```
$ _
```

The selections provided by the N number register sometimes provide exactly the right page-numbering style. However, when you need a style not provided by the N register, you can manually control headings and footers using the .PH, .EH, .OH, .PF, .EF, and .OF macros. These macros control the headings on all, even and odd, headers and footers. They all take a single argument with the following general form:

    .PH "ʹleftʹcenterʹrightʹ"

Note there are *four* single- and *two* double-quote characters in the macro call example. The strings left, center, and right will appear in the obvious places in the heading. The number register P contains the current page number. In any of the .PH etc. macros, references to the P number register must be escaped by four backslashes for reasons too mysterious to go into here.

    .PH "ʹʹ- \\\\nPʹʹ"

The page-heading assignment given above centers the current page number in the heading on all pages.

Let's consider the following as an example. In many bound manuscripts, the page headers must differ between the even and the odd pages, so that the page numbers are always away from the binding. This is accomplished with the following -mm commands.

    .PH "ʹʹʹʹ"
    .EH "ʹ\\\\nPʹʹʹ"
    .OH "ʹʹʹ\\\\nPʹ"

The .PH command clears the default centered page number that usually appears on both even and odd pages, the .EH command places a left-adjusted page number on even pages, and the .OH command places a right-adjusted page number on odd pages.

Two-column mode is invoked with the .2C macro, and one-column format can be resumed using the .1C macro. When you are in two-column mode, there are several options for how -mm will format footnotes and displays. These options are controlled by the .WC (width control) macro. By default footnotes are the column width, displays are as wide as a column, and floating displays cause a break when output on the current page. Here are the options for the .WC macro that allow you to control these features.

N   restores the default settings: -WF, -FF, -WD, and FB.

WF   makes footnotes wide (2 columns wide in .2C mode). The argument -WF (instead of WF) makes footnotes one column wide. -WF is the default.

FF   makes all footnotes on a page the same width as the first footnote. This will override -WF or WF. The argument -FF, the default, will allow a mix of footnote styles on a page.

WD   makes displays wide (2 columns wide in .2C mode). The argument
      -WD, which is the default, makes displays one column wide.

FB   makes floating displays cause a break when they are output on the
      current page. The argument -FB prevents floating displays output
      on the current page from causing a break. FB is the default.

The following command would make both displays and footnotes two columns wide:

.WC WF WD

7.3   PARAGRAPHS AND HEADINGS

Numbered section headings are used in many technical documents to organize the material. In -mm the .H command will produce an automatically
numbered heading. The first argument for .H is the *level* of the heading,
and the second argument is the text of the heading. By default, level 1 and
level 2 headings are in bold, with blank space above and below. Headings
level 3 through 7 are in italics, with blank space above, and the following
paragraph starts on the same line as the heading. Figure 7.1 shows how
heading commands in a typical document are specified and how they are
formatted by -mm.

Although the default -mm heading styles are reasonable, one advantage of
-mm is its extensive array of features for controlling the appearance of headings. For many people the default heading appearance and numbering system are appropriate; those readers should skip ahead in this section to the
discussion of paragraphs.

Ej   The Ej number register can be set so that headings whose level is
      less than or equal to the value in Ej will always be moved to the
      top of the next page. If Ej is set to 2, then level 1 and level 2 head-
      ings will always start a new page. The default value is zero.

Hs   Headings whose level is less than or equal to the Hs number register
      will be followed by a blank line and then the following paragraph.
      The default value for Hs is two.

Hb   Headings whose level is less than or equal to the Hb number register
      will be followed by a break. This will make the following para-
      graph start on the line immediately following. If the heading level
      is greater than both Hb and Hs, the following paragraph will start
      on the same line as the heading. The default value for Hb is 2.

Hi   The Hi number register controls the appearance of the first para-
      graph following each *stand-alone* heading (a heading level whose

INPUT:

```
.nr Cl 3        \" save three levels of heads for toc
.H 1 "The Corpse Created"
.P
On a dark and gloomy night many years before I was born,
there was a tragic affair that forever changed . . .
.P
This tale was first told me by my father, when I was too young
to understand. Years later, when I was near my majority . . .
.nr Pt 1        \" indent all paragraphs
.H 2 "Introduce Sir George, Young Giles, and Lady Gillian"
.P
My father knew Sir George for many years before the tragedy.
Although they were the same age, of course they . . .
.P
But for all his knowledge of the elder, his acquaintance with
young Giles was meagre. For Lady Gillian had kept . . .
.nr Pt 2        \" indent paragraphs except after a heading
.nr Pi 8        \" larger paragraph indent
.H 2 "Tempers Flare over Giles' Behavior"
.P
Some months before the terrible night, young Giles was seen
by several parishioners in the church graveyard late . . .
.P
At first the townsfolk weren't sure it was Giles, because he
had seldom been seen.  But the crest of arms on his cloak . . .
.H 3 "Giles Threatened by His Nanny"
.P
Although she was a slight and nearsighted woman, Giles' Nanny
had an inner strength respected by all. At the trial she . . .
.nr Hc 1        \" center level one heads
.ds HP 12 10 10        \" heading point sizes
.HM I 01 01   \" heading numbering style
.nr Np 1        \" number all paragraphs
.H 1 "Clues Accumulate"
.P
Once the general alarm had been raised, the local constable
arranged for townspeople to aid in the search. . . .
.P
Many refused, because the ghastly nature of the crime
kindled people's superstitions. However, some . . .
.nr Np 0        \" disable auto paragraph numbering
.H 2 "M. Clochet Arrives"
.nP             \" numbered paragraph
```

```
The most famous detective of the day was M. Clochet.
His origin is obscure; in fact, even his date of birth
is a matter of some dispute. . . .
.nP
But one fact about M. Clochet is undisputable. His
powers with women were at least the equal of
his deductive acumen. . . .
```

Figure 7.1(a). Sample headings and paragraphs for the *The Secret Corpse*.

level is less than Hs or Hb). If Hi is zero, the following paragraph will be left-justified. If Hi is 1, the next paragraph will be justified the same as all paragraphs in the document. If Hi is 2, the following paragraph will be indented enough to align with the first word of the heading. The default value for Hi is 1.

Hc   The Hc number register controls heading centering. All stand-alone headings whose level is less than or equal to the value in Hc will be centered. The default value is zero, making all headings left-aligned.

HF   The HF string register stores the default font numbers for the seven heading levels. The default string stored in HF is *3 3 2 2 2 2 2*, meaning that headings level 1 and 2 are in bold (troff font number 3) and headings 3 through 7 are in italic (troff font 2). The following command would make all headings bold:

    .ds HF *3 3 3 3 3 3 3*

If fewer than seven fonts are specified, the trailing fonts are presumed to be font 1, ordinary Roman. Remember that in nroff, italics will print as underlining.

HP   The HP string register stores the default point sizes for the headings. For example, the following string assignment command would make level 1 and level 2 headings 9-point and levels 3 through 7 10-point.

    .ds HP 9 9 10 10 10 10 10 10 10

Remember that point sizes are not effective in nroff. The default values for the HP string register are those shown above.

.HM   The .HM macro controls the style of the heading numbers. Arabic numerals (1, 2, 3, etc.) are the default, but alphabetic labeling (A, B, C, etc.) or Roman numerals (I, II, III, etc.) are also available. The .HM macro takes up to seven arguments to control the labeling style for each of the seven heading levels. The arguments to .HM

OUTPUT:

1. The Corpse Created

On a dark and gloomy night many years before I was born, there was a tragic affair that forever changed . . .

This tale was first told me by my father, when I was too young to understand. Years later, when I was near my majority . . .

1.1 Introduce Sir George, Young Giles, and Lady Gillian

My father knew Sir George for many years before the tragedy. Although they were the same age, of course they . . .

But for all his knowledge of the elder, his acquaintance with young Giles was meagre. For Lady Gillian had kept . . .

1.2 Tempers Flare over Giles' Behavior

Some months before the terrible night, young Giles was seen by several parishioners in the church graveyard late . . .

At first the townsfolk weren't sure it was Giles, because he had seldom been seen. But the crest of arms on his cloak . . .

1.2.1 Giles Threatened by His Nanny Although she was a slight and nearsighted woman, Giles' Nanny had an inner strength respected by all. At the trial she . . .

II. Clues Accumulate

II.01 Once the general alarm had been raised, the local constable arranged for townspeople to aid in the search. . . .

II.02 Many refused, because the ghastly nature of the crime kindled people's superstitions. However, some . . .

II.01 M. Clochet Arrives

01.01 The most famous detective of the day was M. Clochet. His origin is obscure; in fact, even his date of birth is a matter of some dispute. . . .

01.02 But one fact about M. Clochet is undisputable. His powers with women were at least the equal of his deductive acumen. . . .

Figure 7.1(b). Sample output from the input in Figure 7.1(a).

can be 1 (numeral one) to mean ordinary Arabic numerals (the default for all heading levels), 01 (or 001 etc.) to mean Arabic numerals with the given number of digits always printed, A (or a) for uppercase (or lowercase) alphabetic labels, or I (or i) for uppercase (or lowercase) Roman numerals. For example, the following command sets headings level 1 to uppercase Roman, heading level 2 to alphabetic, and the remaining headings to Arabic:

    .HM I A 1 1 1 1 1

The default numeric format for all heading levels is Arabic.

Ht   The Ht number register may be set to 1 to inhibit the usual concatenation of the numbers in heading labels. Ordinarily, a level 3 heading would be printed as 3.1.2., but only the rightmost part (2.) would be present if Ht were set to 1. The default value for Ht is zero.

–mm also has facilities for *unnumbered* headings. The .HU macro introduces an unnumbered heading. Like the .H command, the .HU command takes the heading text as its argument. By default, unnumbered headings are like level 2 headings, except that the number isn't printed. However, each unnumbered heading will increase the level counter by 1. Since unnumbered headings work like numbered headings, all of the controls mentioned above can be used to control their style. You can control the presumed level of an unnumbered heading using the Hu number register. As implied above, the default value of the Hu number register is 2.

Paragraphs in –mm documents are started by the .P command. The default is for paragraphs to have their first line flush left. Paragraphs with an indented first line are produced by supplying an argument to the .P command.

    .P 1.

There are two separate styles of numbered paragraphs. If you set the Np number register to 1, all paragraphs will automatically be numbered. The number will be in two parts, the current number of the level 1 headings followed by the paragraph number. Thus, in the fifth section of a document, the paragraphs will be numbered 5.01, 5.02, etc. Each level 1 heading will increase the heading part of the paragraph by 1 and reset the paragraph number to zero.

The second method of producing numbered headings is using the .nP command to start paragraphs. Each paragraph labeled by a .nP command will also be labeled by a two-part number. The first part of the label will be the level 2 heading value, and the second part of the label will be the paragraph number. The first *two* lines of the paragraph will be indented to make the numbering stand out.

Several number registers allow you to control the appearance of paragraphs.

Pt   The `Pt` number register controls the default format of paragraphs. Setting `Pt` to 1 will indent the first lines of paragraphs. Setting `Pt` to 2 will indent the first lines of paragraphs, except that the first line will be flush left when a paragraph immediately follows a heading. The default value of the `Pt` number register is zero.

Ps   The `Ps` number register controls the spacing between paragraphs. The default spacing is one line for `nroff` and one-half line for `troff`. The units are lines for `nroff` and half lines for `troff`.

Pi   The `Pi` number register controls the indent of paragraphs and many lists. The default value is 3 ens for `troff` and 5 ens for `nroff`, and the units are ens for both formatters.

Np   The `Np` number register controls automatic numbering of paragraphs. When set to 1, paragraphs will automatically be numbered. The default value of the `Np` number register is zero.

Several paragraph styles and options are demonstrated in Figure 7.1.

7.4   CHARACTER FORMATS AND ACCENT MARKS

-mm has several macros that let you switch from one font to another or switch point sizes. If you simply want to switch from one font to another, you can use the .R, .I, and .B macros. Each of these macros will switch to the named font for following text. Since you often want to switch fonts only for a word or two, the .I and .B macros accept arguments. The first argument will be in italic (or bold), the second will be in the surrounding font, the third will be in italic (or bold), etc., up to six arguments. The arguments will be squished together without intervening spaces, so you must use quoted spaces to avoid this feature.

```
.nf
Slurp, scoop, in an ice cream sloop.
.I
Sniffle, wiffle, in a pudding piffle.
.R
.B Eye "lets " is "lets " is lands
lost in the sea.
But plenty to eat for you and me!
```

produces

> Slurp, scoop, in an ice cream sloop.
> *Sniffle, wiffle, in a pudding piffle.*
> **Ey**elets **is**lets **is**lands
> lost in the sea.
> But plenty to eat for you and me!

-mm automatically places a narrow space after italic text to prevent possible collisions.

-mm also has six macros that switch between pairs of fonts. These are similar to the .I and .B macros described above, except the switching is between pairs of fonts rather than between the surrounding font and bold or italic. These six macros are .IB, .BI, .RI, .IR, .RB, and .BR.

-mm has the .SM macro for printing text at a 1-point reduced size. .SM requires either one, two, or three arguments:

1. With one argument, .SM will print that argument 1 point smaller than surrounding text.

2. With two arguments, .SM will print the first smaller and the second in the surrounding size, and the two will be glued together without intervening space.

3. With three arguments, .SM will print the first in the surrounding point size, the second 1 point smaller, and the third in the surrounding size. All three arguments will be glued together without intervening space.

Here is an example of the .SM command:

```
The
.SM UNIX
system originated on minicomputers.
.SM U NIX ""
is a trademark
of AT&T Bell labs \(em it should never be used
as a noun.
```

produces

> The UNIX system originated on minicomputers. UNIX is a trademark of AT&T Bell labs — it should never be used as a noun.

-mm does not have a macro for printing text in a larger point size.

There are seven accent marks in -mm. Each accent mark is produced by placing a three-letter code following the letter to be marked.

NAME	INPUT	OUTPUT	NAME	INPUT	OUTPUT
acute	e*´	é	grave	e*`	è
circumflex	o*^	ô	tilde	n*~	ñ
umlaut	u*:	ü	Umlaut	U*;	Ü
cedilla	c*,	ç			

7.5 LISTS

Lists are the glory of -mm. Lists are important in many scholarly or technical documents, because they are an organizational tool. In most lists there
is a *mark* at the beginning of each item. For example, the list near the end
of the previous section (describing the arguments of .SM) used numbers to
mark each item in the list.

All -mm lists have the same general layout. The overall list is bracketed
by a list-begin, list-end pair of macros, much as a display is bracketed by
display-start, display-end macros. Although there are six different list-
begin macros in -mm, the list-end macro is always the .LE macro. Inside the
list-begin, list-end bracketing macros, each item of the list is introduced by
the .LI macro. Thus all lists have the general form shown in Figure 7.2.

Three of -mm's list types are almost trivially simple. The *bullet list* is
started by a .BL command. Each item in a bullet list is marked by a bullet.
The bullet list's twin is the *dash list*, started by the .DL command, which
substitutes dashes for the bullets. A close cousin of .BL and .DL is the

INPUT:

```
.BL
.LI
Lists start with a list-begin macro, .BL for this bullet list.
.LI
Each item in a list is introduced by a .LI macro.
.LI
Every list ends with the .LE macro.
.LE
```

OUTPUT:

- Lists start with a list-begin macro, .BL for this bullet list.

- Each item in a list is introduced by a .LI macro.

- Every list ends with the .LE macro.

Figure 7.2. All -mm lists have the form shown above.

marked list, which is started by the .ML command. The .ML command takes an argument string that specifies the mark to be used for every item in the list. The argument string should not contain any paddable spaces. An example of a marked list is shown in Figure 7.3.

In glossaries, descriptions of commands, and similar material, the author often wants to mark each item in a list with a different word or phrase. In −mm these lists are called *variable-item* lists, and they are introduced by the .VL command. The first argument to .VL specifies the indentation of the list in ens. There is no default; you must specify an indentation. In a variable-item list, each .LI macro is typically provided with an argument that specifies the mark for that item. An example variable-item list is shown in Figure 7.4.

One interesting feature of −mm is that you can make *exdented* paragraphs using variable-item lists. An exdented paragraph is one in which the first line of the paragraph starts farther to the left than the others. They are often used in glossaries or lists of references. You can make an exdented paragraph by omitting the label on the .LI commands in a .VL list. An example is shown in Figure 7.5.

One powerful feature of −mm′s lists is that they, like headings, can be automatically numbered. This allows you complete freedom to add or delete list entries without having to go through the list manually updating the number that marks each item. The .AL list-begin macro is used to start an automatically numbered list. A related type of list, the *reference* list, is started using the .RL list-begin macro. Reference lists are always labeled by

INPUT:

```
.ML \(dg
.LI
The command \f2.BL\fP starts a \f3bullet\fP list.
.LI
The command \f2.DL\fP starts a \f3dash\fP list.
.LI
The command \f2.ML mark\fP starts a \f3marked\fP list.
.LE
```

OUTPUT:

† The command *.BL* starts a **bullet** list.

† The command *.DL* starts a **dash** list.

† The command *.ML mark* starts a **marked** list.

Figure 7.3. In this example of a marked list, the mark is a dagger, specified by the troff code \(dg.

INPUT:

```
.ce
Forms of Communication
.VL 10
.LI \f2CB\fP
Used primarily by motorists for entertainment.
Also used by boaters and by hobbyists.
.LI \f2HAM\fP
Used primarily by hobbyists for long-distance communication.
.LI \f2Two\0Tin\0Cans\0and\0a\0String\fP
Used primarily by kids learning about science.
Operational distance is strictly limited,
and operator failure (inability to maintain string
tension) is common.
.LE
```

OUTPUT:

Forms of Communication

CB   Used primarily by motorists for entertainment. Also used by boaters and by hobbyists.

HAM   Used primarily by hobbyists for long-distance communication.

Two Tin Cans and a String Used primarily by kids learning about science. Operational distance is strictly limited, and operator failure (inability to maintain string tension) is common.

Figure 7.4. Variable-item lists are often used to define terms. The labels should not contain ordinary spaces; therefore, unpaddable spaces (indicated by the \0 code) are used in the third label. Notice how the overly long label for the third item is formatted. A long label can be prevented from running into the following text by placing a .br command on the following line.

Arabic numerals surrounded by square braces, a style often used for footnotes or other numbered references.

By default, Arabic numerals are used to number the items in an .AL list, but Roman numerals or alphabetic labels may be used. The second argument to .AL specifies the type of the labels: 1 (numeral one) means use Arabic numerals (the default), A (or a) means use uppercase (or lowercase) alphabetic labels, and I (or i) means use uppercase (or lowercase) Roman numerals. Examples are shown in Figures 7.6 and 7.7.

The remainder of this section contains more detailed information about the different -mm lists. You might want to skip to the following section on first reading. In the following descriptions, square brackets surround optional macro arguments.

INPUT:

```
.ce
References
.VL 5
.LI
Gilbert, C., \f2Management Science Applied to
the Scientific Laboratory\fP, The Quarterly
Journal of the Harvard Business School, Spring 1986.
.LI
Katz, L., \f2Law Enforcement Applications of
Microscopic Tracer Beads\fP,
Law Enforcement Today, Vol. 18, No. 3, Jan. 1943.
.LE
```

OUTPUT:

References

Gilbert, C., *Management Science Applied to the Scientific Laboratory*, The Quarterly Journal of the Harvard Business School, Spring 1986.

Katz, L., *Law Enforcement Applications of Microscopic Tracer Beads*, Law Enforcement Today, Vol. 18, No. 3, Jan. 1943.

Figure 7.5. Variable-item lists can be used to make exdented paragraphs. The amount that the paragraph body is indented, 5 ens in this example, is specified in the .VL command.

.BL [indent] [no-space]

.DL [indent] [no-space]

The .BL and .DL macros start bullet or dash lists. They take two optional arguments. The first argument is the indentation amount of the list specified in ens. If specified, the first argument will override the default indentation, which is the same as the indentation of a normal paragraph. If the second argument is specified, it means that items in the list won't be separated by the customary extra half line of space. If you want to specify the second argument while retaining the default indentation, supply the null argument "" for the indentation as follows:

.BL "" 1

.ML mark [indent] [no-space]

The .ML macro starts marked lists, which have one required argument, the mark, and two optional arguments, indent and no-space. The mark should not contain paddable spaces. The indentation and no-space arguments are the same as for bullet lists. The default indentation is the width of the mark plus 1 en.

INPUT:

```
.ce
Versions of the Unix System
.AL I
.LI
V6 (1976) \(em First widely distributed Unix System
.LI
V7 (1978) \(em Bourne shell, the first modern Unix System
.LI
System V
.AL 1
.LI
System V \(em (1983) \(em \f2se\fP screen editor
.LI
System V Release 2 (1984) \(em Consider it Standard
.LI
System V Release 3 (1986) \(em Streams
.LE
.LI
BSD
.AL a
.LI
2.9 (1983) \(em Final PDP-11 System
.LI
4.2 (1983) \(em High Performance and Networking
.LI
4.3 (1986) \(em Windowing and Tuning
.LE
.LE
```

Figure 7.6(a). Automatic lists are numbered automatically in any of five different formats: Roman numerals (upper- or lowercase), Arabic numbers, or alphabetic (upper- or lowercase).

.AL [type] [indent] [no-space]

The .AL macro starts "automatic" lists, which take three optional arguments. The first argument is the type of the list, specified by the keys 1, a, A, i, or I as described above. The indent and no-space arguments have their customary meanings, and the default indentation is 6 ens.

.RL [indent] [no-space]

A reference list is the same as an Arabic format automatic list, except the numbers are placed within square brackets.

OUTPUT:

Versions of the Unix System

   I. V6 (1976) — First widely distributed Unix System

  II. V7 (1978) — Bourne shell, the first modern Unix System

 III. System V

      1. System V — (1983) — *se* screen editor

      2. System V Release 2 (1984) — Consider it Standard

      3. System V Release 3 (1986) — Streams

 IV. BSD

      a. 2.9 (1983) — Final PDP-11 System

      b. 4.2 (1983) — High Performance and Networking

      c. 4.3 (1986) — Windowing and Tuning

Figure 7.6(b). Sample output from the input in Figure 7.6(a).

.VL indent [mark-indent] [no-space]

    A variable-item list uses marks supplied with each item of the list. The indent of the list must be specified (in ens), and there are two optional arguments, with the obvious meanings. Each .LI will have either (1) an argument, which will be used as the mark; (2) a null argument, which means there is no mark; or (3) no argument, which means produce an exdented paragraph.

.LI [mark] [in-front]

    The .LI macro, used to identify each item in a list, has two optional arguments. The first argument is a mark, which will be used instead of the default mark. If a mark and a second argument are used, then the additional mark will appear in front of the default mark instead of replacing it. For an example, see the list in Figure 7.7.

.LE [add-space]

    The .LE macro, used to end a list, has one optional argument. When it is supplied, the .LE will supply a half line of space following the list. This option should be used only when the list is followed by plain text, not when the list is followed by a macro (e.g., .P or .H) that will insert its own extra space.

INPUT:

```
.ce
\f3HOW TO CLEAN UP A REALLY FILTHY HOUSE\fP
.AL A
.LI
Advice for the Extremely Rich
.br
If you are wealthy, so wealthy that you own a Caribbean island
or even a U.S. Senator, stop reading right now.  You don't need
to clean your house; just throw it out and buy a new one.
.LI
Advice for the Moderately Rich
.br
Take a two-week vacation to a quiet, uninhabited island. Before
your departure, hire a dozen trustworthy clean fetishists,
pay them handsomely, and point them to your abode.  On the
plane ride home, read the sequel to this book, \f2How to
Keep a Clean House Clean\fP.
.LI
Advice for the Average Joe
.br
If you are like me, you have grimly come to the realization that you
have to do it yourself.  There are three main things to remember:
.BL "" 1
.LI
Don't put it off.
.LI
Do it all at once, or you'll never finish it.
.LI
Don't try to do anything else, like watch a soap opera,
while you're cleaning.
.LE
With these cautions in mind, you're ready to attack
your personal Disaster Area, the Kitchen:
.AL
.LI
Liquid Supplies
.AL i "" 1
.LI
Glass Cleaner
.LI
Dishwashing Liquid
.LI
Ammonia
.LI
```

```
Chlorine
.LI \\(rh
Never use chlorine and ammonia together. The fumes are
actually mustard gas, of WWI fame.
.LE
.LI
Solid Supplies
.AL i "" 1
.LI
Roach Killer
.LI
Dishwasher Powder
.LE
.LE
.LE
```

Figure 7.7(a). Lists are usually used to organize documents.

7.6 DISPLAYS AND FOOTNOTES

As usual, -mm's support for displays is comprehensive. Unlike the (to me) disorganized approach of -ms, -mm uses just two macros to introduce displays: .DS for static displays and .DF for floating displays. You may remember from the chapter on -ms that a static display always stays at the same spot in the text. If a static display is too big to fit on the current page, it is moved to the next, leaving a hole on the bottom of the page. Conversely, if a floating display is too big to fit on the current page, following text is used to fill the current page, and then the floating display is placed at the top of the following page. Although a floating display won't leave holes in the text, it may move relative to its surrounding text. Both display types use the .DE macro to indicate the end of the display.

The definition of a display in -ms is very narrow. -ms displays are kept together and processed in no-fill mode. The definition of a display is broader in -mm. In -mm, a display is simply a block of text that is kept together and possibly processed in a different style from the surrounding text.

Both display types have three optional arguments—the format, the fill, and the right indent. The *format* code L means don't indent the display, the code I means indent the display, the code C means individually center each line of the display, and the code CB means center the display as a block. If the code is null or omitted, the display will not be indented. Your documents can be made more inscrutable by using the numerical codes 0, 1, 2, or 3 instead of L, I, C, or CB, respectively. The default format is not indented.

OUTPUT:

HOW TO CLEAN UP A REALLY FILTHY HOUSE

A. Advice for the Extremely Rich
If you are wealthy, so wealthy that you own a Caribbean island or even a U.S. Senator, stop reading right now. You don't need to clean your house; just throw it out and buy a new one.

B. Advice for the Moderately Rich
Take a two-week vacation to a quiet, uninhabited island. Before your departure, hire a dozen trustworthy clean fetishists, pay them handsomely, and point them to your abode. On the plane ride home, read the sequel to this book, *How to Keep a Clean House Clean*.

C. Advice for the Average Joe
If you are like me, you have grimly come to the realization that you have to do it yourself. There are three main things to remember:

- Don't put it off.

- Do it all at once, or you'll never finish it.

- Don't try to do anything else, like watch a soap opera, while you're cleaning.

With these cautions in mind, you're ready to attack your personal Disaster Area, the Kitchen:

1. Liquid Supplies

    i.   Glass Cleaner
    ii.   Dishwashing Liquid
    iii. Ammonia
    iv.   Chlorine
    ☛   Never use chlorine and ammonia together. The fumes are actually mustard gas, of WWI fame.

2. Solid Supplies

    i.   Roach Killer
    ii.   Dishwasher Powder

Figure 7.7(b). Sample output from the input in Figure 7.7(a).

The optional *fill* argument allows you to specify that the text in the display will be filled; the default is for no-fill inside a display. If the fill argument is F (or 1), then the display will be filled, but if the fill argument is N or 0 or "" (null) or omitted, then the display will be no-fill.

The optional *rindent* argument can be used to make the right margin of a display indented from the right margin of the surrounding text. The indentation is specified in ens. Several features of displays are illustrated in Figures 7.8 and 7.9.

Footnotes are delimited in -mm by the .FS, .FE pair of macros. Footnotes may not appear within displays, and displays may not occur within footnotes. You can supply your own label for footnotes, or you can have -mm automatically number your footnotes for you.

If you supply the label, you must do it in two places, after the footnoted text and as an argument to the .FS command. Here is an example specification for a manually labeled footnote.

```
casualties at Antietam, but the carnage at Antietam
surpassed that of any other single day in American
combat history.\0[Foot 1965b]
.FS [Foot 1965b]
Foot, Weary. \f2Bull Run to Antietam\fP,
Civil Press, Harrisburg 1965.
.FE
```

Automatically numbered footnotes are produced using the *F string as a label. Each time the string is used, the label is incremented by 1. When you are using automatically numbered footnotes, you should not supply a label argument to the .FS command.

```
casualties at Antietam, but the carnage at Antietam
surpassed that of any other single day in American
combat history.\0\*F
.FS
Foot, Weary. \f2Bull Run to Antietam\fP,
Civil Press, Harrisburg 1965.
.FE
```

With all types of footnotes it is important to make sure that the footnote label, your own or the string *F, is glued onto the word that you want to footnote. If the label and the footnoted word are separated by an ordinary space, a line break may separate the footnote label from the labeled word, producing an extremely odd citation. In the examples above, I have used a digit width space, but you can also omit the space entirely or use an ordinary unpaddable space.

-mm has 12 footnote styles that can be selected using the .FD macro. The options controlled by the .FD macro are whether automatic hyphenation is enabled within a footnote, whether text is adjusted or ragged, whether the

INPUT:

```
.DS C
500 E. 63\urd.\d St., Apt. 14C
New York City, New York, 10021
December 3, 1985
.DE
.sp 2
.DS L
Frederick C. Taylor, Jr.
Secretary
J. M. Smucker Co.
Orrville, Ohio  44667
.DE
.sp
Dear Mr. Taylor,
.P
```

I would like to clear up a problem that has been plaguing me
for about a year. The difficulty arose when my daughter Kari,
age 5, received one share of your stock as a gift. It is her
first investment, and she loves to talk about owning part of
the company whose jam she so greedily enjoys. Unfortunately
her name has been spelled incorrectly from the beginning of
ownership, presenting problems with mail delivery, check
cashing, etc. I realize that Kari is a very small holder,
in size, in age, and in number of shares. However, I feel
that it would be best for all concerned if her name were
spelled correctly.

```
.P
```

The name, as it is currently recorded on account 130-1386520,
is Carl Christian. Her correct first name, as noted above,
is Kari. Please bring this matter to the attention of the
appropriate official at Smuckers so that it can be corrected.

```
.sp
.DS CB
Thank you very much,
.sp 3
Kaare Christian
(Parent and Guardian
of Kari Christian)
.DE
```

Figure 7.8(a). An example letter using the **-mm** macro package and the **nroff** formatter.

OUTPUT:

500 E. 63$^{rd.}$ St., Apt. 14C
New York City, New York, 10021
December 3, 1985

Frederick C. Taylor, Jr.
Secretary
J. M. Smucker Co.
Orrville, Ohio 44667

Dear Mr. Taylor,

I would like to clear up a problem that has been plaguing me for about a year. The difficulty arose when my daughter Kari, age 5, received one share of your stock as a gift. It is her first investment, and she loves to talk about owning part of the company whose jam she so greedily enjoys. Unfortunately her name has been spelled incorrectly from the beginning of ownership, presenting problems with mail delivery, check cashing, etc. I realize that Kari is a very small holder, in size, in age, and in number of shares. However, I feel that it would be best for all concerned if her name were spelled correctly.

The name, as it is currently recorded on account 130-1386520, is Carl Christian. Her correct first name, as noted above, is Kari. Please bring this matter to the attention of the appropriate official at Smuckers so that it can be corrected.

Thank you very much,

Kaare Christian
(Parent and Guardian
of Kari Christian)

Figure 7.8(b). Sample output from the input in Figure 7.8(a).

INPUT:

```
.DS C
.S 12 15
The Persuasive Effect of Brand Names
on Taste Perception
.sp 2
.S D D
.I
Jennifer Stare, Ph.D.
Nigel Biggelthwaite, Ph.D.
.sp 2
.R
New School for Gustatory Research
New York City, New York 10037
.sp 2
.I
Abstract
.R
.DE
.DS I F 2
.S 8 12
The ``taste test'' is a hallmark of our consumer society.
Marketers of food and drink often point to the blind taste
test to prove the superiority of their products.  One
disadvantage of these studies is that they ignore the
powerful effect of packaging on the consumer's perception
of taste. In this study we compare a prestigious carbonated soda
water drink with its low-rent cousin, club soda. The results
of this study reveal the influence that brand names have on
our taste buds.
.DE
.S D D
.H 1 Introduction
The advent of the young urban professional has caused a
dramatic increase in expensive supermarket items. Many are
similar in appearance to cheaper, more common products.  We
emptied the liquid from a case of expensive bottled mineral
water and replaced it with ShopFine club soda.  The soda was
served to customers at The Laughing Parrot, a popular
midtown lunch spot.
```

Figure 7.9(a). The first page of a manuscript formatted using the -mm macros.

OUTPUT:

The Persuasive Effect of Brand Names
on Taste Perception

Jennifer Stare, Ph.D.
Nigel Biggelthwaite, Ph.D.

New School for Gustatory Research
New York City, New York 10037

Abstract

The "taste test" is a hallmark of our consumer society. Marketers of food and drink often point to the blind taste test to prove the superiority of their products. One disadvantage of these studies is that they ignore the powerful effect of packaging on the consumer's perception of taste. In this study we compare a prestigious carbonated soda water drink with its low-rent cousin, club soda. The results of this study reveal the influence that brand names have on our taste buds.

1. Introduction

The advent of the young urban professional has caused a dramatic increase in expensive supermarket items. Many are similar in appearance to cheaper, more common products. We emptied the liquid from a case of expensive bottled mineral water and replaced it with ShopFine club soda. The soda was served to customers at The Laughing Parrot, a popular midtown lunch spot.

Figure 7.9(b). Sample output from the input in Figure 7.9(a).

footnote is indented, and whether the footnote label is left- or right-adjusted. The following table shows what code you should supply as the first argument to .FD to select a given style.

STYLE	HYPHENATION	RIGHT MARGIN	TEXT INDENT	LABEL JUSTIFICATION
0	no	adjusted	yes	left
1	yes	adjusted	yes	left
2	no	ragged	yes	left
3	yes	ragged	yes	left
4	no	adjusted	no	left
5	yes	adjusted	no	left
6	no	ragged	no	left
7	yes	ragged	no	left
8	no	adjusted	yes	right
9	yes	adjusted	yes	right
10	no	ragged	yes	right
11	yes	ragged	yes	right

The default style is 10 for nroff and zero for troff.

If a second argument is supplied to the .FD macro, then footnote numbering will be reset after every first-level heading.

The spacing between footnotes can be controlled with the Fs number register. The default value of the Fs number register is one that means footnotes are separated by a 3-point space. Setting Fs higher than 1 will produce multiples of 3-point spaces.

7.7   TABLE OF CONTENTS

The .TC macro of -mm will output a stored table of contents. -mm automatically collects information for a table of contents from the headings that you create in a document. By default the first two levels of headings are saved, but you can change that by supplying a new value for the Cl (capital C, lowercase ell) number register. For example, setting the Cl number register to 4 means the first four heading levels will be saved for inclusion in a table of contents.

The .TC macro accepts up to nine arguments.

    .TC [slevel] [spacing] [tlevel] [tab] [head ...]

The slevel and spacing arguments control vertical space in the table of contents. spacing blank lines will be placed in front of every entry whose heading level is less than or equal to slevel. For example, if slevel is 3 and spacing is 1, then table of contents entries for level 1, 2, and 3 heads will be preceded by one blank line. (In troff, a blank line is half the current vertical space; it is a full blank line in nroff.) The default for both slevel and spacing is 1.

The `tlevel` and `tab` arguments control the placement of the page number for each entry. Entries whose heading level is less than or equal to `tlevel` will have their page number placed flush right; higher level headings will have the page number follow the heading text. When `tab` is set to zero, then flush-right page numbers will be preceded by a string of dots; otherwise they will be preceded by spaces. The default for `tlevel` is 2, and the default for `tab` is zero.

The remaining arguments supplied to the `.TC` macro are used as headings. They are centered horizontally on the page above the table of contents.

The `Ci` string register controls the indentation for each heading level in the table of contents. By default, each level will align with the text portion of previous levels. The string supplied for `Ci` must contain an indentation amount for each level of saved heading. Thus, if the `Cl` number register is set to 4, there must be four numbers in the string supplied to `Ci`. Numbers supplied to `Ci` should be scaled using one of the usual `troff` scale codes. For example, if there are three levels of saved headings, the following will specify that levels 1 and 2 heads are flush left and level 3 heads are indented 1 centimeter.

```
.ds Ci 0 0 1c
```

A sample table of contents is shown in Figure 7.10. The input for this table of contents comes from Figure 7.1. If you look at the beginning of Figure 7.1, you will see the command

```
.nr Cl 3
```

which means that three levels of headings are saved. In Figure 7.10, the commands before the `.TC` command makes level 3 heads indented.

INPUT:

```
.ds Ci 0 0 6n
.TC 2 1 2 0
```

OUTPUT:

CONTENTS

1. The Corpse Created   1

1.1 Introduce Sir George, Young Giles, and Lady Gillian   1

1.2 Tempers Flare over Giles' Behavior.   1

      1.2.1 Giles Threatened by His Nanny 1

II. Clues Accumulate.   1

II.01 M. Clochet Arrives   1

Figure 7.10. This sample table of contents reflects the headings in Figure 7.1.

CHAPTER 8

Equations and the eqn Preprocessor

Although naked troff has adequate facilities for typesetting mathematical material, its notation is impossibly difficult. The obvious solution to the problem was to extend troff so that its notation for expressing mathematics would be simpler. However, troff was already about as large a program as could fit on the then current PDP-11 architecture. Thus necessity, often called the mother of invention, forced the developers to provide a mathematics notation for troff as a separate program. Thus was born eqn, the first troff preprocessor.

Although eqn is designed expressly as an aid for typesetting mathematical equations, it is abysmally ignorant of math. Instead, eqn is a simple layout language. It knows how to put one group of symbols over another, or how to set a superscript. You describe an equation to eqn much as you might describe it to a graphic artist — take these symbols, put them over these, make this in smaller type, align these equations like this. Although at first blush it seems odd that a program for typesetting mathematics doesn't know anything about the subject, in practice eqn's mathematical ignorance has worked in its favor.

The original references for eqn are *A System for Typesetting Mathematics* and *Typesetting Mathematics — User's Guide*, both by Kernighan and Cherry. A condensed version of these papers appears in the Western Electric *Document Processing Guide*. Beware that the Western Electric guide omits the two large examples from the papers.

8.1   USAGE

eqn is a troff preprocessor. It is used with troff in a UNIX pipeline.

```
$ eqn quarks | troff -ms
$ _
```

In this particular example the -ms macros are also used, but you should keep in mind that eqn and the -ms macros address separate aspects of the formatting process. Either can be used without the other, but they are often used together, as shown above.

Although eqn is best used with troff on high-resolution printers, a version of it called neqn can be used with nroff on more modest printers. neqn accepts the same equation definitions as eqn, but it produces output more suited to the lower-resolution printers used with nroff. Few people use neqn's very modest output quality for anything other than proofing.

```
$ neqn quarks | nroff -ms -T450-12 | q450
$ _
```

In your document the equations are separated from the plain text by the .EQ, .EN delimiters as follows.

```
.EQ
a sup 2 + b sup 2 = c sup 2
.EN
```

Usually just one equation is placed between the eqn delimiters. Within an equation specification, the format is relatively free-form. Spaces must be used to separate the words of the specification, but extra spaces, tabs, and line breaks are ignored. Thus the following specification will produce exactly the same output as the equation specification given above.

```
.EQ
a sup 2 +
   b sup 2 =
      c sup 2
.EN
```

The placement of the equation on the output page depends on what macro package you are using, because each macro package supplies its own definition for the .EQ and .EN macros. If you aren't using a macro package, the equation will be set inline like this: $a^2 + b^2 = c^2$. With the -me or -ms macro package the equation will be centered horizontally in its own space, like this:

$$a^2 + b^2 = c^2$$

However, with -mm, the equation definition must be surrounded by display
macros, and the type of the -mm display will determine whether the equation
is left-adjusted, centered, etc. In -mm, an equation specification for a centered equation looks like the following.

```
.DS C
.EQ
a sup 2 + b sup 2 = c sup 2
.EN
.DE
```

In-line equations can be made with any of the macro packages using the
delim option, as explained in Section 8.10.

With -ms and -me, the .EQ start-equation delimiter accepts two arguments. The first argument should be C (the default), I, or L to indicate a
centered, indented, or left-aligned equation. The second argument is an
optional title for the equation that will be placed at the right margin.

```
.EQ I (III-1)
a sup 2 + b sup 2 = c sup 2
.EN
```

Here is the output:

$$a^2 + b^2 = c^2 \hspace{8cm} \text{(III-1)}$$

With the -mm macro package, the .EQ start-equation delimiter takes just
one argument, an optional title.

The .EQ, .EN delimiters aren't shown in most of the examples in this
chapter. Wherever possible, the eqn input is shown on the left of a display,
and the typeset output is shown on the right, like this:

```
x ~=~ {b +- sqrt{b sup 2 - 4ac}} over 2a
```
$$x = \frac{b \pm \sqrt{b^2 - 4ac}}{2a}$$

When the example input and output won't fit side by side, the eqn input is
usually shown above the resultant output. The components of this equation
will be explained in the latter part of this chapter.

8.2   SUB, SUPER, AND OVER

eqn, with its mathematical ignorance, is primarily a layout language.
Although there are many eqn features for equation layout, just three commands, sub, sup, and over, provide much of the necessary control. sub
and sup are used for subscripts and superscripts. Each level of a sub- or

superscript is printed in a smaller typeface. Thus e sup i sup 2 produces e^{i^2}. If a single item must have both a superscript and a subscript, mention the subscript first. X sub i sup 2 is printed as X_i^2. If you reverse the order, X sup i sub 2, you get X^{i_2}; the 2 becomes a subscript of i, not of X.

The over keyword is used to produce fractions. Thus 1 over 2 produces $\frac{1}{2}$. Notice that eqn arranges for enough space above and below the line so that the extra-height fraction doesn't collide with the surrounding lines. Notice also that eqn is not audacious (mathematical) enough to translate 1 over 2 into 1/2. Think layout; try to put aside thoughts of mathematical meaning.

8.3   KEYWORDS

eqn has many built in keywords that make it easier to specify equations. *Action* keywords, such as over, tell eqn to do something. eqn's action keywords are discussed in the body of this chapter.

Symbol keywords are words that stand in for a mathematical symbol. For example, the inf keyword produces an ∞. eqn's symbol keywords are summarized in Table 8.1. troff doesn't contain special symbols for some Greek letters; use Roman letters as necessary.

Function names are eqn's third type of keyword. Symbols that eqn doesn't recognize are ordinarily set in italics, in accordance with common mathematical practice. However, eqn knows the following function names, and they will be set in a Roman font.

and	arc	cos	cosh	coth	det	exp	for
if	Im	lim	ln	log	max	min	Re
		sin	sinh	tan	tanh		

Any of these keywords can be output in italics by quoting them (see the following section). Conversely, any nonrecognized function name can be output in a Roman font by using the roman keyword (see Section 8.9.1).

Diacritical marks are symbols that appear above letters, or sequences of letters. Here is a table showing eqn's collection of diacritical marks.

a dot	$\dot{a}$	b dotdot	$\ddot{b}$
c hat	$\hat{c}$	d tilde	$\tilde{d}$
e vec	$\vec{e}$	f dyad	$\overrightarrow{f}$
g bar	$\bar{g}$	h under	$\underline{h}$

Table 1. eqn's Symbolic Keywords.

alpha	α	omega	ω
beta	β	omicron	o
chi	χ	phi	ϕ
delta	δ	pi	π
epsilon	ϵ	psi	ψ
eta	η	rho	ρ
gamma	γ	sigma	σ
iota	ι	tau	τ
kappa	κ	theta	θ
lambda	λ	upsilon	υ
mu	μ	xi	ξ
nu	ν	zeta	ζ
DELTA	Δ	PSI	Ψ
GAMMA	Γ	SIGMA	Σ
LAMBDA	Λ	THETA	Θ
OMEGA	Ω	UPSILON	Υ
PHI	Φ	XI	Ξ
PI	Π		
>=	$\geq$	<=	$\leq$
==	$\equiv$	!=	$\neq$
->	$\rightarrow$	<-	$\leftarrow$
<<	$\ll$	>>	$\gg$
+-	$\pm$	approx	$\approx$
inf	∞	partial	∂
half	$\frac{1}{2}$	times	$\times$
prime	$'$	cdot	$\cdot$
del	∇	grad	∇
...	$\cdots$	,....,	$,\ldots,$
sum	$\sum$	int	$\int$
union	$\cup$	inter	$\cap$
prod	$\prod$	nothing	

Notice that eqn does its best to place the diacritical at the right height. The bar and under marks will be extended to fit above (or below) very long inputs. The other marks are centered above their input.

8.4   QUOTES, BRACES, TILDES, AND SPACES

As eqn peruses your equations, its first thought is to separate the keywords from everything else. Keywords are words that eqn knows. For instance, the sup keyword tells eqn that the following word is a superscript. However, eqn's notion of a word may be different from yours. For example, if you say f(x sup 2), you will produce the funny-looking equation $f(x^{2)}$, because the word 2) will be used as the superscript. You can make your notion of a word come closer to eqn's by the liberal application of spaces in the input. The equation specification f(x sup 2) will produce the output $f(x^2)$. The extra space following the 2 makes the difference.

Often the opposite problem arises: you want eqn to take several distinct words and treat them as one. If you surround a group of words with curly braces ({}), the enclosed items will be treated as a group.

sqrt { b sup 2 - 4ac } $\sqrt{b^2 - 4ac}$

e sup {i omega t} $e^{i\omega t}$

1 over { sin sup 2 (alpha t) } $\dfrac{1}{\sin^2(\alpha t)}$

You can override the special meanings of keywords by quoting them. Here is the third example from above, with the keywords sin and alpha quoted.

1 over { "sin" sup 2 ("alpha" t) } $\dfrac{1}{sin^2(alphat)}$

One lesson from this example is that keywords can be stripped of their special meanings by quoting. Another lesson is that eqn places symbols such as alpha and t next to each other, to produce *alphat*. When Einstein writes $e = mc^2$, we recognize the *m* and the *c* as separate symbols, but in the equation above the *alpha* and the *t* need some white space to clarify their meaning. eqn uses the tilde character (˜) to force extra white space into the output. eqn's equations are often too compact, and judicious use of tildes will make your output more aesthetically pleasing. In some cases, such as the following, the extra space is required to clarify the meaning.

1 over { "sin" sup 2 ("alpha" ˜t) } $\dfrac{1}{sin^2(alpha\ t)}$

If you need some extra white space, but not as much as provided by a tilde, you can get a half-width space using a caret (ˆ).

$$\texttt{1 over \{ "sin" sup 2 (\^{} "alpha" \~{}t\^{}) \}} \qquad \frac{1}{sin^2(alpha\ t)}$$

8.5 FROM, TO

Summations and integrals often have bounds expressions written above and below the summation or integral symbol. This effect is achieved in eqn using the keywords from and to.

$$\begin{array}{l}\texttt{sum from i=1 to N} \\ \texttt{\~{}int from \{C sub 1\} f(x,y,z)ds}\end{array} \qquad \sum_{i=1}^{N}\int_{C_1} f(x,y,z)ds$$

The word in front of the from or to keywords can be anything, so constructs such as the following are possible.

$$\texttt{X inter from (inter) Y} \qquad X \underset{(inter)}{\bigcap} Y$$

In this example, the second appearance of the word inter isn't recognized as a keyword because of the surrounding parentheses. If the parentheses had been separated (by white space) from the word inter, then the second inter would need to be quoted (to suppress its meaning as a keyword), and the whole sequence of three symbols would need to be surrounded by braces. As you can see, it is much simpler to glue the parentheses to the word inter. The from keyword is often used with the lim function to identify the limits.

8.6 LEFT, RIGHT

The keywords left and right are used to produce big curly braces, square brackets, parentheses, bars, etc. (In this section the word *bracket* will refer to all of the possibilities: curly braces, square brackets, parentheses, and bars.) If you don't use the left and right keywords, the bracket is printed in the normal size, which is often not what you want. The following example shows both ways.

$$\begin{array}{l}\texttt{bold f cdot [bold i dx over ds} \\ \texttt{+ bold j dy over ds]}\end{array} \qquad \mathbf{f}\cdot[\mathbf{i}\frac{dx}{ds}+\mathbf{j}\frac{dy}{ds}]$$

```
    bold f cdot left [ bold i dx over ds
```

$$\mathbf{f} \cdot \left[\mathbf{i}\frac{dx}{ds} + \mathbf{j}\frac{dy}{ds} \right]$$

```
     + bold j dy over ds right ]
```

Large parentheses or curly brackets may not be attractive, depending on your typesetter font. (The word `bold` in this example is used to print the following word in boldface, rather than in italics. See Section 8.9.1.)

It is permissible to have a `left` brace without using a `right`. However, in this case you should put braces around the following thing so that `eqn` can calculate its height.

```
    left ( { f over { int x sub i sup n }}
```

$$\left(\frac{f}{\int x_i^n}\right.$$

If you want a large `right` brace without a left, you need to put in a phantom left brace as a placeholder.

```
    left "" f cdot int x sub i sup n right ]
```

$$f \cdot \left. \int x_i^n \right]$$

The `""` is a null symbol; it expands into a large left nothing that serves as a placeholder for the following large right bracket.

8.7 PILES AND MATRICES

A `pile` is `eqn`'s way of making a stack of things. The general specification of a pile looks like this:

    `pile { ` *thing* ` above ` *thing* ` above ` *thing* ` · · · }`

The *things* may be anything, and the keyword `above` separates the items in the pile. Here is the input for a longish example:

```
left [
   pile { bold i above partial / partial x above F sub x }
   pile { bold j above partial / partial y above F sub y }
   pile { bold k above partial / partial z above F sub z }
right ]
```

And here is the output:

$$\left[\begin{array}{ccc} \mathbf{i} & \mathbf{j} & \mathbf{k} \\ \partial/\partial x & \partial/\partial y & \partial/\partial z \\ F_x & F_y & F_z \end{array} \right]$$

By default, eqn's piles are centered, and the vertical spacing is compact. eqn has three additional flavors of piles: lpile, which is left-adjusted; rpile, which is right-adjusted; and cpile, which is centered. The vertical spacing of *rlc*piles is slightly larger than that of ordinary piles.

The vertical spacing of adjacent piles isn't set so that the rows line up, as illustrated in the following:

```
left [
   pile { sqrt 2 over 2 above 1 }
   pile { 1 above sqrt 2 over 2 }
right ]
```

$$\begin{bmatrix} \dfrac{\sqrt{2}}{2} & \\ 1 & \dfrac{\sqrt{2}}{2} \end{bmatrix}$$

If you want the rows of piles to align horizontally, you need to use a matrix instead of a pile. The input grammar for a matrix is more complicated than for piles, but then eqn does more alignment work for matrices, so it's a good tradeoff.

```
matrix {
        col { thing above thing above thing  · · · }
        col { thing above thing above thing  · · · }
        col { thing above thing above thing  · · · }
        · · ·
}
```

The *things* can be anything, and the braces are all necessary. (Of course you can also use braces within the *things* as necessary.) Each column must have the same number of elements. Here is the previous example, redone with eqn's matrix facility.

```
left [ matrix {
   col { sqrt 2 over 2 above 1 }
   col { 1 above sqrt 2 over 2 }
} right ]
```

$$\begin{bmatrix} \dfrac{\sqrt{2}}{2} & 1 \\ 1 & \dfrac{\sqrt{2}}{2} \end{bmatrix}$$

eqn matrices can also have left-aligned columns, right-aligned columns, or centered columns using the keywords lcol, rcol, and ccol, respectively.

8.8 MARK AND LINEUP

When several equations appear above one another in a display, you often want them to align at some predetermined point, often (but not always) at an equals sign. This can be accomplished with eqn using the mark and lineup keywords. In the first equation you place the mark keyword at the desired alignment point, and then in the following equations you place the `lineup` keyword at the desired alignment point.

Lineups are calculated as a distance from a left margin (or left point of indentation), so they won't work on material that is centered one line at a time. However, you can use the block centered displays of -mm or -ms to center the equations as a block. You should also beware of specifying a mark in the first equation that is too far to the left for the given lineup in the subsequent equations. eqn doesn't do any lookahead when processing `mark` and `lineup`, and it can only adjust the lineup of subsequent equations by moving them to the right; it has no latitude to move them to the left.

Here is a trio of aligned equations using the -ms or -me macros.

```
.EQ I
int from C ( bold {f cdot t hat} ) ds mark =
    int from C f sub x dx + f sub y dy
.EN
.EQ I
lineup = int from C y ~ dx ~-~ x ~dy
.EN
.EQ I
lineup = int from C
    left ( y dx over ds ~-~ x dt over ds right ) ds
.EN
```

Here is the output.

$$\int_C (\mathbf{f} \cdot \hat{\mathbf{t}}) ds = \int_C f_x dx + f_y dy$$

$$= \int_C y\, dx - x\, dy$$

$$= \int_C \left(y\frac{dx}{ds} - x\frac{dt}{ds} \right) ds$$

8.9 TWEAKS

Although eqn often comes close on its own, for best results it needs some help. To my eye, untuned eqn output looks too dense. I prefer a looser appearance. As a first defense against overcrowding, eqn has the ˜ and ˆ for adding extra horizontal space.

Another problem area is type size and font selection. eqn tries to put function names in Roman and variables in italic. However, eqn's list of known functions is not exhaustive, and some equations should be treated differently. For example, vectors are commonly typeset in bold, not italics, to emphasize their multivalued aspect. eqn's choice of sizes is often ideal, but sometimes an adjustment is helpful.

8.9.1   Fonts and Sizes

The eqn keywords bold, italic, and roman are the most often used font control keywords. Each of these eqn directives affects only the following word. For example, bold i cdot roman dx produces **i**·dx. If you want the i and the dot product mark in bold, you can use braces. The eqn input bold {i cdot} roman dx produces **i**·dx.

A font other than the default troff Roman, italic, or bold can be accessed using the font keyword. The font keyword is followed by a single-digit font number or a single-character font name. The fat keyword is an alternative way to produce an emphasized appearance. The thing following fat is made a touch fatter by overstriking. fat is commonly used to produce emphasized italics, or emphasized special symbols.

The size keyword overrides eqn's choice of type size. The word size is followed by a number giving the absolute size, or by a signed digit indicating a relative size change, followed by the thing whose size is being controlled.

$$\texttt{partial / partial x} \qquad \partial/\partial x$$

$$\texttt{size -2 partial / partial x} \qquad \partial/\partial x$$

$$\texttt{size -2 \{partial / partial x\}} \qquad \partial/\partial x$$

8.9.2   Positioning

The keywords back, fwd, up, and down give you fine control of positioning. Each directive is followed by a number indicating the amount of the motion in hundredths of an em. Thus the command fwd 100 moves to the right about the width of the letter m. Here is a previous example redone to create a more spacious layout.

```
left [ ~
   pile { up 50 bold i above size -2 {partial / partial} x
      above down 50 {F sub x }}
   fwd 50
   pile { up 50 bold j above size -2 {partial / partial} y
      above down 50 {F sub y }}
   fwd 50
   pile { up 50 bold k above size -2 {partial / partial} z
      above down 50 {F sub z }} ~
   right ]
```

Here is the output:

$$\begin{bmatrix} \mathbf{i} & \mathbf{j} & \mathbf{k} \\ \partial/\partial x & \partial/\partial y & \partial/\partial z \\ F_x & F_y & F_z \end{bmatrix}$$

8.10   GLOBAL OPTIONS

Usually what appears between the `eqn` delimiters is an equation, but it is also possible to control several options with statements enclosed in the standard delimiters. The default point size used by `eqn` can be set with the `gsize` statement, and the default font can be set with the `gfont` statement. For example, the following tells `eqn` to set all subsequent equations based on 8-point type.

```
.EQ
gsize 8
.EN
```

When you are using any of the standard macro packages, any equations placed between the `.EQ` and `.EN` delimiters will be set off from the body of the text. If you want your equations to be placed in line, like many of the equations in this chapter, you can select a secondary pair of delimiters using the `delim` keyword. The word `delim` is followed by two characters; the first is the opening delimiter, and the second is the closing delimiter. When `eqn` encounters the opening delimiter in the text, it starts to process an equation, just as if it had encountered the `.EQ` delimiter. The difference is that the equation will be set in line. For example, the following will set both `eqn` delimiters to the currency symbol, a common choice.

```
.EQ
delim $$
.EN
```

If you want to restore the usual meaning of the `eqn` delimiter, you can use the special directive

```
.EQ
delim off
.EN
```

With the delimiters set to the currency symbols, an in-line specification such as `$v del t del S cos theta$` will produce the following in-line equation: $v \nabla t \nabla S \cos\theta$. Beware that some equations are too large to set in line; use the ordinary displays when necessary.

eqn has a simple macro definition facility that allows you to use a name to stand in for some sequence of eqn commands. For example, the following eqn input is a definition.

```
define raise 'up 50 bold'
```

Given this definition, raise becomes an eqn keyword that can be used the same way as any other keyword. Remember to surround raise with spaces so that it is recognized, and remember to quote it if you don't want its special meaning to be used. In this example I have used single quotes to delimit the definition, but any pair of characters can be used, provided the delimiters don't appear in the definition.

Here is the previous example of a complicated pile, somewhat simplified by using definitions.

```
define raise 'up 50 bold'
define part 'size -2 {partial / partial}'
define lower 'down 50'
left [ ~
    pile {raise i above part x above lower {F sub x}}
    fwd 50
    pile {raise j above part y above lower {F sub y}}
    fwd 50
    pile {raise k above part z above lower {F sub z}} ~
right ]
```

Here is the output:

$$\left[\begin{matrix} \mathbf{i} & \mathbf{j} & \mathbf{k} \\ \partial/\partial x & \partial/\partial y & \partial/\partial z \\ F_x & F_y & F_z \end{matrix} \right]$$

The worst thing you can do in a definition is to define something to be itself. For example, if the second definition above had been entered as

```
define partial 'size -2 {partial / partial}'
```

then eqn will report a serious error when the newly minted partial keyword is used.

Occasionally it is necessary to program eqn differently for the typesetter from how you program it for the printer. The keyword tdefine introduces a definition that is only expanded when eqn/troff is used, and ndefine introduces a definition that is only expanded when neqn/nroff is in use.

8.11   TROUBLESHOOTING

Although most eqn troubleshooting must be done by examining the printed output, there are several other debugging aids. The checkeq program will examine a file containing eqn text and report errors in matching eqn's pairs of delimiters.

```
$ checkeq quarks
quarks:
$ _
```

The lack of output indicates that checkeq didn't find any problems.

You can get a list of eqn's error messages without generating any printed output by redirecting eqn's output to '/dev/null'.

```
$ eqn quarks > /dev/null
eqn: fatal error: pushback overflow
file quarks, between lines 180 and 181
$ _
```

The message above shows the approximate location of the error, and the internal symptom. In this case the problem was a macro defined in terms of itself.

CHAPTER 9

Tables and the tbl Preprocessor

tbl is a program that enhances the power of the troff system. It translates an easy-to-use language for specifying tables into the troff codes that actually print the table. tbl automatically calculates column widths, provides several styles of column alignment, and draws lines in the table as necessary.

Before tbl was available, simple tabular data was managed by manually setting troff's tabs appropriately. For a wide column you simply provided a large tab stop. troff provides right-aligning tabs and centering tabs in addition to the traditional left-aligning tabs, so some variety in column alignment style was possible before tbl. The problem with the manual approach is twofold: producing attractive tables was an iterative process because column widths had to be tuned by trial and error, and the process was too hard for most troff users.

tbl makes it easy to produce simple tables, and with some work you can use tbl to produce impressive, complicated tables. tbl is one of the tools that sets the UNIX text-formatting system apart from the easier, but generally less powerful word processors that are used on many personal computers.

Since tbl is a "table specification to troff codes" translator, tbl must process your file before it is sent to troff.

```
$ tbl file | troff -ms
$ _
```

When both the tbl and the eqn preprocessors are needed, tbl should come first.

```
$ tbl file | eqn | troff -ms
$ _
```

In the commands shown above, the -ms macros are present to control the formatting of the nontabular material. tbl doesn't rely on -ms features, although the two systems are often used together.

The original documentation for tbl is *TBL—A Program to Format Tables* by tbl's author, M. E. Lesk. A deteriorated version of Lesk's paper (which fails to credit Lesk as the original author) is found in the *System V Document Processing Guide*. If you plan to use it as a reference, you should find an original copy of the document, containing all 13 examples from the *Examples* section at the end of the paper.

9.1 SIMPLE TABLES

tbl is a troff preprocessor. Like other troff preprocessors, tbl is only concerned with part of the input text, the table description. tbl finds table descriptions within documents by looking for the markers .TS and .TE. Material within the region delimited by .TS and .TE markers is processed by tbl; all other material in the document is untouched.

All table descriptions have the following general structure. After the .TS the general options of the table are described, followed by a semicolon. Then there is a description of the column formats, followed by a period. Finally the table data appear, eventually followed by .TE. Here is a picture of a table description.

```
.TS
options ;
column formats .
data
more data
  . . .
.TE
```

The *options* part of a table description may be omitted if you choose to accept the defaults.

Even though the options are easy to understand, let's postpone them for a while and start with the *column formats*. The column-formats part of a table description tells tbl how many columns of data are present and how you want tbl to format each column. Single-character key letters are used to describe the format of a column. The five major formats are left-adjusted, right-adjusted, centered, numeric, and horizontally spanned. Two other formats, alphabetic and vertically spanned, will be discussed in Section 9.2. The key letters for these column types are shown in the following

table. (Although uppercase letters are shown in the following table, either
upper- or lowercase may be used in table descriptions.)

Key   Column Type
L   Left Adjusted
C   Centered
R   Right Adjusted
N   Numeric
S   Spanned
A   Alphabetic
^   Vertically Spanned

   The data in a table is presented so that one line in the input file contains
the data for one line of the table. The data for each column is delimited
using tabs. So for a two-column table, each line of data would consist of
the entry for the first column, a tab, and then the entry for the second column. Probably the most common error using tbl is to put in too many or
too few entries on a line.
   In this chapter, when I present a figure that shows how a table is constructed, I am going to use the character ⊤ as a *visible tab* character.
Otherwise you wouldn't be able to tell the spaces in a table from the tabs.
It is important to examine carefully the figures in this chapter; textual
descriptions of how to use tbl are at best a substitute for actually examining the table specifications. (When you are editing a table specification with
the vi editor, it is often useful to turn on the list option so that the tabs
in your input are visible on the screen.) Here is the table specification that
produced the simple table shown above.

```
.TS
L C
C L.
Key ⊤ Column Type
L ⊤ Left Adjusted
C ⊤ Centered
R ⊤ Right Adjusted
N ⊤ Numeric
S ⊤ Spanned
A ⊤ Alphabetic
^ ⊤ Vertically Spanned
.TE
```

The first column format key L C, indicating a left-adjusted column and a
centered column, is used for the first line of the table. The second column
format key C L, indicating a centered column and a left-adjusted column, is
used for the second line of data through to the end of the table. If there
are *n* column format lines, they specify the format for the first *n* lines of

the table, and the last column format line is used for line *n* through the end of the table. The way column format lines are used coincides with the way most tables are designed; at the top of a table are headings, where each line has its own format, and then the data follows, where each line has the same format.

The data in a table will be scanned twice by troff. This becomes important when you use a \ to introduce a troff embedded command. Codes such as \(bu (to access the bullet character) or \s-2 (to decrease the point size by 2) work correctly, but embedded commands that access number registers or perform local motions may need an extra backslash on the front. Of course if you are performing local motions inside a table, you must be very careful that your home-brewed local motion produces a zero-sum effect, or following items in the table will be skewed.

9.1.1 Horizontal Spanning

In the table shown above, each column of data has its own heading. Although this is common usage, it is also common to provide an overall heading for the table that spans several columns. That feature is provided by tbl's horizontally spanned heading S format. For example, the table shown above might be clearer if it contained the overall title "Key Letters and Their Meanings." The input and output are shown in Figure 9.1. Notice that instead of the usual two tab-separated entries per line, the data line for the spanned heading contains just one entry. Other example tables with horizontally spanned titles are shown in Figures 9.3 through 9.9.

9.1.2 Numeric Columns

Tables often contain numeric data. One simple approach to handling numeric data is to put it into a right-adjusted column. For a plain column of figures, the simple approach will work fine. A better approach is to use a *numeric* column. In a numeric column, tbl attempts to align the numbers at their decimal point. Here are the rules that tbl uses for finding the decimal point.

- If the data contain periods, tbl will choose the rightmost period.

- Failing that, tbl will choose the rightmost digit.

- Finally, if the data are devoid of periods and digits, tbl will revert to centering the item.

Numeric columns also allow you to force alignment at a given place in an input string by inserting the troff placeholder \&. An example that demonstrates forced alignment is shown in Figure 9.2.

INPUT:

```
.TS
C S
L C
C L.
Key Letters and Their Meanings
Key T Column Type
L T Left Adjusted
C T Centered
R T Right Adjusted
N T Numeric
S T Spanned
A T Alphabetic
^ T Vertically Spanned
.TE
```

OUTPUT:

Key Letters and Their Meanings
Key	Column Type
L	Left Adjusted
C	Centered
R	Right Adjusted
N	Numeric
S	Spanned
A	Alphabetic
^	Vertically Spanned

Figure 9.1. The S key letter makes a heading span several columns of a table.

INPUT:

```
.TS
N.
2
4.0
.6
\&8.
Wh\&o
d\&o
\&we
appreciate?
.TE
```

OUTPUT:

```
    2
   4.0
    .6
   8.
  Who
   do
   we
appreciate?
```

Figure 9.2. Numeric column alignment is useful for numbers or for custom alignment of nonnumeric text by using the **troff** \& placeholder.

9.1.3 Font and Point Size Control

The key letters described above, which describe the overall format of a column, may be combined with other key letters that control several secondary characteristics of a column. Two of the most commonly used secondary controls are F, to make font changes, and P, to make point size changes. The F key letter is followed by a font number or name. (One-character font names should be followed by a space or tab to avoid ambiguity.) The key letter B is an accepted abbreviation for FB, and the key letter I can replace FI.

The key letter P controls point size for a column. P is followed by a signed digit to indicate a relative point size change, or a number to indicate the absolute point size. Figure 9.3 shows both features. Note that the F3 command could have been coded B.

9.1.4   Horizontal and Vertical Lines

Many tables contain horizontal and vertical lines. A *vertical* line in a table is produced by placing a vertical bar (|) between two column specifiers in the format section of the table. A *double vertical* line is produced by doubling the |. A *full-width horizontal* line across a table is produced by placing an underscore (_) alone on a line in the data part of the table. Similarly, a *double full-width horizontal* line is produced by an equals symbol (=) alone on a line in the data part of a table. Lines are joined as necessary; for example, a horizontal line will be joined smoothly to a vertical line extending downward.

Things are slightly more complicated for *columnwide horizontal* lines. If the data for one column consist of a underscore (or equals symbol), then that column will contain a full-width single (or double) horizontal line. It will join any neighboring horizontal or vertical lines. Alternatively, a horizontal line guaranteed *not* to join up with neighboring lines is produced with the data _.

You can fill the full width of a column with something other than a horizontal line by using \Rx as a column data item. The *x* stands for a character code that will be repeated as many times as it fits in the column. For example, the column data \R\(mu will produce a column full of multiplication signs. These options are illustrated and described in Figure 9.4.

INPUT:

```
.TS
CF3P+1 S
LFI CI
C L.
Secondary Keys
Key [T] Usage
F [T] Font Selection
B [T] Bold Font
I [T] Italic Font
P [T] Point Size Selection
.TE
```

OUTPUT:

Secondary Keys

Key	Usage
F	Font Selection
B	Bold Font
I	Italic Font
P	Point Size Selection

Figure 9.3. Fonts and point sizes can be chosen for columns using secondary keys.

9.1.5 Options

The *options* part of a table specification allows you to control the overall format of a table:

center
> makes the table centered between left and right margins. Otherwise, it will align near the left margin. This option has no effect on the vertical position of the table.

expand
> increases the separation between the columns, so that the table width matches the width of text on the page. The default column separation is 3 ens.

box
> encloses the entire table in a box.

doublebox
> encloses the entire table in a double box.

INPUT: **OUTPUT:**

```
.TS
 | CB S S |
 | CB S S |
 | LI CI LI |
 | c | c | c |.

 _
Single-Column
Horizontal Lines
Code T Meaning T Example
 =

\&_ T Joined, single line. T _
\&= T Joined, double line. T =
\&\_ T Orphaned, single line. T \_
\&\Rx T Repeated \f2x\fP. T \Rx

 _
.TE
```

	Single-Column Horizontal Lines	
Code	*Meaning*	*Example*
___	Joined, single line.	
=	Joined, double line.	
_	Orphaned, single line.	
\Rx	Repeated *x*.	xxxxxxx

Figure 9.4. Notice how the | is used in the format section of the table to produce the four vertical lines, and notice how _ and = are used in the body of the table to produce the three full-width horizontal lines. In column 1 of the table, the **troff** placeholder \& is used so that **tbl** places the _, =, and _ characters into the table, rather than using them specially as shown in column three of the table.

`allbox`

> boxes every item in the table. There will be a horizontal line between all of the rows and a vertical line between all of the columns.

`tab(x)`

> specifies an alternate tab character. This option is especially useful when you are constructing tables with many narrow columns, because using tabs makes the lines in your input file wider than most terminals. Common alternate column separators are #, @, %, and _. The column separator should not appear in the table as data.

`linesize(n)`

> specifies an alternate point size for drawing the lines in a table.

`delim(xy)`

> specifies *x* as the start of equation delimiter and *y* as the end of equation delimiter. This is necessary only in a numeric column that contains equations. When `tbl` knows the `eqn` delimiters, it doesn't disturb the equation during its attempt to align a numeric column. Equations are usually placed in left-aligned, centered, or right-aligned columns.

All of `tbl's` options are described in Figure 9.5, which also shows the *box* option in action.

9.2 ADVANCED TABLES

The `tbl` features presented above are sufficient to create serviceable, informative tables. However, `tbl` has several additional features that must be mastered to produce more sophisticated tables. All of the facilities discussed in the following sections are summarized in Figures 9.11 and 9.12, at the end of this chapter.

9.2.1 Alphabetic Columns

An *alphabetic* column is indicated in the format part of a table by the key letter A. Although alphabetic columns are easy to use, they are hard to describe, so the discussion has been deferred until now. An alphabetic column is selected using the A key letter in the column format section of a table description. In an alphabetic column, all entries are aligned on the left, with the longest entry centered in the column. However, the alignment on the left may not actually be at the left edge of the column. When one column contains both left-adjusted rows and alphabetic rows, the alphabetic entries will be indented slightly from the left-adjusted. This allows you to

INPUT:

```
.TS
box;
CB S
L | LP9.
\f9tbl\fP Options

_
center ⊤ Center the table horizontally.
expand ⊤ Expand the width to fit the page.
box ⊤ Draw a box around the table.
doublebox ⊤ Draw a double line around the table.
allbox ⊤ Enclose every data element in a box.
tab(x) ⊤ Use x as the tab character.
linesize(n) ⊤ Use point size n for drawing lines.
delim(xy) ⊤ Use x and y as the \f9eqn\fP delimiters.
.TE
```

OUTPUT:

tbl **Options**	
center	Center the table horizontally.
expand	Expand the width to fit the page.
box	Draw a box around the table.
doublebox	Draw a double line around the table.
allbox	Enclose every data element in a box.
tab(x)	Use x as the tab character.
linesize(n)	Use point size n for drawing lines.
delim(xy)	Use x and y as the eqn delimiters.

Figure 9.5. Notice how the option *box* simplifies the table specification. Only the middle vertical line needs to be mentioned in the format section, and only the interior horizontal line needs to be specified in the table body. Compare the format of this table with that of Figure 9.4.

create columns of tables that are somewhat analogous to indented paragraphs. An example is shown in Figure 9.6.

Alphabetic columns are often used when a wide column is specified manually using the W(n) column format (see Section 9.2.5). This lets the data be aligned on the left but centered overall. The left column format would also give left alignment, but the overall block of data would be left of center.

9.2.2 Subheadings

Tables that contain *subheadings* following part of the data can be produced by inserting an additional format specification in the data part of the table.

INPUT:

```
.TS
box;
CBP+1 S S S
L CP-1 CP-1
L CP-1 CP-1
LBP-1
A N N N.
AUTO SALES DATA

—
 T  Dec. 20-31  T  Dec. 20-31
 T  1985  T  1984  T  %Chg.
CHRYSLER CORP.
Chry-Plym Div.  T  19,453  T  14,892  T  30.6
Dodge Div.  T  11,695  T  9,638  T  21.3
\0\0Total Cars  T  31,148  T  24,530  T  27
.TE
```

OUTPUT:

AUTO SALES DATA			
	Dec. 20-31	Dec. 20-31	
	1985	1984	%Chg.
CHRYSLER CORP.			
Chry-Plym Div.	19,453	14,892	30.6
Dodge Div.	11,695	9,638	21.3
Total Cars	31,148	24,530	27

Figure 9.6. Alphabetic columns are left-aligned, but indented relative to a left column. The \0 is a **troff** digit width space code that is used to indent the *Total* line even farther to the right. (Information adapted from *The Wall Street Journal*, Jan. 7, 1986, page 21.)

The start of the additional format specification is indicated by .T& on a line by itself; then the format specifier lines appear, terminated as usual by a period. Here is a sketch showing a table with one additional format specification (there can be as many as you need).

```
.TS
options ;
column formats .
data
  . . .
.T&
column formats .
data
  . . .
.TE
```

An example of a repeated headings appears in Figure 9.7.

9.2.3   Vertical Spanning

Sometimes you need to span a table entry vertically. Like a horizontally
spanned title, a *vertically spanned* column entry makes it clear that a single
entry in one column is related to several rows of an adjacent column. This
idea will be clearer when you look at the example. There are two ways to
specify vertical spanning. In the data part of a table a \^ as a column entry
means that the entry from the previous row will span down to the current
row. An example appears in Figure 9.8. The second method is to specify
the spanning in the column format part of a table. The ^ column format
key letter indicates that the previous row's data will span the current row.

9.2.4   Text Blocks

Although typical entries in a table are numbers, single words, or short
phrases, occasionally tables are constructed with more verbose entries. tbl
has *text blocks* to manage longer-than-usual entries. A text block is
specified by starting the data for a column with the special T{ code. Following the T{, you can enter the text for the block, starting on the next line
and taking as many lines as are required. A T} at the beginning of a line
marks the end of the text block. If there are additional columns in the
table, you place a tab following the T} and then enter the data for the
remaining columns.

Ordinarily you should manually specify the column width for columns
that contain a text block, because tbl can't determine the width automatically. If you don't manually specify the column width using the W(n) format specifier (see Section 9.2.5), the width will be calculated from the for-
mula $L \times C/(N+1)$, where L is the current line length, C is the number of
columns spanned by the text, and N is the total number of columns in the
text. For a one-column text block in a four-column table, given a line
length of 5 inches, the default width would be 1 inch ($5 \times 1/(4+1)$).

Text blocks are processed separately from the rest of the table. They are
formatted using the font, point size, vertical spacing, etc. that were in effect

INPUT:

```
.TS
box;
CBP+1 S S S
L CP-1 CP-1
L CP-1 CP-1
LBP-1
A N N N.
AUTO SALES DATA
_
⊤ Dec. 20-31 ⊤ Dec. 20-31
⊤ 1985 ⊤ 1984 ⊤ %Chg.
CHRYSLER CORP.
Chry-Plym Div. ⊤ 19,453 ⊤ 14,892 ⊤ 30.6
Dodge Div. ⊤ 11,695 ⊤ 9,638 ⊤ 21.3
\0\0Total Cars ⊤ 31,148 ⊤ 24,530 ⊤ 27
.T&
LBP-1
A N N N.
_
VOLKSWAGEN
\0\0Total Cars ⊤ 2,689 ⊤ 1,632 ⊤ 64.8
.TE
```

OUTPUT:

AUTO SALES DATA			
	Dec. 20-31 1985	Dec. 20-31 1984	%Chg.
CHRYSLER CORP.			
Chry-Plym Div.	19,453	14,892	30.6
Dodge Div.	11,695	9,638	21.3
Total Cars	31,148	24,530	27
VOLKSWAGEN			
Total Cars	2,689	1,632	64.8

Figure 9.7. Additional column format entries may be placed in a table following the .T& command. (Information adapted from *The Wall Street Journal*, Jan. 7, 1986, page 21.)

at the beginning of the table, unless one of these was overridden by a column format specification. If the surrounding text is filled, the text in a text block will also be filled. You can create a text block with a ragged right by using .na as the first line in the text block. You can only have 20 or 30 text blocks in most tables because of internal troff limitations. The table from Figure 9.8 is redone in Figure 9.9 using text blocks.

INPUT:

```
.TS
box;
CP+1B S
C | L.
Text Entry Commands

_
a [T] Append text following
\^ [T] current cursor position.

_
i [T] Insert text before the
\^ [T] current cursor position.

_
o [T] Open up a new line following
\^ [T] the current line and add
\^ [T] text there.

_
O [T] Open up a new line in front
\^ [T] of the current line and add
\^ [T] text there.

_
<ESC> [T] Return to visual command mode.
.TE
```

OUTPUT:

Text Entry Commands	
a	Append text following current cursor position.
i	Insert text before the current cursor position.
o	Open up a new line following the current line and add text there.
O	Open up a new line in front of the current line and add text there.
<ESC>	Return to visual command mode.

Figure 9.8. This table uses vertical spanning to vertically center the command letters next to the command descriptions.

Normally, the vertical spacing inside a text block is the same as for surrounding text. However, the column format key letter **v** followed by a number can override the default, allowing you to control the space between lines in a text block.

INPUT:

```
.TS
box;
CP+1B S
C | LW(2i).
Text Entry Commands

_
a T T{
Append text following current cursor position.
T}

_
i T T{
Insert text before the current cursor position.
T}

_
o T T{
Open up a new line following the current
line and add text there.
T}

_
O T T{
Open up a new line in front of the current
line and add text there.
T}

_
<ESC> T T{
Return to visual command mode.
T}
.TE
```

OUTPUT:

Text Entry Commands	
a	Append text following current cursor position.
i	Insert text before the current cursor position.
o	Open up a new line following the current line and add text there.
O	Open up a new line in front of the current line and add text there.
<ESC>	Return to visual command mode.

Figure 9.9. Text blocks are used for long table entries.

9.2.5 Column Widths

tbl's automatically calculated column widths can be overridden manually as necessary. Two examples have been mentioned above, in the discussions of alphabetic columns and text blocks. The key letter W followed by a number in parentheses indicates the *column width*. If the specified width is smaller than the widest item in the column, then the width of the widest item will be used, so that your columns don't overlap. troff units can be used to indicate the scale; for example, W(2i) indicates a 2 inch column width. The default width unit is ens.

9.2.6 Equal-Width Columns

In some tables you want to have a group of *equally wide* columns, even though the contents of those columns may not be exactly the same width. This is especially important in fully boxed tables. The column format key letter E tells tbl to make all indicated columns equally wide. Thus a column format such as

    L CE CE CE

specifies four columns, with the rightmost three having the same width.

9.2.7 Column Separation

The default separation between columns, except for expanded tables, is 3 ens. You can override this default by placing a number following the column type key letter. The default column separation is often decreased for very dense tables, and it is often increased to provide emphasis for a given column. Thus a column format such as

    L5 L5 C

specifies a three-column table with 5 ens between the columns.

9.2.8 Equations in Tables

You can place an equation in a table. An example is shown in Figure 9.10. When an equation appears in a table, both the eqn and the tbl preprocessors must be run, and it is essential that tbl be first in the pipeline. An equation in a table is recognized by eqn because of its surrounding delimiters. The equation in Figure 9.10 is set off by the % character. At some point in the document preceding that equation, eqn must encounter an equation specification such as the following that sets the delimiter.

```
.EQ
delim %%
.EN
```

Otherwise, the equation won't be recognized by eqn.

It is only necessary to tell tbl what delimiter is used for equations when you place an equation in a numeric column. Notice that in Figure 9.10 tbl doesn't need to know about the equation, because it is in a centered column.

INPUT:

```
.TS
center;
CF9 C.
X inter from (inter) Y ⊤ %X inter from (inter) Y%
.TE
```

OUTPUT:

$$\text{X inter from (inter) Y} \qquad X \underset{(inter)}{\bigcap} Y$$

Figure 9.10. Equations can be included in tables.

	COLUMN TYPE KEY LETTERS
L	Left aligned
C	Centered
R	Right aligned
S	Horizontally spanned
N	Numeric alignment
A	Alphabetic
ˆ	Vertically spanned
—	Single horizontal line
=	Double horizontal line
	MODIFIERS
n	Space between columns
|	Vertical line between columns
||	Double vertical line
T	Put vertically spanned item at top
F	Select font (by number or name)
I	Select italic font
B	Select bold font
Pn	Select point size n
Vn	Select vertical space n in text block
W(n)	Select column width n
E	Equally wide columns marker

Figure 9.11. The column format key letters may be presented in either upper- or lowercase. In this figure, n indicates a number.

FORMAT CONTROLS IN THE DATA

Alone on a Line

—	Draw a horizontal line across the entire table.
=	Draw a double horizontal line across the entire table.

Column Entries.

—	Draw a horizontal line across the column.
=	Draw a double horizontal line across the column.
_	Draw a horizontal line across the column that will not touch adjacent horizontal or vertical lines.
\Rx	Draw a string of repeated x's filling the column. x may be any character.
\^	This will produce a vertically spanned entry constructed from the above data.

Text Blocks

T{	As a column entry, this indicates that the following lines contain a text block. The block is terminated by T} column entry, possibly followed by data for the remaining columns.

Figure 9.12. tbl format controls that are embedded in the data part of a table. troff font, point size, and spacing commands may also be embedded in the data part of table.

CHAPTER 10

References and the refer Preprocessor

Although references form but a small part of business correspondence, they are an important part of most scientific and technical writing. There are several difficulties with typesetting references that are addressed by the body of UNIX programs loosely known as `refer`. One problem is tedium—references are often used in multiple papers and it is tedious to rekey a reference each time it is used. Another difficulty is the formatting that is required by certain journals for references. Yet another problem is finding the correct citation; perhaps you know the name of the author but can't find an accurate title, date, etc.

The refer system is a much more comprehensive tool than the `tbl` and `eqn` preprocessors discussed in Chapters 8 and 9. The `refer` program is a `troff` preprocessor, and there are additional programs for creating a data base of references, sorting the data base, printing the data base, and for independent queries of the data base. Throughout this chapter the term refer *software* will cover the entire group of programs; I will try to say refer *program* when I am talking about the `troff` preprocessor named `refer`.

The refer software is less widely available than the `tbl` or `eqn` preprocessors. The refer software first appeared in Version 7 UNIX, and it is also a standard part of Berkeley UNIX. However, the refer software is not a standard part of UNIX System V, and it is not a standard part of the optional Documenter's Workbench software for System V. Even worse, the `refer` program is supported only by -ms and -me macros, which are not part of System V.

The original description of `refer`'s technology appeared in *Some Applications of Inverted Indexes on the UNIX System*, by Mike Lesk. For users more interested in applications than software technology, there is *Refer—A Bibliography System*, by Bill Tuthill.

162

10.1 THE REFER SOFTWARE SYSTEM

Even if you infrequently format a table or equation, you should learn about tbl and eqn, because the alternative is almost unthinkable. However, the refer software is not necessary for occasional references, because small numbers of references can easily be managed manually.

The advantage of the refer software is productivity. You can cite a multiauthor paper that has an excessively long-winded title with just a few keystrokes. Students can sound as learned as their elders simply by borrowing and citing a seasoned data base. An extensive reference data base is even useful for on-line literature searches.

The refer program is a troff preprocessor. It recognizes an informally phrased reference citation in the input text, examines the reference data bases to find the exact citation, and places the text of the citation into the text in a style amenable to processing by the -ms macro package. Each user can have multiple reference data bases, and there is also a default systemwide reference data base. The reference data bases are maintained separately from documents containing references by the addbib and indxbib programs. Reference data bases can be searched by the lookbib program, and they can be printed using sortbib and roffbib.

10.2 ADDBIB

A reference data base is simply a text file containing a set of references. The format of the text in a reference data base will be described below. There are many ways to organize reference data bases. If you write papers in several disciplines, you may want to maintain separate reference data bases for each subject. In a departmental setting, it may be preferable for each member to maintain his or her own data base, or the members can pool their references and maintain a departmentwide reference data base. refer can search several data bases during one pass through a document, so you can partition your references into separate data bases as necessary.

In a reference data base, each record (citation) is separated from other citations by a blank line. Within a citation, each element (e.g., author, title) of the citation is on a separate line, and each such line starts with a % followed by the citation key letter followed by a blank. Each element in a citation can span multiple lines if necessary. Here is a citation for Charles Darwin's last book, a treatise on worms.

```
%A C. Darwin
%T The Formation of Vegetable Mould, Through
the Action of Worms
%I John Murray
%C London
%D 1881
%K mold
```

In this citation the author field, %A, has the data *C. Darwin*. If there had been a coauthor, then there would have been several %A fields, the first being the name of the principal author. Notice that Darwin's long title is placed on two lines. The %I field is the publisher, and the %C and %D, are the city and date of publication. Other fields often used are %J for the name of a journal containing a paper, %B for the name of a book containing a paper, %V and %N for the volume and number within a volume, %E for the name of a book's editor, and %P for the pages of interest. In some styles of papers, the footnotes sometimes contain preamble commentary (printed before the reference) or concluding commentary, specified using %H

Table 10.1. refer's Field Identifiers.

%H	Header Commentary (printed before reference)	%O	Other Commentary (printed after reference)
%A	Author's Name	%Q	Corporate or Foreign Author
%T	Title	%S	Series Title
%J	Journal Name	%B	Book Name
%R	Report, Paper, or Thesis (unpublished material)	%E	Editor (of book containing article)
%V	Volume Number	%N	Number within Volume
%P	Page Number	%D	Date of Publication
%I	Publisher	%C	City of Publisher
%K	Additional Keywords	%X	Abstract
%L	Label (for alternate refer style)		

The %T keyword is used for the title of an article or a book. If it is the title of an article, the %J or the %B keyword should also be used to identify the source. Don't use both %J and %B in one citation, and don't use %B except to name a book in which the given article appears. Authors identified with the %A keyword may have the last word of the name printed first (when the -a option of refer is invoked); use the %Q keyword for authors whose names can't be reversed sensibly.

and %O, respectively. An abstract of the paper may appear following the %X indicator, and relevant keywords can be specified following the %K. The keyword *mold* was specified in this case, because people would more likely refer to this book using the American spelling than the British spelling (*mould*), which Darwin used in his original title. Unless you write your own macros to support `refer`, you needn't specify keywords that appear elsewhere in the citation. Table 10.1 contains a full list of the `refer` system key letters.

One method of maintaining reference data base files is using `vi` or some other text editor. The data base is a text file, so all you need to do is to stick to the given format. If you choose to maintain these files by hand, there are two things you must do very carefully: you must always leave a blank line between citations, and you must never allow any white space (blanks or tabs) at the end of a line.

`addbib` is a menu program that helps you to enter references into a reference data base. `addbib` is not as flexible as a text editor, but it makes sure that the format of the reference file is maintained. After new entries have been placed into a reference data base file using `addbib`, you can fix minor mistakes using a text editor.

`addbib` prints a series of prompts for the most important citation entries. At each prompt you can enter the requested data, or just hit <CR> to skip to the next field. Entering a hyphen will back up one field, which is useful for repeating the author field. You can continue a long field onto several lines by typing a backslash as the last character on a line. Here is a typical dialogue with `addbib`, showing how the citation listed above was entered.

```
$ addbib darwin
Instructions? n

    Author:      C. Darwin
     Title:      The Formation of Vegetable Mould, Through\
>the Action of Worms
   Journal:
    Volume:
     Pages:
 Publisher:      John Murray
      City:      London
      Date:      1881
     Other:
  Keywords:      mold
  Abstract: (ctrl-d to end)
^D
Continue? n
$ _
```

Other possible answers to the "Continue?" prompt are y or *carriage return* to continue entering references, and ed or vi to call up the ed or vi text editors to patch up the reference file.

If you are creating a bibliography data base for troff use, you will probably want to place accent marks in the names of foreign authors and publications. When the refer program processes the data base, each field, except for the X (abstract) field, is stored in a troff string. This means that you should escape each troff embedded command with an extra leading backslash. The X field is treated as a paragraph, so you don't need to treat embedded commands specially inside the X field.

10.3   SORTBIB AND ROFFBIB

For the purpose of citing references in papers, the order of references in your reference data base file doesn't matter. But if you want a hard-copy listing of the entire file, it is important for the references to be ordered appropriately. The sortbib program sorts a reference data base, producing the sorted version on the standard output. roffbib will print a reference data base, either one sorted by sortbib or one in its natural order. Both sortbib and roffbib are Berkeley additions to the refer software system. They are found on Berkeley UNIX systems but won't necessarily be found on a Version 7 UNIX system.

By default, sortbib sorts a reference data base primarily by author's last name and secondarily by date. Although sortbib's output may be collected in a file, it is often sent to roffbib for printing. roffbib has a host of printing options, perhaps the two most important of which are -T*term* to tell nroff which terminal you are using, and -Q to send the output to the typesetter or laser printer.

Typical usage is to pipe the output of sortbib to roffbib:

```
$ sortbib darwin | roffbib -Q
$ _
```

sortbib's input must be a file or files; it cannot read data from the standard input.

Here is my 'darwin' reference data base, sorted by the default sortbib strategy:

Darwin, C., *The Structure and Distribution of Coral Reefs,* Smith, Elder, London, 1842.

Darwin, C., *On the Origin of Species,* John Murray, London, 1859.

Darwin, C., *The Various Contrivances by Which Orchids Are Fertilized by Insects,* John Murray, London, 1862.

Darwin, C., *Variation of Animals and Plants under Domestication,* John Murray, London, 1868.

Darwin, C., *Different Forms of Flowers on Plants of the Same Species,* John Murray, London, 1877.

Darwin, C., *The Formation of Vegetable Mould, Through the Action of Worms,* John Murray, London, 1881.

Notice that the author part of the citations shown above has been reversed by `roffbib`.

The `-s`*keys* option of `sortbib` can tell `sortbib` to use a different set of primary and secondary sort keys, with up to four keys total. The letters following the `-s` are the sort fields, in order. For example, the option `-sDTA` would make `sortbib` sort primarily by date and then secondarily by title and author. The option `-sID` would sort primarily by publisher and secondarily by date. Here is the 'darwin' data base sorted by title using the `-sT sortbib` option:

Darwin, C., *Different Forms of Flowers on Plants of the Same Species,* John Murray, London, 1877.

Darwin, C., *The Formation of Vegetable Mould, Through the Action of Worms,* John Murray, London, 1881.

Darwin, C., *On the Origin of Species,* John Murray, London, 1859.

Darwin, C., *The Structure and Distribution of Coral Reefs,* Smith, Elder, London, 1842.

Darwin, C., *Variation of Animals and Plants under Domestication,* John Murray, London, 1868.

Darwin, C., *The Various Contrivances by Which Orchids Are Fertilized by Insects,* John Murray, London, 1862.

Notice that `sortbib` does its best to ignore articles (such as *the*) at the beginning of a title while sorting.

10.4   INDXBIB AND LOOKBIB

Before a reference data base can be used efficiently, it must be *indexed*. Indexing speeds access to the data base, and it also makes it possible to search multiple data bases by specifying a single data base. The `indxbib` program can index one or more data bases into a single set of index files. This allows you to maintain your references in several separate data bases, but then search them as if they were one large data base. Index files created by `indxbib` have the same base name as the data base with suffixes `.ia`, etc.

```
$ ls -l darwin*
-rw-r--r--  1 kc        681 Feb 13 22:57 darwin
$ indxbib darwin
$ ls -l darwin*
-rw-r--r--  1 kc        681 Feb 13 22:57 darwin
-rw-r--r--  1 kc       2056 Feb 16 17:37 darwin.ia
-rw-r--r--  1 kc        352 Feb 16 17:37 darwin.ib
-rw-r--r--  1 kc         87 Feb 16 17:37 darwin.ic
$ _
```

Each time a reference data base is updated using addbib (or a text editor), it should be reindexed. If you forget to reindex a data base after an update, then the refer program or lookbib may fail to find references that are in the data base.

lookbib is an interactive program for querying a reference data base. For example, you can ask lookbib to find all papers by a given author in a given year, or all papers mentioning a given keyword, or all papers from a given publisher. You can cite a group of papers by simply mentioning the words that should be matched. For example, you can get all papers published by John Murray by mentioning the word Murray. addbib isn't picky about turning up too many references; for example, the keyword *Murray* might turn up a paper by the author Bill Murray in addition to listing books published by the publisher John Murray.

Most reference citations consist of a handful of words to narrow the focus. The citation will usually list the author and the subject or the author and the date. While using lookbib, it's acceptable (and often desirable) to turn up multiple references for a given query. However, one of the most common uses of lookbib is to determine a query (a set of keywords) that is sufficiently focused to turn up a specific reference, because those keywords can be used in a manuscript to specify a reference for inclusion by the refer program. Figure 10.1 shows a sample lookbib dialogue.

10.5   THE REFER PREPROCESSOR

Although large reference data bases are useful for on-line literature searches, for most people the motivation for creating a reference data base is including citations in their papers. That's what the refer program does. The refer program is a troff preprocessor. It takes a text file containing text and reference citations, and it fills in the reference citations by looking them up in the data base. Once the reference citation has been filled in by refer, the file is passed to troff, where it becomes the responsibility of the troff macro package to format the references correctly. refer merely includes the necessary information in the document; it is the macro package that actually controls the format of the reference.

```
$ lookbib darwin
Instructions? n
> plants
%A C. Darwin
%T Variation of Animals and Plants under Domestication
%I John Murray
%C London
%D 1868
%K domestication

%A C. Darwin
%T Different Forms of Flowers on Plants of the Same Species
%I John Murray
%C London
%D 1877
%K flowers
> plants flowers
%A C. Darwin
%T Different Forms of Flowers on Plants of the Same Species
%I John Murray
%C London
%D 1877
%K flowers

>  ^D
$ _
```

Figure 10.1. A `lookbib` dialogue. Notice that `lookbib`'s prompt is a >. The *plants* query pulls out two references from the data base. Adding the word *flowers* to the query focuses the query to a single book by Darwin.

refer is used similarly to any other troff preprocessor. When refer is used with any of the other preprocessors, it should be first in the pipeline. The most important argument for refer is -p, which is followed by the name of the reference data base file. Other file name arguments are presumed to be the document file(s).

```
$ refer -p darwin galap1.t | tbl | troff -ms
$ _
```

The command shown above uses the 'darwin' data base to resolve the references in the 'galap1.t' document. In this example the document file is presumed to contain tabular data, so the output of refer is sent to the tbl preprocessor and then to the troff formatter for printing, using the manuscript macros.

In a document a reference is cited by placing keywords inside the .[, .] braces. For example, the following citation will pull the full citation of Darwin's most famous work:

```
.[
darwin origin species
.]
```

Of course, this citation is overly precise (overly cautious) for our trivially small 'darwin' data base. However, overspecification is usually a good idea for large data bases, because it protects you from future entries that are similar to an existing one.

refer expects that the keywords will produce a unique citation; it is an error for the keywords to lead to zero references or to more than one reference. By default, the reference will be formatted as a footnote on the page where it appears in the document. This style is shown in Figure 10.2.

Several reference labeling systems are available. The default strategy is to number the citations, starting at 1. The starting point can be controlled by the -f*n* command line argument, where *n* is the starting number. In some manuscript styles, it is best to include the labels in the data base, usually in the %L field. The -k command line argument will use the contents of the %L field as a label. (An arbitrary field can be used as the label using the -k*x* command line argument, where *x* is the key letter of the label field.)

Another labeling style uses the senior author's last name and date of publication as the label. refer will produce this alternate style when the -l*m,n* command line argument is present. (l is lowercase ell.) The *m* specifies the number of characters to take from the author, and the *n* specifies the number of characters to take of the date. If *m* (or *n*) is omitted, the full name (or date) is used. For example, the command line argument -14.2 would produce the label Darw59a for *The Origin of Species*.

Another area of reference control offered by refer is the ordering of the author's names. The default is to print the author names in their natural order—first name (or initials), then last name. However, the -a*n* command line argument of refer can be used to reverse the names of the first *n* authors. If *n* is omitted, then all author names will be reversed.

refer can also produce *endnotes*. You must specify the -e command line argument, and then you must place the special refer citation

```
.[
$LIST$
.]
```

in your document at the place where the endnotes should be placed. When you are using the endnote style, the -s*keys* command line argument can be used to control the ordering of the endnotes (using the same syntax as for the sortbib program). refer's ability to produce endnotes is shown in Figure 10.3.

INPUT:

```
.LP
Although Darwin is known primarily for his voyage on the
Beagle, his discoveries on the Galapagos Islands, and for
his seminal book \f2The Origin of Species\fP,
.[
darwin origin species
.]
we should also remember the methods that he pioneered in
achieving his greatness.  Evolution in the gradeschool sense
is a theory that explains how modern species have formed. But
in a deeper sense the theory of evolution is a method, a
technique for examining and understanding nature.  Before
Darwin's work scientists didn't know how to form or test
hypotheses about the history of natural processes. Darwin
showed that small, easily observable changes are the stuff
from which epochal changes are made. This argument was made
with greatest force in Darwin's last book, the oft
misunderstood \f2The Formation of Vegetable Mould, Through
the Action of Worms\fP.
.[
darwin mold
.]
```

OUTPUT:

Although Darwin is known primarily for his voyage on the Beagle, his discoveries on the Galapagos Islands, and for his seminal book *The Origin of Species*,[1] we should also remember the methods that he pioneered in achieving his greatness. Evolution in the gradeschool sense is a theory that explains how modern species have formed. But in a deeper sense the theory of evolution is a method, a technique for examining and understanding nature. Before Darwin's work scientists didn't know how to form or test hypotheses about the history of natural processes. Darwin showed that small, easily observable changes are the stuff from which epochal changes are made. This argument was made with greatest force in Darwin's last book, the oft misunderstood *The Formation of Vegetable Mould, Through the Action of Worms.*[2]

---

1. C. Darwin, *On the Origin of Species,* John Murray, London (1859).
2. C. Darwin, *The Formation of Vegetable Mould, Through the Action of Worms,* John Murray, London (1881).

Figure 10.2. This example shows how two citations in the body of the text are printed as footnotes using the **refer** preprocessor with the **-ms** macros.

INPUT:

```
.LP
Although Darwin is known primarily for his voyage on the
Beagle, his discoveries on the Galapagos Islands, and for
his seminal book \f2The Origin of Species\fP,
.[
darwin origin species
.]
we should also remember the methods that he pioneered in
achieving his greatness.  Evolution in the gradeschool sense
is a theory that explains how modern species have formed. But
in a deeper sense the theory of evolution is a method, a
technique for examining and understanding nature.  Before
Darwin's work scientists didn't know how to form or test
hypotheses about the history of natural processes. Darwin
showed that small, easily observable changes are the stuff
from which epochal changes are made. This argument was made
with greatest force in Darwin's last book, the oft
misunderstood \f2The Formation of Vegetable Mould, Through
the Action of Worms\fP.
.[
darwin mold
.]
.[
$LIST$
.]
```

Figure 10.3(a). This example shows how two citations in the body of the text are printed as endnotes using the –e option of the **refer** preprocessor with the –ms macros.

Occasionally it is desirable to specify one of the data base fields within a refer style reference in a manuscript. For example, in one context you might want to mention a given page number in one reference to a paper and another page number when referring to that paper in some other context. Or you might want to use the %L (label) field differently in different manuscripts, etc. All of these needs are addressed by the ability to redefine a field within a citation simply by placing a bibliographic style line in the reference. For example, you could cite page 108 of Darwin's *Origin of Species* with the following citation.

```
.[
darwin origin species
%P 108
.]
```

OUTPUT:

Although Darwin is known primarily for his voyage on the Beagle, his discoveries on the Galapagos Islands, and for his seminal book *The Origin of Species*,[1] we should also remember the methods that he pioneered in achieving his greatness. Evolution in the gradeschool sense is a theory that explains how modern species have formed. But in a deeper sense the theory of evolution is a method, a technique for examining and understanding nature. Before Darwin's work scientists didn't know how to form or test hypotheses about the history of natural processes. Darwin showed that small, easily observable changes are the stuff from which epochal changes are made. This argument was made with greatest force in Darwin's last book, the oft misunderstood *The Formation of Vegetable Mould, Through the Action of Worms*.[2]

References

1. C. Darwin, *On the Origin of Species*, John Murray, London (1859).
2. C. Darwin, *The Formation of Vegetable Mould, Through the Action of Worms*, John Murray, London (1881).

Figure 10.3(b). Sample output from the input in Figure 10.3(a).

CHAPTER 11

Pictures and the pic Preprocessor

pic is a troff preprocessor that translates a written specification of a line drawing into the troff codes that actually produce the drawing. Thus, you can have line drawings and text in a single document. The basic elements of a pic drawing are circles, ellipses, arcs, splines, boxes, lines, and text. Here is a simple pic drawing.

This drawing contains four objects, three circles and a semicircle. It is not surprising that the pic input used to create this picture is also four lines long.

```
.PS
C: circle radius .5i
arc from C.c + (-.25,0) to C.c + (.25,0) radius .25i
circle radius .05i at C.c + (-.2,.2)
circle radius .05i at C.c + (.2,.2)
.PE
```

In this drawing the sizes and placements are defined explicitly. However, in many drawings pic's default sizes and placement rules will produce an acceptable result.

pic is distributed as part of the AT&T's *Documenter's Workbench*. Thus, it is not a standard part of most UNIX distributions, but it is available for an extra charge. pic has some compatibility with the original version of troff, but for most purposes the newer device independent ditroff, another component of the Documenter's Workbench, is required. It makes little sense to use pic if your only output device is a daisy wheel printer. Either a laser printer with graphics capability or a true typesetter is required. When pic was first written, suitable output devices were rare. Today, many UNIX systems have a pic-capable laser printer.

The original description of pic is *PIC—A Graphics Language for Type-setting, User Manual*, by Brian Kernighan. A more technical description of pic by Kernighan appears in "PIC—A Language for Typesetting Graphics," in the January 1982 issue of *Software Practice and Experience*.

When pic is used with other preprocessors, it should be used after the refer preprocessor but in front of both tbl and eqn. The -T*term* argument can be used to tell pic what typesetter you are using. In most installations, pic is set up so that its default typesetter is correct; the -T option is usually used only at installations with more than one typesetter.

11.1   SHAPES AND DIRECTIONS

pic's three closed shapes are circles, ellipses, and boxes. Any of these shapes can contain text by placing the quoted text after the name of the shape. Ordinarily, one object, together with all of its attributes, is described on a single line of pic input. However, one description can be continued onto a following line using a backslash at the end of the first line, and multiple descriptions can appear on one line if they are separated by semicolons.

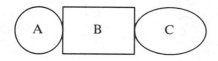

```
.PS
circle "A" ; box "B" ; ellipse "C"
.PE
```

The default movement is to the right, and by default the objects touch each other. There are several ways to refine this operation. One way is to use the move keyword.

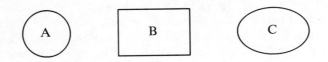

```
.PS
circle "A" ; move ; box "B" ; move ; ellipse "C"
.PE
```

Another way to separate objects is to create an intervening object that is invisible. An advantage of this technique is that the invisible object can contain very visible text.

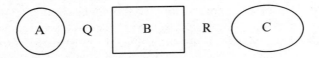

```
.PS
circle "A" ; circle "Q" invis ; box "B"
circle "R" invis ; ellipse "C"
.PE
```

Although the default movement direction is to the right, you can move in any direction. Once a direction is chosen, it sticks until another direction is chosen. The direction commands are up, down, right, and left.

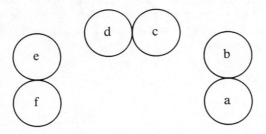

```
.PS
up
circle "a" ; circle "b"
move left
circle "c" ; circle "d"
move left
down
circle "e" ; circle "f"
.PE
```

Directions can be complete commands or they can modify a command such as move. Both usages are shown in the example above.

11.2   LINES, ARCS, AND SPLINES

Lines, arcs, and splines are visible paths from one place to another. Arrowheads can be affixed to either or both ends of an arc, line, or spline using the notations <-, -> and <->.

A line is simply a line that travels in a given direction. The word line must always be followed by a direction. One cannot establish a direction and then draw a line; rather, the line command must mention the direction.

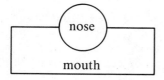

```
.PS
line right ; circle "nose" ; line right
line down
line left ; line left "mouth" above ; line left
line up
.PE
```

The keyword above in this example moves the text above the line; without this directive, the word mouth would intersect the line. (For more information about text placement, see Section 11.4.)

Arrows can make this composition more lifelike.

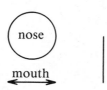

```
.PS
move right ; circle "nose" ; move right
line down
move left ; line left "mouth" above <-> ; move left
line up
.PE
```

A line can be composed in several separate commands, or it can be composed in a single command from segments joined using the then keyword. Here is a four-segment line, followed by two equivalent descriptions.

```
.PS
# four separate lines
line up ; line down right ; line up right ; line down
.PE
.PS
# one line consisting of four segments
line up then down right then up right then down
.PE
```

Notice that the direction given for a line can contain two directions, and notice that a # introduces a pic comment.

Lines and boxes can be dashed or dotted, using the keywords dotted and dashed in the object description. pic's curved objects cannot be dotted or dashed.

An *arc* is a section of a curve. The default pic arc is a quarter of a circle, with the standard circle radius, running in a counterclockwise direction. Arcs can be drawn with different angular extent or radial dimension using size and placement controls discussed in later sections. Clockwise arcs can be drawn using the cw keyword in an arc description.

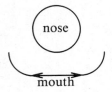

```
.PS
circle "nose" ; arc invis cw
arc cw
line left "mouth" below <->
arc cw
.PE
```

A *spline* is a smooth, curved path fitted to a series of points. In pic you specify the path for a spline just as you would for a line. Splines, like arcs and lines, can have arrows at either or both ends. Here is the previous example of a segmented line, redone as a spline:

```
.PS
spline up then down right then up right then down
.PE
```

11.3   SIZES AND VARIABLES

All the pictures produced up to this point (except the smiley face) have used the default sizes. Naturally, pic allows you to control sizes, either by explicitly mentioning a size each time you specify a picture or by changing the default size selections. The following table details the default sizes (in inches).

arcrad	0.25		
arrowht	0.1	arrowwid	0.05
boxht	0.5	boxwid	0.75
circlerad	0.5		
dashwid	0.1		
ellipseht	0.5	ellipsewid	0.75
lineht	0.5	linewid	0.5
moveht	0.5	movewid	0.5

Any of these sizes can be changed by assigning it a new value.

```
.PS
lineht = 0.25
.PE
```

Once changed, the new value remains until another change is made.

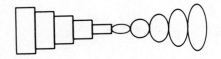

```
.PS
boxwid = 0.2i ; ellipsewid = 0.2
box
boxht = 0.4 ; box
boxht = 0.3 ; box
boxht = 0.2 ; box
boxht = 0.1 ; box
ellipseht = .1 ; ellipse
ellipseht = .2 ; ellipse
ellipseht = .3 ; ellipse
ellipseht = .4 ; ellipse
ellipseht = .5 ; ellipse
.PE
```

Notice that in the example above the default box and ellipse width are changed at the outset. The new values are used to draw all the boxes and ellipses in the picture.

Changing the default values is appropriate when several objects will be drawn using the new value, but it is cumbersome to change the default before drawing each object. Therefore pic allows you to specify the height, width, etc. in each object specification. Here is a redo of the previous example, using defaults to adjust the widths and using commands in each object's specification to adjust the heights.

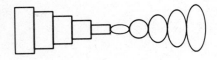

```
.PS
boxwid = 0.2i ; ellipsewid = 0.2 ; boxht = .5
box
box height 0.4
box height 0.3
box height 0.2
box height 0.1
ellipse height .1
ellipse height .2
ellipse height .3
ellipse height .4
ellipse
.PE
```

Boxes and ellipses can have their height and width specified; circles and arcs can have their radius specified. As a somewhat peculiar special case, you can control the height and width of an arrowhead on an arc, line, arrow, or spline using the height and width keywords. Here is an example showing all the possibilities:

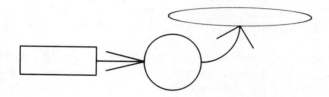

```
.PS
box height .3 width .8
arrow right height .4 width .2
circle radius .3
arc -> height .2 width .4 radius .4
ellipse width 1.5 height .2
.PE
```

All the size specifications we have used in previous examples have been literal numbers. When we wanted an ellipse an inch and a half wide, the number 1.5 appeared in the specification. pic also allows you to provide a symbolic name for a dimension. For example, you could define a variable named stdwidth to have the value 0.5. Then anytime you use the name stdwidth as a dimension, you will get something a half inch in size. Placing standard dimensions in variables makes it easy to establish parameters for a drawing. If like objects are all scaled using a common variable, then an entire drawing can be scaled by changing just a few variable assignments. Variables that you create are assigned values just like pic's standard, built-in variables.

ERR	OR	FR	P	RESERVED	RECEIVED DATA BITS

```
.PS
.ps 8
onebit=.25
fourbits=4*onebit
eightbits=8*onebit
boxht=onebit
boxwid=onebit
box "ERR" ; box "OR" ; box "FR" ; box  "P"
box width fourbits "RESERVED"
box width eightbits "RECEIVED DATA BITS"
.ps 10
.PE
```

Notice that the entire drawing can be scaled up or down by changing the value of the onebit variable. You should also notice that you can embed a troff command in a pic drawing, although you need to be careful. Trying to add extra vertical space will lead to disaster, but point size changes and font changes are allowed. (Note: variable names must start with a lower-case letter. Words starting with uppercase letters are reserved as labels; see Section 11.5.)

Some pic users prefer to avoid changing the values of the built-in pic variables boxht and boxwid, because the changes persist from one drawing in a document to the next. For example, the drawing above changed the box size variables. If I enter a simple pic command such as

```
.PS
box "kc"
.PE
```

then I won't get a standard size box, I'll get a small one.

The main reason to change the default sizes of objects is to make it easier to specify several objects of a given size. An alternative way to do that is to use the same keyword to specify that the current object should be the same size as the previous. Here is the example from above, showing how same works:

ERR	OR	FR	P	RESERVED	RECEIVED DATA BITS

```
.PS
.ps 8
onebit=.25
fourbits=4*onebit
eightbits=8*onebit
box "ERR" width onebit height onebit
box same "OR" ; box same "FR" ; box same "P"
box same width fourbits "RESERVED"
box same width eightbits "RECEIVED DATA BITS"
.ps 10
.PE
```

The major advantage of this technique is that subsequent pictures aren't affected. Notice that explicitly specifying a parameter (e.g., width in the *RESERVED* box) overrides part of the same dictum. Notice also that the keyword same preceded the width override; the opposite order would not have worked.

11.4 TEXT

All of pic's shapes and lines can have text labels. By default, the text is placed at the center of the object, although text can also be attached to sides, corners, etc. Another default is that text is ordinarily centered at the given position. Other possibilities are placing the text above or below the given position, or placing the left or right edge of the text at the given position. Vertical adjustments are made with the above and below keywords, and the horizontal placement is controlled with the ljust and rjust keywords. Only one keyword can be applied in any given situation. The keyword center is also available, although it is seldom used, because it is the default.

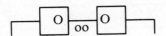

```
.PS
linewid = .3 ; boxwid = .3 ; boxht = .3
line up linewid/2 ; line right
box "O" ljust
line right "oo" below
box "O" rjust
line right ; line down linewid/2
.PE
```

To understand this example, remember that ljust means that the left edge of the text lies at the center of the box.

If you supply several pieces of text for a given object, they will be stacked one above the other.

```
         i
        XX
       OXX
      XXOXO
     XOXXOX
    OXOOXXX
   XOXXOXOX
        Z
   = = = = =
```

```
.vs 7
.ps 9
.PS
box height 1 width .75 "i" "xx" "oxx" "xxoxo" "xoxxox" \
    "oxooxxx" "xoxxoxox" "z" "====="
.PE
.vs
.ps
```

The stack of text in this example is somewhat contrived, but it illustrates the idea. Notice that the point size and line spacing were set outside of the diagram, to avoid all chance of confusing troff. Notice also that in this particular example the vertical spacing is set less than the point size, a choice that is reasonable only because the text consists entirely of lowercase letters without ascenders.

11.5 PLACEMENT

pic offers much finer control of object placement than that shown so far. Simple but effective drawings can often be made with the facilities discussed so far, but more elaborate drawings need to use pic's positional fine tuning. One aid is the ability to *label* an object, so that its position can subsequently be referenced. A refinement of this capability allows you to refer to the sides and corners of objects. Even if an object's position isn't saved in a label, the positions of the most recently drawn objects can be referred to using the keyword last. Another tool is *location arithmetic*, an x,y offset can be added to a position. pic also allows you to place something *fractionally* between two other positions.

Any object may be labeled by placing a capitalized word followed by a colon in front of the object definition. Labels always start with a capital letter to distinguish them from variable names. The keyword at tells pic where to place an object.

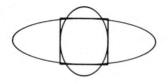

```
.PS
Home: box height .5 width .5
ellipse height .5 width 1.5 at Home
ellipse height .75 width .5 at Home
.PE
```

You can refer to a previous object using the keyword last. last must be followed by the type of whatever you are talking about. The previous example could have been coded equivalently as follows:

```
.PS
box height .5 width .5
ellipse height .5 width 1.5 at last box
ellipse height .75 width .5 at last box
.PE
```

pic also understands constructs such as 2nd last box or 3rd last ellipse, but referring too far back in this way is hazardous. Usually it is better to use a label if you need to refer to the position of any but the previous object. Whereas phrases such as 3rd last box refer to a box three back from the current one, you can also refer to the 1st box or third ellipse. Without the keyword last, counting starts at the first item, not the last. In my opinion, referring to items by their position in a drawing (second, third, last, etc.) is best used only in simple situations. It is usually preferable to use labels. Remember that adding (or subtracting) items to a drawing will change the relative ordering.

A label for an object refers to the geometric center of a box, circle, ellipse, or arc, and it refers to the starting point of a line, arrow, or spline or the starting point of a motion.

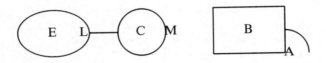

```
.PS
E : ellipse ; L : line ; C : circle
M : move    ; B : box  ; A : arc cw
"E" at E    ; "L" at L rjust
"C" at C    ; "M" at M ljust
"B" at B    ; "A" at A ljust
.PE
```

You can also refer to the "corners" of an object. The suffix ne refers to the northeast corner, the suffix e refers to the east corner, etc. Here is a picture showing the corners on a box, circle, and ellipse:

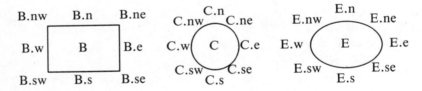

```
.PS
movewid = movewid * 1.5
B: box; move
C: circle ; move
E: ellipse
BB: box invis at B width 1.4 * boxwid height 1.4 * boxht
CC: circle invis at C radius 1.5 * circlerad
EE: ellipse invis at E \
            width 1.5 * ellipsewid height 1.5 * ellipseht
"B" at B         ; "C" at C          ; "E" at E
"B.n" at BB.n    ; "C.n" at CC.n    ; "E.n" at EE.n
"B.ne" at BB.ne ; "C.ne" at CC.ne ; "E.ne" at EE.ne
"B.e" at BB.e   ; "C.e" at CC.e    ; "E.e" at EE.e
"B.se" at BB.se ; "C.se" at CC.se ; "E.se" at EE.se
"B.s" at BB.s   ; "C.s" at CC.s    ; "E.s" at EE.s
"B.sw" at BB.sw ; "C.sw" at CC.sw ; "E.sw" at EE.sw
"B.w" at BB.w   ; "C.w" at CC.w    ; "E.w" at EE.w
"B.nw" at BB.nw ; "C.nw" at CC.nw ; "E.nw" at EE.nw
.PE
```

In this picture I used a trick to make placement of the text easier. I used invisible objects slightly larger than the objects being labeled and placed the text on the phantom corners, not on the real corners. Alternatively, I could have used the text placement keywords ljust, above, etc., but in this instance it seemed easier to use a trick.

The suffixes t (top), b (bottom), r (right), and l (left) are synonyms for n, s, e, and w, respectively. I use the compass notation exclusively, because I find it easier to remember.

Besides an object's corners and center, which refer to positions, an object also has a height and width (and radius for curves) which can be referenced. For example, I can draw a box around the previous design by referring to the heights and widths of the objects in that design, using the suffixes ht and wid.

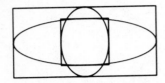

```
.PS
Home: box height .5 width .5
ellipse height .5 width 1.5 at Home
ellipse height .75 width .5 at Home
box width 1st ellipse.wid height 2nd ellipse.ht at Home
.PE
```

One advantage of this technique is that you can change the sizes of the ellipses, and the surrounding box will still be drawn correctly. Perhaps more importantly, you can use blocks (see Section 11.6) to enclose a group of objects and then refer to the size of that part of your drawing.

One common use of corners is to control how objects are placed relative to each other. It is possible to place the corner of one object so that it touches a given corner of another object by using the with keyword. Here is an example.

```
.PS
ellipse width 1 height .5
ellipse width .8 height .4 with .sw at last ellipse.sw
ellipse width .6 height .3 with .w at last ellipse.w
ellipse width .4 height .2 with .nw at last ellipse.nw
ellipse width .2 height .1 with .n at last ellipse.n
.PE
```

Given pic's flexible ability to refer to previous locations, it is natural that it can also perform arithmetic on coordinates. For example, you might want to place something above or below a previously located corner. You can add an offset to a location by adding (or subtracting) a parenthesized pair of numbers. For example, the following pic expression refers to a point 1 inch to the right and 0.5 inch above the center of the previous ellipse:

```
last ellipse + (1, .5)
```

Here is a larger example that contains address arithmetic:

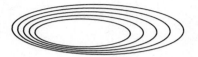

```
.PS
ellipse width 1i height .3i
ellipse width 1.2i height .36i at last ellipse + (.04,.01)
ellipse width 1.4i height .42 at last ellipse + (.04,.01)
ellipse width 1.6i height .48 at last ellipse + (.04,.01)
ellipse width 1.8i height .54 at last ellipse + (.04,.01)
.PE
```

Corners are very useful when you are drawing lines from one object to another as well as when you are positioning objects. Here is a simple example that makes extensive use of corners:

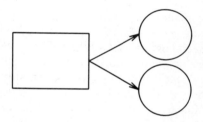

```
.PS
box height .6 width .8
circle radius .275 at last box.ne + (.8,0)
circle same at last box.se + (.8,0)
arrow from last box.e to 1st circle.w
arrow from last box.e to 2nd circle.w
.PE
```

One difficulty with this drawing is that the lines to the circles don't head toward the center of the circle; rather they head toward the western corner. Ideally, the line would head directly toward the center of the circle, ending wherever it landed on the edge. You can achieve this effect in pic with the chop directive. chop tells pic to chop off part of a line. At the beginning of the line, we don't want to chop off anything, so we specify chop 0, but for the end of the line we specify chop .275 to chop 0.275 inch off of the line.

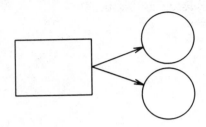

```
.PS
box height .6 width .8
circle radius .275 at last box.ne + (.8,0)
circle same at last box.se + (.8,0)
arrow from last box.e to 1st circle chop 0 chop .275
arrow from last box.e to 2nd circle chop 0 chop .275
.PE
```

If you just specify chop without a dimension, then the line will be chopped by circlerad, and if you just specify one chop instead of two, then both ends will be chopped the same amount.

Although most pic drawings are specified using relative motions, you can also specify absolutely where something goes. For most drawings where pic is an appropriate tool, relative movements are usually preferred. However, situations occasionally arise where absolute locations are required. A specification of an absolute coordinate doesn't refer to page coordinates but rather to pic's own coordinate system. If you place one object at (0,0) and another at (2,0), they will be 2 inches apart, but their placement on the page will be determined by the surrounding text, whether pic drawings are centered, etc. Also keep in mind that pic drawings too wide to fit on the page are scaled to fit.

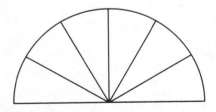

Table 11.1. Not all `pic` attributes (listed in the left column) are usable with all of `pic`'s graphical objects

	Box	Circle Ellipse	Arc	Line Arrow	Spline	Move	Text	Block
height								
width	•	•	•	•	•			•
from			•	•	•			
to			•	•		•		
at	•	•	•				•	•
then				•	•			
dotted								
dashed	•			•				
chop				•	•			
radius								
diameter		•	•					
cw			•					
up								
down								
left			•	•	•	•		
right								
– >								
< –			•	•	•			
< – >								
same	•	•		•		•		•
invis	•	•	•	•	•			
text	•	•	•	•	•	•	•	•
with	•	•						•

```
.PS
arc from (-1,0) to (1,0) cw
line from last arc to (-1,0)
line from last arc to (-.866,.5)
line from last arc to (-.5,.866)
line from last arc to (0,1)
line from last arc to (.5,.866)
line from last arc to (.866,.5)
line from last arc to (1,0)
.PE
```

chop, like `pic`'s other attributes, can only be applied to certain types of objects. chop can shorten a line or a spline, but it is irrelevant to `pic`'s other graphical objects. Table 11.1 shows which attributes can be applied usefully to which objects. For example, the line labeled chop contains bullets in the line and spline columns, indicating that those objects can be chopped. No other objects can be chopped.

Although I don't find absolute coordinates very useful for drawings that I specify by hand, I have found them to be very useful for machine-generated pic code. There are several translators that convert drawings coded in a foreign format into pic code, and these translators make heavy use of absolute coordinates.

The last method of placement I'm going to discuss is pic's ability to place an object some fraction of the way between two places. The syntax for specifying a fractional placement is somewhat difficult, but the basic idea is very simple. For example, to place a circle one-third of the way between a place labeled A and a place labeled B, you would use the following pic directive:

```
circle at 1/3 <A,B>
```

Naturally, the place identifiers can be labels, as shown in the previous example, or corners, absolute locations, expressions, etc. Here is a previous example, with some additional text that is placed below the figure using fractional commands:

ERR	OR	FR	P	RESERVED			RECEIVED DATA BITS								
15	14	13	12	11	10	9	8	7	6	5	4	3	2	1	0

```
.PS
.ps 8
onebit=.25
fourbits=4*onebit
eightbits=8*onebit
boxht=onebit
boxwid=onebit
A: box "ERR" ; B: box "OR" ; C: box "FR" ; D: box  "P"
E: box width fourbits "RESERVED"
F: box width eightbits "RECEIVED DATA BITS"
"15" at A.s below
"14" at B.s below
"13" at C.s below
"12" at D.s below
"11" at 1/8 <E.sw, E.se> below
"10" at 3/8 <E.sw, E.se> below
"9" at 5/8 <E.sw, E.se> below
"8" at 7/8 <E.sw, E.se> below
"7" at 1/16 <F.sw, F.se> below
"6" at 3/16 <F.sw, F.se> below
"5" at 5/16 <F.sw, F.se> below
"4" at 7/16 <F.sw, F.se> below
"3" at 9/16 <F.sw, F.se> below
"2" at 11/16 <F.sw, F.se> below
"1" at 13/16 <F.sw, F.se> below
"0" at 15/16 <F.sw, F.se> below
.ps 10
.PE
```

Note that the fraction can be less than zero or greater than 1.

11.6   BLOCKS AND DEFINITIONS

pic has several features that make it more convenient to specify complicated drawings. *Definitions* give pic a simple macro capability. They
reduce the number of keystrokes for repetitive drawings, and they have a
few other benefits as well. Another useful feature is the *block*. pic has
two kinds of blocks, one that provides some isolation between the block
and the surrounding text, and one for grouping statements together so they
can be treated as a unit.

pic's definitions allow you to give a name to a chunk of text. Each time
you use the name, pic throws in the entire chunk of text. A pic definition
is written using the following syntax:

define *name* X *replacement* X

The replacement text may have new lines, and X is any character that doesn't appear in the replacement text. Definitions can have parameters, but first let's consider a simple example. In a previous picture we showed a tree enclosed in a box. Here is how we can use definitions to make multiple copies of the picture:

```
┌──────────┬──────────┬──────────┬──────────┬──────────┐
│    i     │    i     │    i     │    i     │    i     │
│   XX     │   XX     │   XX     │   XX     │   XX     │
│   OXX    │   OXX    │   OXX    │   OXX    │   OXX    │
│  XXOXO   │  XXOXO   │  XXOXO   │  XXOXO   │  XXOXO   │
│  XOXXOX  │  XOXXOX  │  XOXXOX  │  XOXXOX  │  XOXXOX  │
│ OXOOXXX  │ OXOOXXX  │ OXOOXXX  │ OXOOXXX  │ OXOOXXX  │
│ XOXXOXOX │ XOXXOXOX │ XOXXOXOX │ XOXXOXOX │ XOXXOXOX │
│    Z     │    Z     │    Z     │    Z     │    Z     │
│ = = = =  │ = = = =  │ = = = =  │ = = = =  │ = = = =  │
└──────────┴──────────┴──────────┴──────────┴──────────┘
```

```
.vs 7
.ps 9
.PS
define tree X
box height 1 width .75 "i" "xx" "oxx" "xxoxo" "xoxxox" \
     "oxooxxx" "xoxxoxox" "z" "====="
X
tree ; tree ; tree ; tree ; tree
.PE
.vs
.ps
```

Obviously, using a definition is much simpler than rewriting the original text several times.

Definitions can have parameters so that each invocation of the definition can behave differently. Inside the definition the words $1, $2, etc. are used to refer to the parameters. When the definition is invoked, the parameters are supplied as a parenthesized list. Any parameters referenced in a definition but not supplied in the actual parameter list simply vanish. Here is a very simple example of a parameterized definition:

```
.PS
define rect Z
box height $1 width 2 * $1 ;
Z
rect(.2) rect(.3) rect(.4) rect(.3) rect(.2)
.PE
```

pic has two ways to delimit a block in a picture, with {} (curly braces) and with [] (square braces). Curly braces are used to enclose a diversion, a part of a picture whose placement shouldn't interrupt the main flow of the picture. When a curly-brace block is encountered, the current position and direction are saved, the drawing inside the curly block is performed, and then the position and direction are restored. I often use curly-brace blocks around text labels that directly follow an object. This lets me place the text relative to the previous object without altering the placement of the next real object. Here is part of the previous example showing how labels can be placed near text but redone with text blocks to make it simpler.

ERR	OR	FR	P
15	14	13	12

```
.PS
.ps 8
onebit=.25
boxht=onebit
boxwid=onebit
box "ERR" ; { "15" at last box.s below }
box "OR" ; { "14" at last box.s below }
box "FR" ; { "13" at last box.s below }
box "P" ; { "12" at last box.s below }
.ps
.PE
```

Without the curly braces, the second, third, and fourth boxes would have been drawn in the wrong place, because the text labels change the current location. Here is how the drawing looks with the curly braces omitted.

Square braces are used to collect a group of objects together. This allows the objects to be treated almost as if they were a single box. You can refer to the center, the corners, the height or width of the last square-bracketed object, using terminology such as `last [].ne` or `last [].wid`.

```
.PS
[
    ellipse height .75 width .3
    move right .2
    ellipse same
    move right .2
    ellipse same
]
box at last [] width last [].wid height last [].ht
.PE
```

A square-bracketed object can be placed at a given place using the at or with keywords.

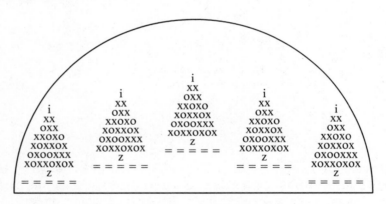

```
.vs 7
.ps 9
.PS
define tree X
     box invis height 1 width .75 "i" "xx" "oxx" "xxoxo" \
        "xoxxox" "oxooxxx" "xoxxoxox" "z" "=====" \
        with .w at $1 <last box.e, last box.ne>
X
[
     box invis height 0 width 0
     tree(0)
     tree(1/3)
     tree(1/3)
     tree(-1/3)
     tree(-1/3)
]
arc cw from last [].sw to last [].se
line from last [].sw to last[].se
.PE
.vs
.ps
```

In this example, the height of each tree is adjusted by placing its western corner at some fractional distance between the previous box's eastern and northeastern corners. Of course, negative fractions work as expected. The curious, invisible, zero-height, zero-width box is a placeholder that the first tree uses.

Labels and variables within a block are private to that block. If you use the name A inside and outside of a block, they refer to two different labels with two distinct values. However, it is possible to obtain the value of a block's private variables; for example, last [].A would refer to A within the last block. Blocks can be nested, but you can't access the private variables in any but the outermost (from your current vantage point) block. Two long examples, containing extensive use of blocks, are found in Figures 11.1 and 11.2.

Control Box

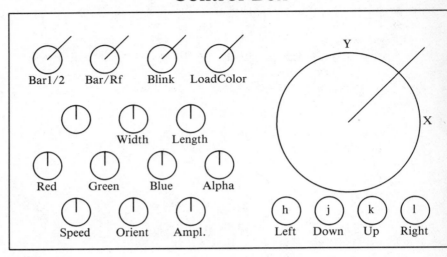

```
.PS
.ps 9
circlerad=.15
rowspace = -.5
[
    # TOGGLE SWITCHES
    handlen = .25
    define togsw X
        [
            A: circle
            $1 at A.s below
            line at A.c to A.c + (handlen,handlen)
            move to A.w + (4*circlerad,0)
        ]
    X
    Tog: togsw("Bar1/2")
    togsw("Bar/Rf")
    togsw("Blink")
    togsw("LoadColor")

    # JOYSTICK
    move to Tog + (2.25,1.5*rowspace)
    Joy: circle diam 1.5
    line from Joy up .8 right .8
    "Y" at last circle.n above
    " X" at last circle.e ljust
```

```
# POTS
define pot X
    [
        A: circle
        $1 at A.s below
        line at A.c to A.n
        move to A.w + (4*circlerad,0)
    ]
X
move to Tog.sw + (0,1*rowspace)
move right 2*circlerad
pot(" ")
pot("Width")
pot("Length")
move to Tog.sw + (0,2*rowspace)
pot("Red")
pot("Green")
pot("Blue")
pot("Alpha")
move to Tog.sw + (0,3*rowspace)
Pot8:move right 2*circlerad
pot("Speed")
pot("Orient")
pot("Ampl.")

# PUSH SWITCHES
colsep = circlerad
move to Pot8 + (2.5,0)
P0:circle "h" ; move right colsep
P1:circle "j" ; move same
P2:circle "k" ; move same
P3:circle "l"
"Left" at P0.s below
"Down" at P1.s below
"Up" at P2.s below
"Right" at P3.s below
]
box ht last [].ht + .5 wid last [].wid + .5 at last []
"\s16Control Box\s0" at last [].n + (0,.4)
.ps 10
.PE
```

Figure 11.1. A longer pic sample showing extensive use of blocks and definitions.

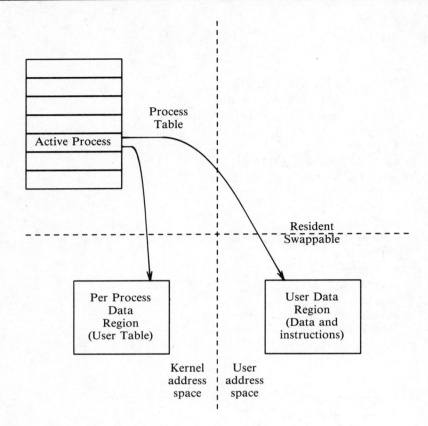

```
.PS
QA:[    # upper left quadrant
        box invis width 1 height .2
        box invis same with .n at last box.s
        box same with .n at last box.s
        box same with .n at last box.s
        box same with .n at last box.s
        box same with .n at last box.s
        A: box same with .n at last box.s "Active Process"
        box same with .n at last box.s
        box same with .n at last box.s
        box invis same with .n at last box.s
        box invis same with .n at last box.s
        box invis height .5i width 1 with .sw at A.e \
                "Process" "Table"
]
QB:[    # lower left quadrant
        B: box height .8i width 1 "Per Process" "Data" \
                "Region" "(User Table)"
] same with .n at QA.s
QC:[    # lower right quadrant
        C: box same "User Data" "Region" "(Data and" \
                "instructions)"
] same with .w at QB.e
line dashed from QA.ne to QB.se
line dashed from QB.nw to QC.ne
"Resident" at 3rd [].n above
"Swappable" at 3rd [].n below
box invis height .4 width .6 with .se at 2nd [].se \
        "Kernel" "address" "space"
box invis same with .sw at 3rd [].sw \
        "User" "address" "space"
spline -> from .5 <QA.A.ne,QA.A.e> right .85 \
        then to QC.C.nw + (.2,0)
spline -> from .5 <QA.A.e,QA.A.se> right .2 \
        then to QB.B.ne - (.2,0)
.PE
```

Figure 11.2. This pic example shows how blocks can manage the placement of the major sections of a drawing and how internal locations in a block can be accessed from outside the block.

CHAPTER 12

Other Document Preparation Utilities

Several additional tools contribute to the UNIX document preparation system. With them you can check your document, display it on your screen, and track your productivity. All of these programs are simple, useful utilities that are used by most people who prepare documents.

12.1 SPELL

spell checks your document for spelling errors. It takes an ordinary text file, strips out all troff commands, and then compares the words in your document with the words in a standard dictionary. Prefixes and suffixes are stripped so that only the roots of words need to be in the dictionary. This means that spell usually isn't fooled by plurals, possessives, etc. If the root word is in the dictionary, then spell will accept derivations; otherwise, spell will flag the word as a possible spelling error. spell also checks through a special dictionary, called a *stop list*, that deals with words that don't follow the normal rules for adding suffixes and prefixes.

The -b option instructs spell to follow rules for British spelling. Beware, as the manual page advises that the British spelling was done by an American.

The -v option instructs spell to explain what suffixes and prefixes were applied to make a word in the dictionary match a word in your document. For example, in the first edition of my UNIX book I routinely misspelled the word *grammar* as *grammer*, even though the manuscript was checked by spell. The -v option of spell explains why:

```
$ echo grammer | spell -v
+m+er    grammer
$ _
```

The answer is obvious—*grammer* is derivable from the word *gram* by dou-
bling the final consonant and adding the suffix *er*. It is often interesting
and useful to use the -v option on short documents, but for long documents the output is too verbose.

spell is capable of automatically saving its output in a log file. This feature is engaged by default on UNIX System V and it is turned off by default
on Berkeley systems. The purpose of the log file is to enable system admin-
istrators to add correct but frequently flagged words to the master dictionary so that spell will be more attuned to local needs. Avoid checking sen-
sitive documents with spell, especially if you are a poor speller. The
records kept in the log file can be very revealing.

Both the Berkeley version of spell and the System V version allow you
to create a private dictionary containing correctly spelled words that are
nevertheless flagged by spell. I'm going to discuss the System V method
first because it is simpler. The System V spell allows you to maintain your
own file of correctly spelled words. The +*local_dict* option specifies that
spell should accept all of the words in the 'local_dict' file as correct. You
must maintain the 'local_dict' file yourself. It must contain one word per
line, and it must be sorted.

```
$ echo rugby | spell
rugby
$ echo rugby > mydict
$ echo rugby | spell +mydict
$ _
```

Subsequent entries in 'mydict' must be added in place so that the file stays
sorted.

With Berkeley UNIX systems you can create your own customized dictionary by using the spellin program. spellin combines a list of words supplied one per line on the standard input with the dictionary named as an
argument and then writes the new dictionary to the standard output. By
default, Berkeley dictionaries are kept in the '/usr/dict' directory. You
should add only roots of words to your personal dictionary because the
spell program will derive related words by adding suffixes and prefixes.

Here is how you would create your own dictionary on a Berkeley system,
containing the standard words (from the standard American dictionary
'/usr/dict/hlista') plus the word *workstation*:

```
% echo workstation | spell
workstation
% echo workstation | spellin /usr/dict/hlista > mydict
% ls -l mydict
-rw-r--r-- 1 kc      50000 Jul  7 22:32 mydict
% echo workstation | spell -d mydict
% _
```

The -d *filename* option of Berkeley spell shown in the last command
above tells spell to use the named file as a dictionary instead of using the
default dictionary. You need to use this option whenever you use spell if
you want to access your personal dictionary. The similar -s *filename*
option tells spell to use the named file instead of the usual stop list.

To add additional words to your personal dictionary, you must create a
new dictionary from your existing one and then rename the new one:

```
% echo filename | spell -d mydict
filename
% echo filename | spellin mydict > mydict.1
% mv mydict.1 mydict
% echo filename | spell -d mydict
% _
```

The spellout program is used on Berkeley systems to see if a given word
is in a dictionary. It reads words from the standard input and reports those
that aren't in the given dictionary. Unlike spell, it doesn't apply
suffix/prefix rules, and it doesn't handle the stop list dictionary specially. It
simply examines the named dictionary file to see if the words found in the
standard input are present. For example, the following shows how you can
search the standard stop list and the standard dictionaries to see if either
contains the word *gram*:

```
% echo gram | spellout /usr/dict/hstop
gram
% echo gram | spellout /usr/dict/hlista
% _
```

The output reveals that *gram* isn't in the stop list dictionary but it is in the
main dictionary. Thus spell is justified (but incorrect) when it accepts the
word *grammer*.

12.2   LOOK

The Berkeley look utility is a useful way to discover the spelling of a word
when you know the first few letters. It takes its argument and then reports
all words in the file '/usr/dict/words' that have the same initial letters. For

example, you can discover whether *aberrant* has one *r* or two using `look`.

```
$ look aber
Aberdeen
Abernathy
aberrant
aberrate
$ _
```

Obviously it has two.

The name of a sorted file other than the default can be specified on the command line. Note that `look` and `spell` use different dictionaries; thus they can occasionally disagree.

12.3   CHECKEQ—CHECKNR—CHECKMM

`checkeq`, `checknr`, and `checkmm` are tools for checking documents prior to formatting by `nroff` or `troff`. `checkeq` is available on both System V and Berkeley Unix, while `checknr` is available only on Berkeley and `checkmm` is available only on System V.

`checkeq` checks the `eqn` delimiters in documents. It will complain if each start of equation delimiter isn't matched by an end of equation delimiter. It doesn't check the actual equation specifications in the document.

`checknr` is a Berkeley program that checks documents containing `-ms` or `-me` constructs. `checknr` will issue a warning message if any of the following are found:

- A command other than those recognized by `nroff`, the `-me` macro package, or the `-ms` macro package.

- Font changes such as `\f2` or `\f3` that aren't followed by a `\fP` to restore the previous font selection.

- Point size changes such as `\s-2` that aren't followed by a `\s0` command to restore the previous point size selection.

- Paired macros such as `.DS` and `.DE` that aren't paired correctly.

Documents must be prepared with the `checknr` style of font and point size changes. Other document preparation styles may produce the desired result, but they can't be checked by `checknr`. For example, a switch from Roman to italics to bold and then back to Roman must be coded as `\f2italic stuff\fP\f3Roman stuff\fP` to avoid complaints by `checknr`.

The `-c` command line option allows you to add additional macros to `checknr`'s list of known commands; the format is -c.*xy*, where *xy* is the name of a macro. The `-a` option allows you to specify additional paired macros; the format is -a.*xy.xz*, where *xy* is the opening macro name and *xz* is the closing macro name. The -f command line option turns off checking of font changes, and the -s option turns off checking of point size changes.

checkmm is used on UNIX System V to check documents prepared for the -mm macro package. It performs all of the checkeq program plus additional checks appropriate for the -mm macros.

12.4   WC

The wc (word count) program can count the number of words, lines, and characters in your documents. Ordinarily a tally of lines, words, and characters is printed for each file mentioned on the command line or for the standard input. The -l command line option tells wc to report line counts, the -w option tells wc to report word counts, and the -c option tells wc to report characters. The default is as if all three options were specified. Here is a tally of several chapters of this book:

```
$ wc chvi*
       817     4978    28104 chvione.t
       422     3237    18909 chvithree.t
      1042     6990    40205 chvitwo.t
      2281    15205    87218 total
 $ _
```

For writers, the wc program often provides a more informative appraisal of a file than the ls program.

12.5   DEROFF AND SOELIM

deroff removes troff constructs from a file. It converts a file containing troff commands into a plain ASCII file that lacks all troff commands. deroff follows the .so and .nx file inclusion and file switch commands. It is used by UNIX document tools such as spell that need your text without the troff embellishments. The -w option tells deroff to output a file of words from your document. Ordinarily the punctuation and line layout of your document is preserved.

```
$ cat oneline
.PP
This is a \f3very\fP \s-2short\s0 file.
$ deroff oneline

This is a   very   short file.
$ deroff -w oneline
This
very
short
file
$ _
```

soelim makes it more convenient to prepare a document in small chunks that are later processed as a whole. For example, it is often best to prepare tbl or eqn specifications in a separate file to make them easy to develop and debug. Once a table or equation is complete and correct, it can be literally included in the main document, or it can be referenced using the .so command. If it is referenced with the .so command, the document must be preprocessed with soelim before tbl or eqn because they don't follow the troff file inclusion commands.

Suppose the file 'jones1a.t' uses the .so command to include the table specification file 'proteins.tbl'. If you try to print 'jones1a.t' without using soelim, the table will be included after tbl's preprocessing—thus it won't be formatted correctly. It will print correctly if you do the following.

```
$ soelim jones1a.t | tbl | troff -ms
$ _
```

soelim is available only on Berkeley systems.

12.6   COL AND COLCRT

People often want to preview nroff output on a terminal. This is useful for debugging your document format commands, proofreading, etc. Unfortunately printers and video terminals have different characteristics. Although plain vanilla nroff output will display correctly, there are some cases that can cause trouble. nroff output that contains half-line motions (superscripts or equations) or backspacing (bold) or reverse line feeds (tables) probably won't display correctly on a terminal. The solution is to use col to convert nroff's printer-style output to a form suitable for terminals. col is also often used to convert nroff output to a form suitable for printers that don't have reverse line feed capability.

Printers use double striking to embolden, most printers can perform half-line motions, and most printers are capable of moving the platen forward or backward as necessary. Video terminals don't overstrike; rather each character replaces the previous. Video terminals never have half-line motions, and the operation of reverse line motions is different than on printers.

col, an exemplary filter, reads from the standard input and writes to the standard output. It keeps track of forward or reverse line feeds, and half-line motions (and backspaces) so that it can send output to the terminal that contains just forward line feeds. For example, on a line containing backspaces col will determine what will be printed on top and then just the top characters will be sent to the display. col does the same for lines with reverse line feeds or lines with half-line motions.

col is usually used as an nroff output filter.

```
$ nroff -ms -T37 jason.let | col
```

— The Document is printed on the terminal—

```
$ _
```

Notice that the terminal type was specified as a 37, which produces control codes for a Teletype Corp. model 37 terminal. Although many printers use the same sequences (<ESC>7 for reverse line feed, <ESC>8 for reverse half-line feed, and <ESC>9 for forward half-line feed), it is best to specify -T37 or for previewing output through col on the screen. If the ultimate output device doesn't support half-line motion, try previewing using the -Tlp terminal selection.

col accepts several command line options:

-b   col will filter lines so that they don't contain backspaces. If two or more characters are slated to appear at the same position, col will display the last one on the terminal.

-f   col will produce output for a device that allows forward half-line motions. col will rearrange the text so that it contains only forward half-line motions.

-x   When you specify this option, col will refrain from converting white space to tabs to speed printing. Use this option when the output terminal doesn't have hardware tab stops.

-p   This option tells col to produce a printable version of any unknown escape sequence found in the input. Normally col simply ignores unknown escape sequences. (This option is present only on System V.)

colcrt is a Berkeley program that also adapts nroff output to a terminal. The advantage of colcrt is that it attempts to preserve the appearance of underlining, superscripts, and subscripts by using extra lines on the display. For example, if there is a superscript on a given line, colcrt will open up the line above and place the superscript there. Like col, colcrt also filters out reverse line feeds.

The following example shows the difference between col and colcrt.

```
$ cat super
An equation:
.br
x\uy\d = 1
.br
.ft 2
After the equation.
$ nroff super | col | uniq
An equation:
xy = 1
After the equation.

$ nroff super | colcrt | uniq
An equation:
 y
x  = 1
After the equation.
----- --- --------

$ _
```

In both of these examples the uniq program is used to collapse multiple blank lines to one so that the output doesn't scroll off the top of the screen. (The -s option of more accomplishes the same thing.)

APPENDIX I

vi Command Reference

The following table lists vi commands that are accessible from visual mode. Except for a few commands, vi doesn't echo the command itself on the screen—only the result is visible. This feature makes it very hard to discover what went wrong when the result is unexpected, because the screen doesn't contain a record of what you typed. At most points in a vi dialogue you can enter <ESC> to return to a normal state. During a text insertion, <ESC> will terminate the insertion and put you in visual command mode; otherwise <ESC> should terminate any partially entered command and ring the terminal's bell.

Since vi has several modes, it is possible for the novice to move unwittingly from one to the other. All of the commands in this reference assume that you are in vi visual command mode. That's where you want to be, unless you care to learn the powerful ex line-editing commands. If you accidentally get into ex command line mode (you know you are in ex command line mode if a : is printed each time you hit <CR>, or if <ESC> is echoed as ^[ ), enter the command vi<CR> to reenter visual mode. (If that doesn't work, try <CR>.<CR>vi<CR>.) If you accidentally get into open line editing mode (you know you are in open line editing mode when cursor movement commands constantly redraw the bottom line of the screen), enter the command Q to move to ex command line mode, and then enter the command vi<CR> to return to visual mode.

Before using vi, the environment variable $TERM must be correctly set for your terminal. If $TERM isn't set, then vi will complain when it starts to run, and you will be put in ex command line mode. If $TERM is set incorrectly, then when vi starts it is likely that your screen display will be garbled. If either of these two problems arises, you should probably enter the command :q<CR> and get help. Since there are several families of similar terminals, it is possible for $TERM to be wrong but for everything to work correctly until you enter a command that exercises a feature that varies within that family of terminals. Such a problem is best left to the experts.

Commands that start with a : or a ! are displayed on the bottom line of the screen as they are entered. For these commands you can use the backspace to make corrections as you enter the command, you can abort the command by striking the interrupt character (usually ^C or <DEL>), and you must hit <CR> (carriage return) when the command has been completely entered.

Many vi commands accept an optional numeric prefix. Usually, if you don't enter a numeric prefix, the command will be executed once; a numeric prefix will repeat the command that many times. The exact meaning of the numeric prefix is detailed below only when it does something other than repeat the command. Commands that accept a numeric prefix are indicated in the following table with a bullet in front of the citation. As you enter a numeric prefix, vi sits there silently, refusing to acknowledge the value visually on the screen. Type carefully.

The commands c, y, d, <, >, and ! are often called *operators*, because they operate on regions of text. An operator must be followed by a suffix, symbolized by § in the following table, that indicates the text region. The suffix may be any of the CURSOR MOVEMENT COMMANDS, any of the TEXT SEARCH COMMANDS, or either of the *go-to* MARKED TEXT COMMANDS. (The suffix need not be a single keystroke.) The <, >, and ! operators always affect whole lines, so they only allow suffixes that specify line positions. When an operator is doubled, it affects entire lines. Thus, cc will change the current line, and 5yy will yank five lines starting with the current line.

Several conventions are used in this appendix. The notation ^X means Ctrl-*X*, where *X* may be any character. The notation <CR> signifies a carriage return, <DEL> is the delete key, <ESC> is the escape key, and <SPACE> is the space key. The notation *text* in the TEXT ENTRY COMMANDS means any printable characters, any escaped (using ^Q or ^V) control character, or tab, space, or carriage return. While you are entering *text*, only the controls described under DURING AN INSERTION are available. You must terminate the insertion before using the full visual command set.

1. CURSOR MOVEMENT COMMANDS

h j k l	•Cursor left, down, up, right.
← ↓ ↑ →	•Cursor left, down, up, right.
ˆH ˆN ˆP \<SPACE\>	•Cursor left, down, up, right.
ˆJ	•Cursor down.
+ \<CR\>	•Cursor to first nonblank on following line.
-	•Cursor to first nonblank on previous line.
G	•Go-to line (go-to end without preceding count).
w b e	•Move forward word, backward word, or to end of word. (A *word* is a sequence of letters and digits, or group of punctuation symbols.)
W B E	•Move forward word, backward word, or to end of word. (A *word* is any text delimited by whitespace.)
0	Cursor to beginning of line.
ˆ	Cursor to first nonblank on line.
|	•Cursor to column 1, or column specified by count.
$	•Cursor to end of line, or if count is not supplied, then cursor to end of count'th following line.
( )	•Cursor moves backward or forward to beginning of sentence.
{ }	•Cursor moves backward or forward to beginning of paragraph.
[[ ]]	•Cursor moves backward or forward to beginning of section.
H M L	•Move cursor to home (top), middle, or lowest line. For H, a count means move to that many lines from top; for L, a count means move to that many lines from bottom.

2. MARKED TEXT

m*a*	Mark location with mark named *a*.
"	Go to line from previous context.
´*a*	Go to line marked *a*.
``	Go to character position from previous context.
`*a*	Go to character position marked *a*.

3. TEXT SEARCHES

f*c* F*c*	•Move cursor forward or reverse to character *c* on current line.
t*c* T*c*	•Move cursor forward or reverse to position left of character *c* on current line.
;	•Repeat last intraline search.
,	•Repeat last intraline search backward.
/*pat*<CR>	Forward search for pattern *pat*.
?*pat*<CR>	Reverse search for pattern *pat*.
n N	Repeat last search in same or opposite direction.
%	Search for balancing parenthesis () or brace {} when cursor is positioned on parenthesis or brace.

4. SCREEN MANAGEMENT

^F ^B	•Forward or backward screenful.
^U ^D	•Up or down one-half screenful. (Preceding count, which is remembered, specifies how many lines to scroll.)
^Y ^E	•Up or down one line.
z<CR> z. z-	•Current line to top, middle, or bottom of screen. A numeric prefix before z specifies which line; a numeric prefix after z specifies a new window size.
^R	Redraw screen. Closes up empty screen lines created during editing on dumb terminals.
^L	Completely rewrite screen. Needed after a transmission error or after some other program writes to the screen.

5. TEXT ENTRY COMMANDS

r*c*	•Replace character under cursor with *c*.
a*text*<ESC>	•Append *text* following current cursor position.
A*text*<ESC>	•Append *text* at the end of the line.
i*text*<ESC>	•Insert *text* before the current cursor position.
I*text*<ESC>	•Insert *text* at the beginning of the current line.
o*text*<ESC>	Open up a new line following the current line and add *text* there.
O*text*<ESC>	Open up a new line in front of the current line and add *text* there.
s*text*<ESC>	•Substitute *text* for character under cursor.
c§*text*<ESC>	•Change the given object to *text*. § is any character position specifier.
C*text*<ESC>	•A synonym for c$. Replaces from cursor position to end of line with *text*.
S*text*<ESC>	•A synonym for cc. Replaces lines with *text*.
R*text*<ESC>	•Replace (overtype) the original material with *text*.
>§	•Shift lines right. § is a line specifier.
<§	•Shift lines left. § is a line specifier.
=	•Reindent line according to lisp standard.
J	•Join lines together.
!§*unixcmd*<CR>	•Filter lines of text through a UNIX pipeline. The pipeline's output replaces the original text. § is a line specifier.
.	•Repeat the last change.

6. DURING AN INSERTION

^Q ^V	Quote the next character. For example, in text insert mode ^V^L will put a line-feed (^L) in the text.
^W	Erase last entered word.
^H	Erase last entered character.
^T	In autoindent mode, indent shiftwidth at beginning of line.
<ESC>	Terminate insertion.

7. TEXT DELETION COMMANDS

x	•Delete character under cursor. (Preceding count repeats, but only on current line.)
X	•Delete character to left of the cursor. (Count repeats, but only on current line.)
d§	•Delete the given object. § is any position specifier.
D	A synonym for d$. Deletes from the cursor to the end of the line.
u	Undo last change.
U	Restore line.

8. BUFFERS

y§	•Yank text into buffer. § is any position specifier.
Y	•A synonym for yy. Yanks lines of text into a buffer.
p P	Put back text from buffer and place it after or before current line or character position.
"*a*	A prefix to yank (y), delete (d), put (p), or change (c) to indicate that the buffer named *a* should be used.

9. SHELL ESCAPES

:!cmd<CR>	Escape to perform one UNIX command.
:sh<CR>	Start a subshell. You may enter commands, then exit from the subshell to return to vi.

10. STATUS

^G	Display file name, modified message, line number, and percentage location in file.
^Z	On UNIX systems that support job suspension, this will suspend vi.
Q	Change from vi mode to ex mode.
<DEL>	Return to vi command mode from a search or from inserting text.
<ESC>	Sound bell or terminate insertion.
:set<CR>	List options set differently from default.

`:set all<CR>`	List settings of all options.
`:set opt=val`	Set option named *opt* to *val*.

11. MACROS

`@b`	Execute the commands stored in the buffer named *b*.
`:map key repl<CR>`	Create a command macro that will be invoked when you hit *key*. *key* is a single keystroke, the escape code generated by a function key, or *#n*, which means function key *n*. When you hit the key, the commands stored in *repl* will be executed. Use `^V` to escape special characters (e.g. ESC, CR) in *repl*.
`:map<CR>`	List the current command macros.
`:unmap key<CR>`	Delete a command macro.
`:map! key repl<CR>`	Create an insertion macro that will be invoked when you hit *key* in insert mode. *key* is coded as detailed for map. *key* becomes a single-keystroke abbreviation for *repl*.
`:map!<CR>`	List the current insertion macros.
`:unmap! key<CR>`	Delete an insertion macro.
`:ab word repl<CR>`	Create an abbreviation for *word*. During a text insertion, whenever you type *word* surrounded by white space or new lines, it will be replaced with *repl*. *word* can be more than one character. Use `^V` in *repl* to escape special characters.
`:ab<CR>`	List the current abbreviations.
`:unab word<CR>`	Delete an abbreviation.
`#n`	Manually simulate a function key on a terminal that lacks function keys.

12. FILE MANIPULATION

`:w<CR>`	Write edit buffer to original file.
`:w filename<CR>`	Write edit buffer to named file.
`:w! filename<CR>`	Write edit buffer to named file. Overwrite existing file.
`:e filename<CR>`	Start editing a new file. A warning will be printed if edit buffer has been modified but not yet saved.
`:e! filename<CR>`	Start editing a new file regardless of whether buffer has been saved since it was last modified.
`:r filename<CR>`	Add a file to the edit buffer.
`:q<CR>`	Quit. (A warning is printed if a modified edit buffer hasn't been saved.)
`:q!<CR>`	Quit. (No warning.)
`ZZ`	Save edit buffer and quit.

Index of vi Command Characters in ASCII Order

CHAR	SECT.	CHAR	SECT.	CHAR	SECT.	CHAR	SECT.
^@		<SP>	1.	@	11.	`	2.
^A	4.	!	5.	A	5.	a	5.
^B	4.	"	8.	B	1.	b	1.
^C		#	11.	C	5.	c	5.
^D	4.	$	1.	D	7.	d	7.
^E	4.	%	3.	E	1.	e	1.
^F	4.	&		F	3.	f	3.
^G	10.	'	2.	G	1.	g	
^H	1. 6.	(	1.	H	1.	h	1.
^I		)	1.	I	5.	i	5.
^J	1.	*		J	5.	J	1.
^K		+	1.	K		k	1.
^L	4.	,	3.	L	1.	l	1.
<CR>	1.	−	1.	M	1.	m	2.
^N	1.	.	5.	N	3.	n	3.
^O		/	3.	O	5.	o	5.
^P	1.	0	1.	P	8.	p	8.
^Q	6.	1		Q	10.	q	
^R	4.	2		R	5.	r	5.
^S		3		S	5.	s	5.
^T	6.	4		T	3.	t	3.
^U	4.	5		U	7.	u	7.
^V	6.	6		V		v	
^W	6.	7		W	1.	w	1.
^X	4.	8		X	7.	x	7.
^Y	4.	9		Y	8.	y	8.
^Z	10.	:	9-12.	Z	12.	z	4.
<ESC>	5. 6. 10.	;	3.	[	1.	{	1.
		<	5.			|	1.
		=	5.	]	1.	}	1.
		>	5.	^	1.	~	
		?	3.	_		<DEL>	10.

APPENDIX II

vi Options Reference

OPTION	ABB.	MEANING
autoindent	ai	autoindent makes vi automatically add the current amount of leading white space to new lines. ˆD at the beginning of a line will cause the indent to retreat left one stop. ˆˆD will retreat to the left margin. The default is noai.
autoprint	ap	When autoprint is set, lines are printed after they are modified by one of the following ex commands: d, c, J, m, t, u, <, or >. This option only applies in line-editing mode; the effect is as if a trailing p were added to each of the above ex commands. The default is ap.
autowrite	aw	When autowrite is set, vi will automatically write out the current file before executing commands that might switch to another file or before executing a shell escape command. The default is noaw.
beautify	bf	beautify tells vi to discard all control characters (other than tab, new line, and form-feed) from the input. The default is nobf.
directory	dir	directory tells vi where to place its temporary files. The default is /tmp.
edcompatible		Makes the ex substitute command more closely resemble ed's. The default is noedcompatible.

OPTION	ABB.	MEANING
errorbells	eb	errorbells tells vi to ring the terminal's bell for a larger set of errors. The default is noeb.
hardtabs	ht	hardtabs defines the hardware tab stops for your terminal. The default is 8.
ignorecase	ic	ignorecase tells vi to ignore case distinctions in searches and substitutions. The default is noic.
lisp		lisp alters the indent strategy in indent mode for lisp programs. The default is nolisp.
list	li	list mode displays tabs and line feeds explicitly. The default is noli.
magic		In magic mode, all regular expression characters are active. In nomagic mode, only ˆ, $, and \ are metacharacters. In nomagic mode, a metacharacter (e.g., ?) can be restored its power by preceding it with a backslash (e.g., \?). The default is magic.
mesg		mesg allows messages to be written on your screen during vi sessions. The default is nomesg.
number	nu	number numbers lines on the display. The default is nonu.
open		open mode allows you to issue the open or visual commands from ex line-editing mode. noopen prevents these commands, so that novices will be less confused by modes. The default is open.
optimize	opt	optimize uses cursor positioning at the end of each line to move to the beginning of the next line. This is more efficient on many terminals. The default is opt.
paragraphs	para	paragraphs tells vi the names of the paragraph macros. When you move to the beginning or end of a paragraph (using the { or } commands), vi searches for the closest paragraph marker in the paragraphs list or for a blank line. In the list, pairs of characters are macro names (e.g., IP). The default is IPLPPPQPP LIbp, which covers standard -ms or -mm paragraphs, -mm list items, and manual page breaks.

OPTION	ABB.	MEANING
prompt		prompt tells vi to print the : prompt when it is waiting for line-editing commands. The default is prompt.
readonly	ro	When readonly is set, the editor will refuse to write to a file (unless you use the w! command). readonly can be set like any other option, or it can be set by invoking vi with the -R command line option. The default is noreadonly.
redraw		redraw tells vi to keep the screen display up to date, even on dumb terminals. This option generates much output on a dumb terminal. The default is noredraw.
remap		remap makes vi repeatedly scan the text of macros to see if any further macros are invoked. noremap scans each only once, making it impossible for one macro to invoke another. The default is remap.
report		When a command modifies more than report lines, vi prints a message. The default is 5.
scroll		scroll is the number of lines the display scrolls in ex mode when you type the EOF character. The default is ½ window.
sections		sections is a list of macro names that vi searches for when you enter the [[and]] commands to move to beginning and end of the section. In the sections list, pairs of characters denote macro names (e.g., SH). The default is SHNHH HU, which covers the heading start commands of -ms and -mm.
shell	sh	shell contains the name of the default shell. When vi starts to execute, shell is copied from the $SHELL environmental variable.
shiftwidth	sw	shiftwidth is the size of the software tab stop. The default is 8.

OPTION	ABB.	MEANING
showmatch	sm	When showmatch is set, vi will automatically move the cursor to the matching (or { for 1 second each time you type a) or }. This is useful for programmers, especially for lisp programmers. The default is nosm.
slowopen	slow	The slowopen mode is an alternate output strategy for open or visual mode. It improves vi on dumb terminals by reducing the amount of screen updating during text inputs. Its value depends on your terminal type. The default is terminal-dependent.
tabstop	ts	Tab characters in the input file produce movement to the next tabstop boundary. Reducing tabstop to 2 or 4 often makes it easier to view heavily indented material, such as C programs. The default is 8.
taglength	tl	taglength is the number of significant characters in a tag. Zero means the entire tag is significant. The default is 0.
tags		tags is a list of files containing tags. The default list is '/usr/lib/tags'.
term		term is the name of the output terminal. Its initial value comes from the $TERM environmental variable.
terse		terse makes vi produce shorter error messages. The default is noterse.
timeout		When timeout is set, the complete character sequence invoking a macro must be entered within 1 second. The default is timeout.
warn		When warn is set vi will warn you if you enter a ! (shell) command without first saving your text. The default is warn.

OPTION	ABB.	MEANING
window		window is the size of the text display in visual mode. The default varies according to the baud rate. It is eight lines at speeds less than 1200 baud, sixteen lines at 1200 baud, and the full screen at more than 1200 baud.
w300		w300 is a synonym for window, but it is only effective if the baud rate is less than 1200. The default is 8.
w1200		w1200 is a synonym for window, but it is only effective if the baud rate is 1200. The default is 16.
w9600		w9600 is a synonym for window, but it is only effective if the baud rate is higher than 1200. The default is full screen.
wrapscan	ws	wrapscan makes vi search the entire file every time. Searches always start from the current line and proceed to the end (or beginning) of the file. When wrapscan is set and a vi search reaches the end (or beginning) of the file, the search continues from the beginning (or end) to the current line. The default is ws.
wrapmargin	wm	wrapmargin is the distance from the right margin at which text is moved automatically to the following line. 0 disables automatic margin insertion. The default is 0.
writeany	wa	When writeany is set, vi will allow you to overwrite existing files without warning you. The default is nowa.

APPENDIX III

nroff/troff Command Line Options

When you format a document with nroff or troff, most format control information is embedded in the text. However, to control the general operation of the formatters, you use ordinary command line options. Like most UNIX commands, the general syntax is

    nroff [options] [files]

The options must precede the files. The standard input is assumed if no file names are present, and the file name "-" means the standard input.

The following command line options apply to both nroff and troff:

-o*list*
>   Output is produced for the pages mentioned in the *list*. The *list* is a comma-separated list of pages, or page ranges. (A page range is n-m, which means from page *n* through page *m*.) For example, the option -o1,3,5,11-19 means pages 1, 3, 5, and 11 through 19.

-n*N*
>   The first page of the document is numbered *N*.

-s*N*
>   The output process is stopped every *N* pages so that you can change the paper. Not functional on all versions of troff.

-m*name*
>   Use the standard macro package *name*. The most common uses of this option are -ms to access the manuscript macros, -mm to access the memorandum macros, -me to access the -me macros, and -man to access the manual macros.

-c*name*
>   Use the compacted version of the standard macro package *name*. Compacted macros require less processing than the uncompacted

macros invoked with the -m option. Use -cm to access the -mm macros. System V UNIX only.

-ra*N*

The nroff/troff internal register named *a* is set to the value *N*. *a* is any single-character register name, and *N* is any value.

-i Read the standard input after the files are processed.

-q Echoing is suppressed during .rd insertions. This is necessary to prevent scrambled output when input and output are attached to the terminal.

The following command line options are only for nroff:

-T*name*

nroff prepares output for the named terminal. On most systems, nroff is set up so that its default terminal matches the locally available terminal. You can see what terminals are supported on your system by listing the contents of the '/usr/lib/term' directory.

-e nroff prepares output that uses the full resolution of the output device. This may result in slower printing.

-h nroff uses tab characters to possibly reduce the size of the output.

The following command line options are only for troff:

-t Send output to the standard output rather than directly to the type-setter. This option is needed when a postprocessor is used to adapt troff to a particular printer.

-a Send an ASCII version of the output to the standard output. This option is useful for various purposes, including checking hyphenation without producing printed copy.

-p*N*

Produce output in point size *N*. All spacing and character placement will be the same as the final copy. This option is useful for producing output quickly.

APPENDIX IV

troff Escape Codes for Special Characters

TYPOGRAPHIC SYMBOLS

●	\(bu	Bullet	○	\(ci	Circle
□	\(sq	Square	¢	\(ct	Cent Sign
®	\(rg	Registered	©	\(co	Copyright
☛	\(lh	Left Hand	☞	\(rh	Right Hand
†	\(dg	Dagger	‡	\(dd	Double Dagger
§	\(sc	Section	|	\(br	Box Vertical Rule
′	\(fm	Foot Mark	°	\(de	Degree
—	\(em	¾ Em dash	-	\(hy	Hyphen
—	\(ru	Rule	_	\(ul	Underrule
′	\(aa	Acute Accent	`	\(ga	Grave Accent
/	\(sl	Slash	\	\e	Backslash
	\0	Digit Width Space		\(sp)	Unpaddable Space
	\^	Narrow Space		\\|	Very Narrow Space

BRACKET BUILDING SYMBOLS

⌈	\(lt	Left Top	⌉	\(rt	Right Top
⌈	\(lc	Left Ceiling	⌉	\(rc	Right Ceiling
{	\(lk	Left Center	}	\(rk	Right Center
⌊	\(lb	Left Bottom	⌋	\(rb	Right Bottom
⌊	\(lf	Left Floor	⌋	\(rf	Right Floor
|	\(bv	Bold Vertical			
√	\(sr	Square Root	‾	\(rn	En-width Root Extender

226

GREEK LETTERS

α	\(*a	alpha		A	\(*A	Alpha
β	\(*b	beta		B	\(*B	Beta
γ	\(*g	gamma		Γ	\(*G	Gamma
δ	\(*d	delta		Δ	\(*D	Delta
ϵ	\(*e	epsilon		E	\(*E	Epsilon
ζ	\(*z	zeta		Z	\(*Z	Zeta
η	\(*y	eta		Y	\(*Y	Eta
θ	\(*h	theta		Θ	\(*H	Theta
ι	\(*i	iota		I	\(*I	Iota
$\varkappa$	\(*k	kappa		K	\(*K	Kappa
λ	\(*l	lambda		Λ	\(*L	Lambda
μ	\(*m	mu		M	\(*M	Mu
ν	\(*n	nu		N	\(*N	Nu
ξ	\(*c	xi		Ξ	\(*C	Xi
o	\(*o	omicron		O	\(*O	Omicron
π	\(*p	pi		Π	\(*P	Pi
ρ	\(*r	rho		P	\(*R	Rho
σ	\(*s	sigma		Σ	\(*S	Sigma
ς	\(ts	terminal sigma				
τ	\(*t	tau		T	\(*T	Tau
υ	\(*u	upsilon		Υ	\(*U	Upsilon
ϕ	\(*f	phi		Φ	\(*F	Phi
χ	\(*x	chi		X	\(*X	Chi
ψ	\(*q	psi		Ψ	\(*Q	Psi
ω	\(*w	omega		Ω	\(*W	Omega

MATHEMATICAL SYMBOLS

+	\(pl	Plus	—	\(mi	Minus
×	\(mu	Multiply	÷	\(di	Divide
±	\(+-	Plus-Minus	¬	\(no	Not
*	\(**	Times	=	\(eq	Equals
≥	\(>=	Greater or Equal	≤	\(<=	Less or Equal
≡	\(==	Identically Equal	≃	\(~=	Approximately Equal
~	\(ap	Approximates	≠	\(!e	Not Equal
→	\(->	Right Arrow	←	\(<-	Left Arrow
↑	\(ua	Up Arrow	↓	\(da	Down Arrow
∪	\(cu	Cup (union)	∩	\(ca	Cap (intersection)
⊂	\(sb	Subset	⊃	\(sp	Superset
⊆	\(ib	Improper Subset	⊇	\(ip	Improper Superset
∞	\(if	Infinity	∅	\(es	Empty Set
∫	\(es	Integral	∂	\(pd	Partial Derivative
√	\(sr	Square Root	∇	\(gr	Gradient
∝	\(pt	Proportional To	∈	\(mo	Member Of
|	\(or	Or	¼	\(14	One-Quarter
½	\(12	One-Half	¾	\(34	Three-Quarters

APPENDIX V

Summary of the -ms Macros

−ms **MACRO COMMANDS**

HEADINGS AND PARAGRAPHS

`.NH n`
text
`.LP`
	Numbered heading. *n* is the heading level, *text* is the heading text, followed by any paragraph command.

`.SH`
text
`.LP`
	Section heading. *text* is the heading text, followed by any paragraph command.

`.PP`	Start a normal paragraph. First line is indented.
`.LP`	Start a normal paragraph. All lines are flush left.
`.IP label`	Start an indented paragraph. All lines are indented on the left. The optional *label* is printed to the left of the first line.
`.XP`	†Start an exdented paragraph. All lines but the first will be indented on the left.

† Berkeley enhancements.

–ms **MACRO COMMANDS**

OVERALL DOCUMENT FORMAT

.1C
.2C
Switch to one-column (the default) or two-column format.

.DA date
The date will be printed at the bottom of the page. This is the default with nroff but not with troff. The optional *date* argument overrides the current date.

.ND
The date will not be printed at the bottom of the page.

.OH 'L'C'R'
.EH 'L'C'R'
.OF 'L'C'R'
.EF 'L'C'R'
†These macros produce *H*eaders and *F*ooters on *O*dd or *E*ven pages. Each three-part header consists of text *L* for the left, *C* for the center, and *R* for the right. In a header or footer % will print the page number.

.AM
†Use at the beginning of any document that uses the new accent marks.

TYPE STYLES

.R
.I wd1 wd2
.B wd1 wd2
Switch font to Roman, italic, or bold. For I or B, if *wd1* is supplied, it alone will be in italic or bold. If *wd2* is supplied, it will follow *wd1*, without a separating space, and be in the surrounding font.

.SM
.NL
.LG
Switch to a smaller, normal-size, or larger typeface. .SM or .LG can be repeated to increase the size change.

.UL word
Underline a single *word*.

† Berkeley enhancements.

-ms MACRO COMMANDS

DISPLAYS AND FOOTNOTES

.DS x
text
.DE
Display *text* in no-fill mode. *text* will be moved to the following page, leaving a blank region, if it doesn't fit. Optional argument *x* may be L for a flush-left display, I for a slightly indented display, C for a line-by-line centered display, or B for a block centered display. The default is an indented display.

.LD
.ID
.CD
Display multipage *text*.
  .LD replaces .DS L
  .ID replaces .DS I
  .CD replaces .DS C

.KS
text
.KE
text will be moved to the following page if it doesn't fit. A blank space may be produced at the bottom of the current page.

.KF
text
.KE
text will float to the start of the following page if it doesn't fit on the current page. Following text may be moved forward to fill the bottom of the page.

.EQ x n
text
.EN
text will be processed by the eqn preprocessor. Optional argument *x* may be I for an indented equation, L for a flush-left equation, or C for a centered equation. Centered is the default. An argument *n* may follow the equation type. It will be placed flush left to identify the equation.

.TS
text
.TE
text will be processed by the tbl preprocessor.

.RS
text
.RE
text will be shifted to the right.

.FS
text
.FE
text is a footnote that will be placed at the bottom of the page. Berkeley -ms allows ** to number footnotes automatically.

−ms **MACRO COMMANDS**

FIRST PAGE FORMATS

`.RP`	Use AT&T Released Paper style.
`.TM`	Use Berkeley Thesis style.
`.TL` *text*	Use *text* as the title.
`.AU loc ext` *text*	*text* specifies an author's name, and optional arguments *loc* and *ext* specify the author's address and phone number.
`.AI` *text*	*text* specifies the author's institution.

`.AB`
text
`.AE`
	Use *text* as the abstract.

`.SG`	Insert the author's name (signature) in the text.

TABLE OF CONTENTS

`.XS n`
text
`.XE`
	†*text* will be stored internally, to be used later as an entry in the table of contents, with *n* the page number. *n* defaults to the current page.

`.XA n` *text*	†Within an `.XS`, `.XE` pair of macros, `.XA` will store *text* to be used later in the table of contents.
`.PX`	†Print the stored table of contents.

† Berkeley enhancements.

-ms NUMBER REGISTERS

NAME	USE	TAKES EFFECT	DEFAULT VALUE (nroff)	DEFAULT VALUE (troff)
HM	Header Margin	Next Page	1i	1i
FM	Footer Margin	Next Page	1i	1i
PO	Page Offset	Next Page	0	26/27i
CW	Column Width (Two-column style)	Next .2C	7/15 LL	7/15LL
GW	Gutter Width (Space between columns)	Next .2C	1/15 LL	1/15LL
PD	Paragraph Drop	Next Para.	1v	0.3v
DD	†Display Drop	Next Display	1v	0.5v
PI	Paragraph Indent	Next Para.	5n	5n
QI	Quote Para. Indent	Next Para.	5n	5n
PS	Point Size	Next Para.	10p	10p
VS	Vertical Spacing	Next Para.	12p	12p
LL	Line Length	Next Para.	6i	6i
LT	Title Length	Next Para.	6i	6i
FI	†Footnote Indent	Next .FS	2n	2n
FL	Footnote Length	Next .FS	11/12 LL	11/12 LL
FF	†Footnote Format	Next .FS	0	0

-ms FORMATTER DEPENDENT STRINGS†

NAME	INPUT	nroff OUTPUT	troff OUTPUT
Dash	*-	--	—
Left Quote	*Q	"	''
Right Quote	*U	"	''

† Berkeley enhancements.

-ms HEADER STRINGS

NAME	USE	NAME	USE	NAME	USE
LH	Left Header	CH	Center Header	RH	Right Header
LF	Left Footer	CF	Center Footer	RF	Right Footer

-ms ACCENT MARKS†

NAME	INPUT	OUTPUT	NAME	INPUT	OUTPUT
Acute	e*´	é	Grave	e*`	è
Circumflex	o*^	ô	Cedilla	c*,	ç
Tilde	n*~	ñ	Umlaut	u*:	ü
Haček	c*v	č	Underdot	s*.	ṣ
Macron	a*_	ā	Angstrom	a*o	å
Slash	o*/	ø			

-ms SPECIAL SYMBOLS†

NAME	INPUT	OUTPUT	NAME	INPUT	OUTPUT
Question	*?	¿	Exclamation	*!	¡
Digraph s	*8	β	Yogh	kni*3t	kni3t
Thorn	*(Th	Þ	thorn	*(th	þ
Eth	*D-	Ð	eth	*d-	ð
AE ligature	*(Ae	Æ	ae ligature	*(ae	æ
OE ligature	*(Oe	Œ	oe ligature	*(oe	œ
Hooked o	*q	ǫ			

These accent marks and special characters are only available on Berkeley versions of -ms, and they will only work if the macro command .AM is placed at the beginning of the document. A smaller set of accent marks that works with all versions of -ms is detailed in Section 6.4. (Note that the original accents will be unavailable after using the .AM command.)

† Berkeley enhancements.

APPENDIX VI

Summary of the -mm Macros

-mm **MACRO COMMANDS**

HEADINGS AND PARAGRAPHS

`.H N text`	Numbered heading. *N* is the heading level, *text* is the heading text.
`.HU text`	Unnumbered heading. *text* is the heading text.
`.P`	Start a paragraph in the prevailing style.
`.P 0`	Start a flush-left paragraph.
`.P 1`	Start an indented paragraph.
`.nP`	Start an automatically numbered paragraph.

-mm MACRO COMMANDS

TYPE STYLES

.R	The commands .R, .I, and .B switch font
.I A B C D E F	to Roman, italic, or bold. For I or B,
.B A B C D E F	optional arguments can be supplied to make
.IB A B C D E F	a temporary switch. If A is supplied, it
.BI A B C D E F	alone will be in italic or bold. If B is also
.RB A B C D E F	supplied, it will follow A, without a sepa-
.BR A B C D E F	rating space, and be in the surrounding
.RI A B C D E F	font. If C is supplied, it will immediately
.IR A B C D E F	follow B in italic or bold, etc. .IB, .BI, etc.

are similar except that the fonts alternate between the two fonts specified in the macro name rather than between a named font and the surrounding font.

.SM A	Print A in (1 pt.) smaller text.
.SM A B	Print A smaller followed by B normal.
.SM A B C	Print B smaller sandwiched between A and C normal.
.S p v	Set the default point size and vertical spac-

ing. The optional argument p controls the point size, and v controls vertical spacing. By default the point size is 10, and the vertical spacing is the point size plus 2. The arguments may be:

number — set the point size to that number

±*number* — change the size by that amount

P — restore the previous size

D — restore the default size

C — maintain current size

-mm **MACRO COMMANDS**

DISPLAYS AND FOOTNOTES

.DS t f i
text
.DE

.DF t f i
text
.DE

.DS and .DF start regular and floating displays. All displays are ended by the .DE command. Both display types accept three optional arguments. The first argument, *t*, specifies the type of the display. It must have the value I for an indented display, C for individually centered lines, CB for centered as a block, or L for left flush (the default). If the fill argument is F, the display will be filled instead of the default no-fill. The third argument, if present, will right-indent the display that many ens.

.EQ label
text
.EN

text will be processed by the eqn preprocessor. Unless *text* is a define or a delimiter, it must be surrounded by a display. An optional *label* argument to .EQ will be printed as an equation label (usually) on the right.

.TS
text
.TE

text will be processed by the tbl preprocessor. Displays must surround the table if you want it kept together.

.FS label
text
.FE

text is a footnote that will be placed at the bottom of the page. In the main text, the string *F can be used to number the citation automatically. Optional *label* should be used when footnotes aren't numbered automatically.

–mm MACRO COMMANDS

LISTS

`.BL i ns`
list
`.LE`

Each item in a bullet list is marked with a bullet (●). Optional arguments *i* and *ns* specify an indent and no-space (no extra space between list elements) mode.

`.DL i ns`
list
`.LE`

Each item in a dash list is marked with a dash (−). Optional arguments *i* and *ns* specify an indent and no-space mode.

`.ML M i ns`
list
`.LE`

Each item in a marked list is identifed by the mark *M*. Optional arguments *i* and *ns* specify an indent and no-space mode.

`.AL t i ns`
list
`.LE`

Item marks in an automatic list are sequenced automatically. The optional argument *t* must be 1 (numeral one) for Arabic numerals, a or A for lower- or uppercase alphabetic, or i or I for lower- or uppercase Roman numerals. The default type is numeric. Optional arguments *i* and *ns* specify an indent and no-space mode.

`.VL I mi ns`
list
`.LE`

A variable-item list uses marks supplied with each `.LE` macro. The argument *i* that specifies the indent must be supplied. Optional arguments *mi* and *ns* specify the indent for the mark and no-space mode. Exdented paragraphs are produced if the `.LI` macros don't have marks.

`.LI m if`

Each item in a list follows a `.LI` macro. The argument *m* specifies the mark. The optional argument *if* specifies that the supplied mark should appear in front of the customary mark.

TABLE OF CONTENTS

`.TC`

Print the stored table of contents. Optional arguments are described in Section 7.7.

-mm MACRO COMMANDS

OVERALL DOCUMENT FORMAT

.1C .2C	Switch to one-column (the default) or two-column format.
.WC X	Control width of displays and footnotes in two-column mode. The *X* argument is explained in the text.
.PH "'L'C'R'" .OH "'L'C'R'" .EH "'L'C'R'" .PF "'L'C'R'" .OF "'L'C'R'" .EF "'L'C'R'"	These macros produce *H*eaders and *F*ooters on all, *O*dd or *E*ven pages. Each three-part header consists of text *L* for the left, *C* for the center, and *R* for the right. In a header or footer, \\\\nP will print the page number.

-mm ACCENT MARKS AND STRINGS

ACCENT MARKS

NAME	INPUT	OUTPUT	NAME	INPUT	OUTPUT
Acute	e*'	é	Grave	e*`	è
Circumflex	o*^	ô	Tilde	n*~	ñ
Umlaut	u*:	ü	Umlaut	U*;	Ü
Cedilla	c*,	ç			

FORMATTER DEPENDENT STRINGS

NAME	INPUT	nroff OUTPUT	troff OUTPUT
Bullet	*(BU	⊕	●
em dash	*(EM	--	—

-mm **NUMBER REGISTERS**

OVERALL FORMAT NUMBER REGISTERS

D † Debug flag.

   0 No debugging.

   1 Debugging. Continue on error.

Hy   Hyphenation control. Default is 0.

   0 Do not hyphenate main text.

   1 Hyphenate main text.

L † Length of page. Units are lines (nroff) or scaled numbers (troff). Default value is 66 (nroff) or 11i (troff).

N † Page numbering style.

   0 All pages get prevailing header.

   1 Prevailing header used as footer on page 1; all other pages get prevailing header.

   2 Page 1 doesn't get a header; all other pages get prevailing header.

   3 All pages get section page number in footer.

   4 If a user header is specified with .PH, it will appear on pages 2 onward. Otherwise no page header will appear.

   5 All pages get section page number in footer.

O † Page offset. The left margin will be offset from the edge of the page by the amount specified in the O number register. The units for O are ens (nroff) or scaled numbers (troff). The default is 7 ens (nroff) and 0.5i (troff).

P † Page number. The P number register may be set on the command line or reset in the document to alter the page-numbering sequence.

S † Point size for troff. The default is 10.

U † nroff underline style for headings. The default is 0.

   0 Continuous underline.

   1 Underline only letters and digits.

W † Text width. The units are ens (nroff) or scaled numbers (troff). The default is 6 inches. Note that for nroff the width of an en is 0.1i in 10-pitch and 0.08333i in 12-pitch.

  † These number registers must be set before the -mm text is processed. They are usually set on the command line.

-mm NUMBER REGISTERS

HEADING FORMAT NUMBER REGISTERS

Ej   Heading eject. Headings at this level or lower will always appear at the top of the page. Default value 0.

Hb   Heading break level. Headings of this level or less will be followed by a break, making following text start on a new line. The default value is 0.

Hc   Heading centering level. Headings of this level or less will be centered. The default value is 0.

Hs   Heading space level. Headings of this level or less will be followed by a blank line (nroff) or a half vertical space (troff). The default is 2.

Ht   Heading type.

   0   Heading numbers will contain as many parts as the level of the heading; e.g., a level 3 head would appear as 4.2.12.

   1   Heading numbers will contain only the rightmost part. For example, the heading mentioned above would be written as 12.

Hu   Heading level for unnumbered (.HU) headings. Unnumbered headings will be treated as if they were at this level for formatting and for incrementing the heading counters.

PARAGRAPH FORMAT NUMBER REGISTERS

Np   Paragraph numbering style. The default is 0.

   0   Paragraphs will not be numbered.

   1   Paragraphs will be numbered.

Pi   Paragraph indent.. Indented paragraphs, bullet lists (.BL), and dash lists (.DL) are indented by the amount specified in the Pi number register. The units are ens, and the default is 5 (nroff) or 3 (troff).

Pt   Paragraph type. Paragraphs started by the command .P (no argument) will be the type specified by the Pt number register. The default is 0.

   0   The first line of all default paragraphs will be left-justified.

   1   The first line of all default paragraphs will be indented by Pi.

   2   The first line of all default paragraphs will be indented by Pi unless they immediately follow a heading, list, or display.

-mm **NUMBER REGISTERS AND STRING REGISTERS**

DISPLAY FORMAT NUMBER REGISTERS

De   Floating display eject flag.

   0 Text may appear on page following a floating display.

   1 Floating displays will always be followed by a page eject.

Ds   The amount of extra space that is placed above and below a static display. Units of lines for nroff and half vertical spaces for troff. Default value is 1.

Eq   Equation label placement. Default is 0.

   0 Label will be placed flush right.

   1 Label will be placed flush left.

Si   Standard display indent. Units are ens, and the default is 5 (nroff) or 3 (troff).

LISTS

Li   List indent. Automatic lists (.AL) and reference lists (.RL) will be indented by the amount specified in the Li number register. The indent is specified in ens, and the default amount is 6 (nroff) or 5 (troff).

Ls   List spacing. Lists that are nested Ls deep or less will have an extra line (nroff) or half vertical space (troff) placed before the list and before each item in the list. If Ls is zero, lists won't be preceded by extra vertical space; if Ls is 1, then only outer lists will be preceded by extra vertical space, etc. The default is 6.

HEADING FORMAT STRING REGISTERS

HF   The string stored in this register contains up to seven font codes, one for each heading level. The default string is 3 3 2 2 2 2 2, which means that level 1 and 2 heads will be bold and other heads will be underlined (nroff) or italic (troff).

HP   The string stored in this register contains up to seven point size codes, one for each heading level. The default is for bold stand-alone heads to be printed 1 point smaller than the text and for other heads to be the same size as the text.

APPENDIX VII

---

mm/mmt Command Line Options

On System V UNIX you can use the mm or mmt programs to format and print your -mm documents. mm formats a document with nroff for ordinary printers, and mmt formats a document with troff for more sophisticated printers such as laser printers or typesetters. mm and mmt were designed to simplify text processing, but some people find them confusing, because they present yet another interface to an already complicated system.

The general syntax for mm and mmt is

```
mm [ options ] [ file . . . ]
mmt [ options ] [ file . . . ]
```

The options must precede the file names, and the special file name "-" can be used to force mm or mmt to read from the standard input. By default, the input is processed using the compacted version of the -mm macros.

The following options are common to both mm and mmt.

-e Preprocess the input with eqn.

-t Preprocess the input with tbl.

-y Use the noncompacted version of the -mm macros instead of the compacted version.

Any unrecognized options will be passed along to nroff or troff. Here are a few of the common nroff/troff options that are used on the mm or mmt command line.

-o*list*

Output is produced for the pages mentioned in the *list*. The *list* is a comma-separated list of pages, or page ranges. (A page range is n-m, which means from page *n* through page *m*.) For example, the option -o1,3,5,11-19 means pages 1, 3, 5, and 11 through 19.

-n*N*

   The first page of the document is numbered *N*.

-s*N*

   The output process is stopped every *N* pages so that you can change the paper. Not functional on all versions of troff.

-ra*N*

   The nroff/troff internal register named *a* is set to the value *N*. *a* is any single-character register name, and *N* is any value.

The following command line options apply only to mm:

-T*term*

   Prepare output for the terminal named *term*. A list of supported terminals can be generated by listing the files in the '/usr/lib/term' directory. If this option is not specified, then output will be generated for the terminal listed in the $TERM environment variable. When all else fails, output will be for a model 450.

-c The col program will be invoked as an output filter. col is automatically invoked for some terminals.

-12

   Produces output in 12-pitch if possible.

-E Produce equally spaced lines on capable printers. Equivalent to the nroff's -e option.

Index